OXFORD WC

THE SIDN

T0115584

PHILIP SIDNEY (1554–86) stu
Church, Oxford. In his Continental travels, he was widely celebrated
but held no aristocratic title at home. Granted minor favours by
Queen Elizabeth, Philip never attained the position for which he had
been educated, and his opposition to her planned French
marriage forced him to retire temporarily from court. His works
include *The Countess of Pembroke's Arcadia*, *Astrophil and Stella*, and
The Defence of Poetry, as well as *The Lady of May* (an entertainment
for Elizabeth). MARY SIDNEY (1561–1621) studied at home, and was
invited to court by Queen Elizabeth. Her marriage to Henry Herbert,
2nd Earl of Pembroke, gave her the title and wealth that eluded her
brother. Mary supervised the posthumous fashioning of Philip's
reputation and completed the metrical Psalter that he had begun.
In addition to Psalms, her works include translations from French
(*A Discourse on Life and Death* and *Antonius*) and Italian (*The Triumph
of Death*), an elegy for her brother, and a pastoral entertainment for
Elizabeth's proposed visit to Wilton.

HANNIBAL HAMLIN (Associate Professor of English at The Ohio
State University) is the author of *Psalm Culture and Early Modern
English Literature* (Cambridge, 2004). MARGARET P. HANNAY
(Professor of English at Siena College), NOEL J. KINNAMON (Professor
of English at Mars Hill College), and MICHAEL G. BRENNAN
(Professor of Renaissance Studies at the School of English, University
of Leeds) have together edited *The Collected Works of Mary Sidney
Herbert, Countess of Pembroke* for the Oxford English Texts series
(Oxford, 1998) and *Selected Works of Mary Sidney Herbert, Countess
of Pembroke* (Tempe, Ariz., 2005).

OXFORD WORLD'S CLASSICS

*For over 100 years Oxford World's Classics have brought
readers closer to the world's great literature. Now with over 700
titles—from the 4,000-year-old myths of Mesopotamia to the
twentieth century's greatest novels—the series makes available
lesser-known as well as celebrated writing.*

*The pocket-sized hardbacks of the early years contained
introductions by Virginia Woolf, T. S. Eliot, Graham Greene,
and other literary figures which enriched the experience of reading.
Today the series is recognized for its fine scholarship and
reliability in texts that span world literature, drama and poetry,
religion, philosophy, and politics. Each edition includes perceptive
commentary and essential background information to meet the
changing needs of readers.*

OXFORD WORLD'S CLASSICS

The Sidney Psalter
The Psalms of
Sir Philip and Mary Sidney

Edited with an Introduction and Notes by
HANNIBAL HAMLIN,
MICHAEL G. BRENNAN,
MARGARET P. HANNAY, and
NOEL J. KINNAMON

OXFORD
UNIVERSITY PRESS

OXFORD

UNIVERSITY PRESS

Great Clarendon Street, Oxford OX2 6DP

Oxford University Press is a department of the University of Oxford.
It furthers the University's objective of excellence in research, scholarship,
and education by publishing worldwide in

Oxford New York

Auckland Cape Town Dar es Salaam Hong Kong Karachi
Kuala Lumpur Madrid Melbourne Mexico City Nairobi
New Delhi Shanghai Taipei Toronto

With offices in

Argentina Austria Brazil Chile Czech Republic France Greece
Guatemala Hungary Italy Japan Poland Portugal Singapore
South Korea Switzerland Thailand Turkey Ukraine Vietnam

Oxford is a registered trade mark of Oxford University Press
in the UK and in certain other countries

Published in the United States
by Oxford University Press Inc., New York

© Hannibal Hamlin, Michael G. Brennan, Margaret P. Hannay, and Noel J. Kinnamon 2009

The moral rights of the authors have been asserted
Database right Oxford University Press (maker)

First published as a World's Classics paperback 2009

British Library Cataloguing in Publication Data

Data available

Library of Congress Cataloging-in-Publication Data

Data available

Typeset by Cepha Imaging Private Ltd., Bangalore, India
Printed in Great Britain
on acid-free paper by
Clays Ltd., Elcograf S.p.A.

ISBN 978-0-19-921793-9

7

ACKNOWLEDGEMENTS

We are most grateful to Viscount De L'Isle, MBE, DL, for his generosity and support in allowing us access to his unique collection of family papers. We are also grateful for expert advice to the staff of the Centre for Kentish Studies, Maidstone, where the Sidney papers are now preserved. Shortly before his death, the late Dr Bent Juel-Jensen kindly allowed us to make a final check of the Tixall manuscript then in his possession. J. C. A. Rathmell's pioneering work on the Sidney Psalter, especially his 1963 edition, has been invaluable, and several of the editors are grateful for more personal expressions of support from Dr Rathmell over the years. All the editors express gratitude to their academic institutions: The Ohio State University, the University of Leeds, Siena College, and Mars Hill College. Hannibal Hamlin is also grateful to the directors and staff of the Folger Shakespeare Library, and would like to thank Cori Martin for both her editorial judgement and her keen understanding of poetic form. Noel Kinnamon would like to thank Rebeccah Neff, Jason Pierce, Nina Pollard, Betty Hughes, Diane Hutt, Susan Kiser, Naomi Ferguson, Joe Blair, and Lora Coomer. Special thanks are due to Ruth Hannay for assistance with glosses and to Gary A. Stringer, General Editor of the John Donne Variorum, who kindly provided the edited text of Donne's 'Upon the Translation of the Psalms'. Finally, we would like to thank Judith Luna, Commissioning Editor of Oxford World's Classics, for her support of this project.

CONTENTS

THE SIDNEY PSALTER

INTRODUCTION

Psalms and Metrical Psalms

The history of the Sidney Psalter must begin with the biblical Psalms themselves. The book of Psalms consists of 150 texts, ranging in length from two verses (117) to one hundred and seventy-six (119), written over the course of many centuries, from at least 1000 BCE to as late as 450 BCE, though their roots lie earlier still in the literary traditions of the ancient Middle East. Though traditionally attributed to King David, the Psalms in fact had many authors, none of whom can be identified with any certainty. Early biblical editors attached headnotes to many Psalms, some identifying particular texts as a Psalm 'of David' (28, 41, 86), 'of Solomon' (72), 'of Asaph' (73, 74), or 'of Moses' (90), but the Hebrew in such phrases could also mean 'for', 'in the manner of', or 'suitable to'. The word 'Psalm' is Greek, and means a song sung to a plucked string instrument. The Hebrew words for these texts are *mizmor* ('song') and *tehilla* ('praise'), and the book as a whole is called *Tehillim* ('Praises'). As Philip Sidney put it, 'the name *Psalms* . . . being interpreted, is nothing but songs'.[1] The Psalms have indeed been sung by Jews and Christians in public worship and in private devotion for several thousand years, but they have also been read, silently and aloud, in public and in private, communally and individually.

The appeal of the Psalms has been partly their variety. There are Psalms of praise and blame, Psalms of cursing and lamentation, Psalms of joy and exaltation, Psalms that recount history, and Psalms that describe Creation or divine law. John Calvin called the Psalms 'an anatomy of all the parts of the soul, in as much as a man shall not find any affection in himself, whereof the Image appeareth not in this glass'. Richard Hooker asked, 'What is there for man to know that the Psalms are not able to teach?' John Donne preached that the Psalms were the 'Manna of the Church', since, just 'as Manna tasted to every man like that that he liked best, so do the Psalms minister instruction, and satisfaction, to every man, in every

---

[1] Sir Philip Sidney, *A Defence of Poetry*, in *Miscellaneous Prose of Sir Philip Sidney*, ed. Katherine Duncan-Jones and Jan van Dorsten (Oxford: Clarendon Press, 1973), 77.

emergency and occasion'.² And not only could the Psalms suit every occasion, but they were perfectly designed to be appropriated by people of all sorts: written consistently in the first person, the book of Psalms is the only biblical book in which the writer addresses himself directly to God. As the Renaissance translator Anthony Gilby put it, 'whereas all other scriptures do teach us what God saith unto us, these prayers . . . do teach us, what we shall say unto God'.³ When the English Protestants exiled in Geneva during the reign of Queen Mary compiled *The Whole Booke of Psalms*, they included 'A Treatise made by Athanasius' in tabular form, 'wherein is set forth, how, and in what manner ye may use the Psalms, according to the effect of the mind'.⁴ Name your condition or mood ('effect of mind'), and Athanasius provided the Psalm for it; there was a Psalm for everyone and every occasion.

However, one problem for sixteenth-century readers of the Psalms was that the Hebrew Psalms were not written in metre or any recognizable poetic form. Since the time of Jerome, it had been widely accepted that indeed the Psalms were 'poems', and that they were somehow in metre, but exactly how this was so was not clear. Philip Sidney asserted that the book of Psalms 'is fully written in metre, as all learned hebricians agree, although the rules be not yet fully found'.⁵ The mystery of Hebrew poetry was not discovered by English scholarship until the eighteenth-century lectures of Robert Lowth.⁶ It was based on a principle of formal parallelism. Most simply, a statement is made, then a second statement follows with roughly the same meaning but different words. For example, Psalm 33 contains the verse, 'A horse is a vain help, and shall not deliver any by his great help', in which the second clause expresses the same idea

² *The Psalmes of David and others. With M. John Calvins Commentaries*, trans. Arthur Golding (London, 1571), *6ᵛ; Richard Hooker, *Of the Lawes of Ecclesiastical Polity*, Book V, in the Folger Library edition, *The Works of Richard Hooker*, vol. ii, ed. W. Speed Hill (Cambridge, Mass., and London: Belknap Press of Harvard University Press, 1977), 150; John Donne, *Prebend Sermons*, ed. Janel Mueller (Cambridge, Mass.: Harvard University Press, 1971), 91.

³ Théodore de Bèze, *The Psalms of David*, trans. Anthony Gilby (London, 1581), a3ᵛ.

⁴ *The Whole Booke of Psalmes* (London, 1562), *7ᵛ.

⁵ Sidney, *Defence of Poetry*, 77.

⁶ See James Kugel, *The Idea of Biblical Poetry: Parallelism and Its History* (New Haven and London: Yale University Press, 1981); Robert Alter, *The Art of Biblical Poetry* (New York: Basic Books, 1985).

with greater intensity and detail.[7] More complex kinds of parallelism vary the original statement in subtle ways, developing, qualifying, or even contradicting it. Psalm 128, for instance, says, 'Thy wife shall be as the fruitful vine upon the walls of thine house: thy children like the olive branches round about thy table', where the metaphors for prosperity are similar, and the elements in each clause are parallel: wife and children, vine and branch, walls and table. This is not a formal principle that sixteenth-century English readers would have recognized as 'verse', however. Thus, many English translations of the Psalms (like those in the major English Bibles) resulted in prose—artful and stylized prose perhaps, but prose none the less. Translating the Psalms into English metre was an attempt to recapture the 'poetic' quality of the Hebrew originals, even if this quality was only a notional one.

Another reason for translating Psalms into metre was that this made them easier to sing and easier to remember. Martin Luther, Calvin, and other Protestant Reformers recognized the usefulness of sung, metrical Psalms as a means of spreading Reformed doctrine, and some of Luther's earliest works were Psalm translations, often relatively loose, Christianized paraphrases like '*Ein feste Burg ist unser Gott*' (Psalm 46) and '*Aus tiefer Not*' (Psalm 130). Calvin also wrote metrical versions of the Psalms, though the most popular French Psalter was the work of Clément Marot and Calvin's successor in Geneva, Théodore de Bèze (commonly known as Beza). Metrical Psalms also existed in Dutch, Hungarian, Polish, Italian, English, and most other European languages, typically (following Luther) set to pre-existing popular or catchy melodies which made them easy to remember. In England, Miles Coverdale tried his hand at metrical singing Psalms, but the version that proved most popular, both for singing in church and at home, was another product of the Geneva exiles, *The Whole Booke of Psalms*, or 'Sternhold and Hopkins' (named after its first two translators). Hundreds of editions of 'Sternhold and Hopkins' were printed after its first appearance in 1562. Many other English versions of the Psalms circulated in the sixteenth century as well. Some were, like 'Sternhold and Hopkins', good for public singing but fairly dull and clumsy as poetry. Others, however, had literary

---

[7] Unless otherwise noted, citations from the Psalms are from the translation of Miles Coverdale for the Great Bible (1539), incorporated into the Book of Common Prayer, slightly modernized.

ambitions, and were not designed for church singing. Indeed, metrical Psalms began to gain a prominent place in sixteenth-century English poetry. One reason is that the Psalms were well known and well loved, and also central to personal religious devotions. But the existence of biblical poetry also provided authoritative justification for writing verse at a time when that was seen by many as both idle and morally suspect: but if David could write poems, then so might others (at least if they stuck to the proper subject matter).[8]

Like sonnets, metrical Psalms were also part of the movement to create a national literature to rival those already flourishing in France and Italy. Thinking probably of French metrical Psalms, Donne lamented that 'Psalms are become so well attired abroad, so ill at home'.[9] Not surprisingly, most important figures in the sixteenth-century development of English poetry were also writers of metrical Psalms. Before the Sidney Psalter, for example, Sir Thomas Wyatt wrote a complex metrical version of the Penitential Psalms (6, 32, 38, 51, 102, 130, 143), based on Italian models; the Earl of Surrey experimented with Psalms in various metres, including blank verse hexameters; George Gascoigne, another literary innovator, wrote a version of Psalm 130 ('Out of the deep') in richly alliterative stanzas. The Anglo-Irish poet Richard Stanyhurst tried a number of Psalms in classical, quantitative metres, using his own innovative spelling system. Among many others who wrote metrical Psalms, two of the Sidneys' uncles, Robert and John Dudley, translated Psalms 94 and 55 respectively while they were imprisoned in the Tower after the failed attempt to crown Lady Jane Grey. Translating Psalms into metre was therefore not an unusual thing to do in sixteenth-century England. In fact, the metrical Psalm rivalled the Petrarchan love poem as the popular lyric mode for English poets.

The Sidneys and Their Psalms

By the late 1570s, when Philip Sidney was in his early twenties, he already seemed likely to achieve prominence beyond the modest expectations of his birth. Although without title, he was the presumptive heir of two of the richest and most powerful noblemen, his

---

[8] See Peter C. Herman, *Squitter-Wits and Muse-Haters: Sidney, Spenser, Milton and Renaissance Antipoetic Sentiment* (Detroit: Wayne State University Press, 1996).

[9] See below, p. 4.

uncles, Ambrose Dudley and the aforementioned Robert Dudley, respectively Earls of Warwick and Leicester, neither of whom had children. Philip had made a considerable impression among Continental scholars and courtiers during a European tour, and he seemed a promising figure in the English court, as well as a skilled athlete, excelling at jousting. Succeeding his father, he was made Royal Cupbearer in 1576, and he was given his first diplomatic mission in 1577 as ambassador to the Holy Roman Emperor Rudolph II, to the Elector Palatine Louis VI, and to Louis's brother Prince Casimir. In 1578 Philip wrote *The Lady of May* as an entertainment for Queen Elizabeth when she visited Leicester at his house in Wanstead. Shortly after this, however, his prospects began to unravel. In 1579 the queen discovered Leicester's clandestine marriage to Lettice Knollys, and the earl found himself in considerable disfavour. Philip himself was forced to leave the court after a heated public quarrel at a tennis court with the Earl of Oxford over precedence and Elizabeth's plans for a French marriage. Moreover, in 1580 or 1581, Leicester had a son, which brought an end to Philip's great expectations of inheritance and as a result may also have ruined his prospects of marrying Penelope Devereux, daughter of the Earl of Essex. Philip later married Frances, the daughter of the influential, but non-aristocratic, Sir Francis Walsingham. He was knighted in the same year (1583), but only as a formality enabling him to participate in the Order of the Garter ceremony for Prince Casimir. Philip's heroic participation in the war in the Netherlands might have brought him the kind of position to which he aspired, but a bullet and gangrene killed him in 1586, aged 32, before he could achieve it.

If public disappointments kept Philip away from court, these times of forced leisure allowed him to write the works (published only after his death) on which his subsequent literary reputation rests: *The Countess of Pembroke's Arcadia* (1590), *Astrophil and Stella* (1591), and the *Defence of Poetry* (1595). The *Arcadia*, a prose romance interspersed with pastoral lyrics, and by far Philip's largest work, was written at Wilton, one of the estates of Henry Herbert, 2nd Earl of Pembroke, husband of Philip's sister, the Countess of Pembroke. Philip spent a good deal of time at Wilton, and it proved a congenial place to read and write, especially since Mary seems to have been an intellectual kindred spirit. Philip began to write the *Arcadia* (its first version now known as *The Old Arcadia*) and the *Defence of Poetry* at

Wilton in 1580. Over the next several years, he finished these works, as well as the sonnet-sequence *Astrophil and Stella*; he also began a much expanded revision of the *Arcadia*, and embarked on the metrical translation of the Psalms. Neither of the last two projects was completed.

By the time of his death, Philip had completed translations of Psalms 1–43. As recent critics have recognized, the Sidney Psalter was, like the '*New*' *Arcadia*, one of Philip's major literary works. Unlike any previous English psalm translator, Philip translated the Psalms into sophisticated verse, selecting or inventing a different metre or stanza form for each Psalm. These were not primarily Psalms for singing or for use in church worship. A few were set to music in the seventeenth century, and, like any religious writing, they probably had a devotional purpose—both for the writer and the reader—but these comprised a fundamentally literary work, a demonstration not only of the mastery of Philip as a poet, but of the lyric possibilities of English poetry, in a sense a practical accompaniment to his *Defence of Poetry*.[10] Mary Philip, in essence her brother's literary executor supervising the posthumous, authorized (by her) publication of his works, continued the Psalter project, translating the remaining 107 Psalms and revising many of Philip's.

Mary Sidney Herbert, Countess of Pembroke, was seven years younger than Philip, but they seem to have been remarkably close (two intervening siblings died young). Although, as a woman, Mary could not attend university or travel in Europe as did Philip, she was nevertheless well educated, being fluent in French, Italian, and Latin. As her later writings demonstrate, she was also learned in classical and contemporary literature as well as the Bible, and was an accomplished musician and skilled at needlework. Like any woman of her position, she also studied the more practical subjects of household management and medicine. After a brief period as a lady in waiting to the queen, Mary achieved the kind of wealth and status of which Philip could only dream when at the age of 16, in 1577, she married the Earl of Pembroke. The earl was about thirty years older than his

---

[10] Psalms 51 and 130 are set for high voice and lute in BL Additional MS 15117, and several were adapted for use in *All the French Psalm Tunes with English Words* (1652). The simplified, accentual-syllabic versions of Psalms 120–7 may also have been adapted for the purpose of singing. See *The Collected Works of Mary Sidney Herbert, Countess of Pembroke*, ed. Margaret P. Hannay, Noel J. Kinnamon, and Michael G. Brennan, 2 vols. (Oxford: Clarendon Press, 1998), i. 47, 52.

young bride, but the marriage brought the Sidneys into close alliance with the powerful Herbert family, and gave Mary the wealth and prestige that enabled her to become the first English woman to be widely celebrated as literary patron and writer. The couple had four children, two of whom (sons William and Philip) inherited, in succession, their father's title and property. In addition to managing her brother's posthumous publications and reputation, Mary wrote not only the greater part of the Sidney Psalter and its two dedicatory poems, 'Even Now That Care' and 'To the Angel Spirit of the Most Excellent Sir Philip Sidney', but she also wrote translations of Robert Garnier's closet drama *Antonius* (a translation that influenced Shakespeare's *Antony and Cleopatra*), *A Discourse of Life and Death* by Philippe Duplessis-Mornay, and Petrarch's *The Triumph of Death*. She also composed a pastoral dialogue-poem and (perhaps) a pastoral elegy for her brother, 'The Doleful Lay of Clorinda'.

Given her wealth and aristocratic status, Mary attracted the attentions of many other writers who sought her patronage or approval. Edmund Spenser, for instance, dedicated to her his *Ruins of Time*, in part an elegy for Philip, and Abraham Fraunce wrote for her both *The Countess of Pembroke's Ivychurch* and *The Countess of Pembroke's Emmanuel*. Her son William Herbert and her niece Mary, later Lady Wroth, both wrote verse inspired by Mary's model, as well as that of Philip and their brother Robert. Although her contemporaries mentioned additional works by Mary, no writings except correspondence survive after the death of her husband in 1601. Her role as literary patron was largely assumed by her son William after he inherited the earldom. She died from smallpox in 1621.

Once the completed Psalter of Philip and Mary Sidney was in circulation (in manuscript), its privileged early readers acknowledged it as a masterwork. Donne wrote that 'Though some have, some may, some Psalms translate | We thy Sidneian Psalms shall celebrate' and that 'they tell us why, and teach us how to sing'. In a verse epistle praising Mary, Samuel Daniel wrote of 'Those Hymns that thou dost consecrate to heaven, | Which Israel's Singer to his God did frame'. 'This monument cannot be overthrown,' Daniel continued, arguing that the Sidney *Psalms* would be a more lasting monument than Wilton House.[11] Thomas Heywood, Francis Meres, and Michael

---

[11] p. 4; Daniel, *Delia & Cleopatra*, quoted in Pembroke, *Works*, i.46.

Drayton all likened Mary to Sappho, the pre-eminent woman poet of antiquity (Mary's Psalm 125 is written in the Sapphic metre, perhaps self-consciously). Much of the praise of the Sidney *Psalms* was directed to Mary, of course, since by the time they were read Philip was dead, but the work was always recognized as a collaboration, most defini-tively in Mary's own dedicatory poem to her brother:

> To thee, pure sprite, to thee alone's addressed
>   This coupled work, by double interest thine:
>   First raised by thy blest hand, and what is mine
> Inspired by thee, thy secret power impressed. (p. 8)

Even though the Sidney Psalter was never printed in the sixteenth or seventeenth centuries, the number of surviving manuscript copies testifies to its wide popularity. The earliest manuscripts of the Sidney Psalter were copied and recopied over the decades, and some Psalms circulated individually as well. At first, readership was largely controlled by Mary and confined to her circle of acquaintance. Sir John Harington possessed manuscripts, for instance, as apparently did Sir Walter Aston; Harington's godfather was Mary's husband, and Aston was a friend of William Herbert, Mary's son. The *Psalms* were also clearly known to poet-members of Mary's family (Lady Mary Wroth, for instance, and George Herbert, a distant cousin) and her household, including Samuel Daniel, tutor to William Herbert, and Thomas Moffett, Mary's physician. By the mid-seventeenth century, however, the Sidney *Psalms* had passed into wide manuscript circulation.[12]

A number of contemporary readers regretted that the Sidney *Psalms* were not printed (perhaps because Mary thought she would have greater control of them through manuscript circulation),[13] including Francis Davison, the poet, anthologist, and literary entre-preneur, who listed them in his papers as a manuscript he wanted to acquire for printing. Another was Sir John Harington, who wrote that 'it is pity they are unpublished, but lie still enclosed within those

---

[12] For complete details on the manuscripts and their provenance, see the extensive commentary in *The Poems of Sir Philip Sidney*, ed. William A. Ringler, Jr. (Oxford: Clarendon Press, 1962), and Pembroke, *Works*.

[13] See Margaret P. Hannay, 'The Countess of Pembroke's Agency in Print and Scribal Culture', in George Justice and Nathan Tinker (eds.), *Women's Writing and the Circulation of Ideas: Manuscript Publication in England, 1550–1800* (Cambridge: Cambridge University Press, 2002), 17–49.

walls like prisoners, though many have made great suit for their liberty'.[14] Of course, the idea of the Sidney *Psalms* imprisoned at Wilton was fanciful, since, even if they were not in print, they were clearly in wide circulation. Further evidence of this is the observable influence they had on subsequent English poetry, both metrical Psalms and religious lyrics. Although singing psalters continued to be produced for worship and devotion, many poets writing metrical Psalms in the seventeenth century followed the Sidneys in casting the Psalms into sophisticated verse. The Psalms of Francis Davison, Phineas Fletcher, Thomas Carew, and John Milton were indebted to the Sidneian model. The Sidney Psalter also shaped religious poetry more generally. Donne's appreciation for the Sidney *Psalms* is clear from his poem praising them; they were also the principal model for George Herbert's *The Temple*, which was in turn the model for subsequent lyric collections, including Christopher Harvey's *The Synagogue* and Henry Vaughan's *Silex Scintillans*. Both Herbert and Vaughan included metrical Psalms in their collections. The Countess of Pembroke was a particularly powerful model for younger women poets, and both Aemilia Lanyer and Lady Mary Wroth acknowledged their debt to her.

In the nineteenth century, interest in the Sidney Psalter was revived by its first print publication, the Chiswick Press edition of 1823 based on the Penshurst manuscript (*A*), apparently instigated by James Boswell, Shakespeare scholar and son of Samuel Johnson's biographer. Select Psalms appeared in a number of subsequent anthologies, and John Ruskin published forty-four of them in his *Rock Honeycomb: Broken Pieces of Sir Philip Sidney's Psalter* (1877). As Ruskin's title indicates, he gave little credit for the work to Mary, and this chauvinistic bias was shared by most Victorian editors and readers. Only in the twentieth century has Mary been restored to her proper role as the principal author and editor of the Sidney Psalter.[15]

---

[14] Quoted in Pembroke, *Works*, i.48.

[15] J. C. A. Rathmell's 1963 edition of the Psalter rekindled interest in the work, as did Coburn Freer's seminal study of the influence of the Sidney *Psalms* on Herbert, *Music for a King* (1972). Critical studies of the Sidney *Psalms* were also spurred on by the publication of the Oxford English Texts editions of Philip Sidney by William A. Ringler in 1962 and of Mary Sidney by Margaret Hannay, Noel Kinnamon, and Michael Brennan in 1998, and by the 1990 biography of the Countess of Pembroke by Margaret Hannay. Individual Sidney Psalms can now be found in standard collections like *The Norton*

The Psalms: Content

Donne praised the Sidney *Psalms* as achieving the 'highest matter
in the noblest form', which may be a good working definition of
any great poetry. Separating out 'matter' and 'form', however, espe-
cially in works of translation, is not easy. Obviously, the primary
'matter' of the Sidneys' poems is that of the biblical Psalms, but even
this is not straightforward. Neither of the Sidneys was expert in
Hebrew (though Mary may have known a little through her chap-
lain Gervase Babington), so they were working from prior transla-
tions into English, French, and Latin. In English, they used the
prose versions of the Book of Common Prayer (from Coverdale's
1539 Great Bible translation) and the Geneva Bible. In French, the
artful verse translations of Marot and Beza in *Les CL. Pseaumes de
David, mis en rime Françoise* (1562) were an important source. In addi-
tion, they consulted the Psalms commentaries of Calvin and Beza,
available in English translation: *The Psalms of David and others. With
M. John Calvins Commentaries*, trans. Arthur Golding (1571), and
[Théodore de Bèze], *The Psalms of David, truly opened and explained
by Paraphrasis*, trans. Anthony Gilby (1581). The extensive marginal
notes in the Geneva Bible provided another source of scholarly com-
mentary. The Sidneys also read and occasionally incorporated details
from the Matthew, Bishops', and other English Bibles, the psalters of
Sternhold and Hopkins, Robert Crowley, and Matthew Parker, select
Psalms translations by George Gascoigne and Anne Vaughan Lock
(and those of George Buchanan into Latin), and the Latin commen-
taries of Victorinus Strigelius (available in English translation by
Richard Robinson, after Philip's death), Franciscus Vatablus, and
Immanuel Tremellius.

With so many sources pouring into the Sidney *Psalms*, whose
voices are we hearing when we read them? Are we still hearing
David's (or an original psalmist's) voice? The voices of all those inter-
vening translators and commentators? The voices of the Sidneys?
Our own voice, given Athanasius' argument that the words of the
Psalms become our own as we need them? In his poem on the Sidney
Psalms Donne was perceptive in using harmony as his prevailing

Anthology of English Literature, which suggests that they are coming to be accorded the
position they deserve among the great literature of the English Renaissance.

metaphor. He describes how 'heaven's high holy Muse' (the Holy
Spirit) whispers the Psalms to David, then 'David to the Jews',

> And David's successors, in holy zeal,
> In forms of joy and art do re-reveal [them]
> To us so sweetly and sincerely too . . . (pp. 3–4)

In Donne's view, all the voices blend into one harmonious song: from
the Sidneys back through the Christian commentators and translators
to the Jewish tradition to David and the first Psalmists and finally to
the Holy Spirit. More practically, however, while the primary content
of the Psalms—their topics, their images, their metaphors, and their
organization from verse to verse—is that of their Hebrew authors, the
strongest voices we hear are those of the Sidneys, since they chose the
specific English words, decided on their particular order, the arrange-
ment of their sounds and shapes, and elaborated the figurative lan-
guage of the originals. Although individual words, phrases, metaphors,
and structures may have derived from this translation or that com-
mentary, the final combination was indeed exclusive to the Sidneys.
To take one example, Rivkah Zim has shown that in Philip's Psalm 6,
the main source is Coverdale, from the Book of Common Prayer
(BCP), especially his choice of the words 'displeasure' and 'beauty' in
lines 2 and 21. The 'worm' and 'moth' of lines 1 and 21, however, are
taken from the Geneva Bible's marginal gloss and the Geneva text for
Psalm 39. 11 (which expresses a similar sentiment to Psalm 6). Other
images or word choices seem to come from the paraphrase of Beza
(Théodore de Bèze), either in the original Latin or (in certain cases)
in Gilby's translation. And yet the final arrangement of this material
is Sidney's own, as are the remaining aspects of the composition that
cannot be traced to an earlier source—for example, the use of affective
apostrophes and imperatives, as Zim argues.[16]

The Sidney *Psalms* exhibit numerous literary qualities admired in
better-known English Renaissance poems. Donne and other seven-
teenth-century poets, for instance, are praised for their metaphysical
wit, what Samuel Johnson called 'the most heterogeneous ideas . . .
yoked by violence together'.[17] Johnson disliked this in Donne, but

---

[16] Rivkah Zim, *English Metrical Psalms: Poetry as Praise and Prayer, 1535–1601*
(Cambridge: Cambridge University Press, 1987), 160–4.

[17] Samuel Johnson, *Life of Cowley*, quoted in Hannibal Hamlin, *Psalm Culture and
Early Modern English Literature* (Cambridge: Cambridge University Press, 2004), 130.

modern readers admire it, and the same wit can be found in the Sidney *Psalms* (no doubt one reason Donne enjoyed them). This can be observed in Mary's Psalm 139, one of her most anthologized poems. The Psalm meditates on God's omniscience and the mysteries of creation, especially the creation of human beings in the womb. In Mary's words, the Psalmist acknowledges:

> Thou how my back was beam-wise laid
> And raft'ring of my ribs dost know:
> > Know'st every point
> > Of bone and joint,
> How to this whole these parts did grow,
> In brave embroid'ry fair arrayed,
> Though wrought in shop both dark and low.

Coverdale's BCP translation is powerful in its own right, but lacks Mary's rich architectural metaphor (coupled with the alliterative hammering) of the 'beam-wise' back and 'raft'ring' of ribs, as well as the shift from construction imagery to 'embroid'ry fair arrayed', a metaphor derived from women's crafts. If the body is metaphorically a building, raftered like a Tudor hall, then the 'embroid'ry'—skin? hair?—may suggest a tapestry covering its walls. The implication of the womb as a subterranean smithy existed previously in Coverdale ('and fashioned beneath in the earth'), but Mary's 'dark and low' adds an epistemological and moral connotation to the physical location. Here, Mary wreathes 'iron pokers into true-love knots' (as Coleridge described Donne's metaphorical habits), though the love is sacred rather than secular.[18]

Another quality we admire in Renaissance lyric is psychological realism, the ability to represent complex inward thought in verse, as Shakespeare did in his soliloquies and sonnets. The Sidneys exhibit this interiority repeatedly. Psalm 73 is a theodicy, an intellectual struggle with the problem of evil, but in the Bible or BCP versions it is expressed with little emotional depth: 'Truly God is loving unto Israel: even unto such as are of a clean heart. Nevertheless, my feet were almost gone, my treadings had well nye slipped.' By contrast, through colloquial diction, broken syntax, with frequent self-interruptions, corrections, and repetitions, and a skilful use of line

---

[18] Samuel Taylor Coleridge, *Poetical Works*, ed. Ernest Hartley Coleridge (Oxford: Clarendon Press, 1969), 433.

breaks, Mary creates a vivid persona in a state of puzzled anxiety, which captures the emotional and psychological implications of the Psalm's content—surprise, doubt, fear' anger, and relief:

> It is most true that God to Israel,
>> I mean to men of undefilèd hearts,
>> Is only good, and naught but good imparts.
> Most true, I see, albe almost I fell
>> From right conceit into a crooked mind
>> And from this truth with straying steps declined:
> For, lo, my boiling breast did chafe and swell
>> When first I saw the wicked proudly stand,
>> Prevailing still in all they took in hand.

Mary also uses metaphor to represent the psychological or spiritual progress described by the Psalmist as a literal journey: she almost 'fell' and with 'straying steps' had almost wandered from the 'right' to the 'crooked'. (Placing 'fell' at the line end and enjambing the line also matches the visual arrangement of the poem on the page to its content, as the reader's eye 'falls' from one line to the next.) Similarly, in her Psalm 130, Mary develops the psychological implications of the opening figure ('Out of the deep have I called unto thee O Lord'), clarifying that the perhaps literal 'deep' of the original (in many Psalms, the Psalmist is in danger of falling into snares and pits) is actually a figurative 'depth of grief':

> From depth of grief
>> Where drowned I lie,
> Lord, for relief
>> To thee I cry:
> My earnest, vehement, crying, praying,
> Grant quick, attentive hearing, weighing.

Here again, Mary's line breaks intensify the impression of the Psalmist's fervent desire for relief, as does the breathless asyndetic (without conjunctions) repetition of parallel adjectives and gerunds in the last two lines.

The Sidneys also inflect their Psalms with their own political and personal concerns, and at these moments their voices cut through the polyvocal harmony of these translations. Elements of Renaissance courts and courtiers, for instance, at times create a sense of courtly complaint or satire. Slander seems always to have been a danger at courts, and in Psalm 64 the Psalmist prays for deliverance from the swordlike tongues of his enemies; Mary adds non-biblical but very Elizabethan 'spies' to several additional Psalms (56, 71, 92). In Psalm 33 the biblical tabernacle is converted into a royal-sounding 'pavilion', and in Psalm 86, the Psalmist becomes God's 'client', whose prayers to him are described as 'careful suits', adopting the language of courtly politics. In Psalm 65, the Psalmist says to God that the blessed man will 'dwell in thy courts', but in Mary's version he is actually signed onto the court payroll:

> Oh, he of bliss is not deceivèd,
>> Whom chosen thou unto thee takest:
> And whom into thy court receivèd
>> Thou of thy check-roll number makest.

In Psalm 123, when Mary writes of 'a waiter's eye on a graceful master' and 'the look of waitress fixed on a lady', she has in mind not a restaurant but the hierarchical society of an Elizabethan court, where those below wait, attend, or pay court to their superiors.

Several of Mary's Psalms reflect not just Elizabethan society but the special experience of a woman. Part of the power in her description of the womb in Psalm 139 may be due to the fact that she is one of the few Renaissance Psalm translators to have actually given birth. Similarly, Mary's experience with childbirth lends visceral detail to the curses of Psalm 58:

> So make them melt as the dishousèd snail
> Or as the embryo, whose vital band
>> Breaks ere it holds, and formless eyes do fail
> To see the sun, though brought to lightful land.

But Mary emphasizes women's experience not only in references to birth. Several critics have noticed that Mary's Psalm 68 gives women a more active role than the biblical original. The reference in Coverdale to those who 'have lain among the pots'—women in kitchens—becomes in Mary's version a 'virgin army' singing God's 'triumphant song', and the 'damsels playing with the timbrels' become 'battle maids'. In a less martial context, Mary elaborates the description of women in the epithalamion (marriage song) of Psalm 45. The Psalm describes how women derive honour from the king, but Mary (in her youth a lady-in-waiting to Queen Elizabeth) adds that the queen herself advances 'her maids of honour', suggesting that the queen's chamber is a place of power and nobility in its own right, apart from the world of men.

The Psalms: Form

The constraints of translation, especially translation of Scripture, which had divine authority, is undoubtedly one reason the Sidneys experimented more with schemes than tropes. It was the tropes, after all—the figures of thought, metaphors, images—that they derived from the biblical Psalms, and no translator could change these radically without passing into some broader genre like biblical 'meditation' or 'adaptation'. Schemes, on the other hand—figures of speech or verbal and visual patterns like alliteration, assonance, rhyme and metre, stanza form, enjambment and caesura, chiasmus, anaphora, polyptoton, and the rest of the rhetorician's handbook—were fair game, since they could be applied and manipulated without greatly altering the fundamental content. Furthermore, the schemes of the original Hebrew poetry (dependent upon the sounds and shapes of that language) were in any case unattainable, as noted above.

The Sidney Psalter is nothing if not various in its forms and schemes. As one critic put it, the Sidney Psalter is 'a School of English Versification',[19] and the elegantly penned title of one of the manuscripts announces that the Psalms it contains are 'translated into diverse and sundry kinds of verse, more rare and excellent, for the method and variety than ever yet hath been done in English'. The Psalter contains 150 Psalms, including the 22 sections of the long Psalm 119, and among these 172 poems the Sidneys repeat only one form (both stanza and metre) exactly. The Sidneys wrote in both iambic and trochaic metres. Trochaics were previously relatively uncommon in English verse, and to combine the two in one poem as the Sidneys did (in 48, for example) was rarer still. The line lengths of the Sidney *Psalms* stretch from tiny dimeters to broad hexameters. The metres and verse forms are imitated from multiple languages. From the English tradition, the Sidneys used rhyme royal (an invention of Chaucer, used in 51, 63), the common metre stanza of 'Sternhold and Hopkins' (19, though with feminine rhymes in odd lines), and both Spenserian and Sidneian sonnets (100 and

[19] Hallett Smith, 'English Metrical Psalms in the Sixteenth Century and Their Literary Significance', *Huntington Library Quarterly*, 9 (1946), 269.

150 respectively). Sonnets were an Italian import, of course, but the
Sidneys also borrowed *terza rima* (7; the metre was previously used
in English by Wyatt in his Penitential Psalms) and *ottava rima* (78)
from that country. From classical verse, Mary appropriated quantita-
tive elegiacs (123), hexameters (122), anacreontics (127), and sap-
phics (125), and 'phaelacian hendecasyllables' (121);[20] she also
imitated the alphabetical forms of the Hebrew Psalms (111 and also
119, the latter according to the first letter of each section). A number
of stanza forms were borrowed or adapted from the Marot–Beza
Psalter (e.g. 1, 14, 32, 40), and Mary's Psalms borrow some stanza
forms that Philip invented for his secular poems in *Astrophil and
Stella*, *Certain Sonnets*, and the *Arcadia* (99, 142, 143, 146).[21] The
Sidneys also experimented with feminine rhyme and tail rhyme (141;
the latter was popular in France as *rime couée*), and Mary wrote one
Psalm in a pentameter version of leonine rhyme (140, where the last
word of one line rhymes with a word in the middle of the next). Many
of the Sidneys' stanza forms appear to be their own inventions, how-
ever, and this formal ingenuity shaped the subsequent poetry of
Herbert, Vaughan, and their imitators.

One of the most ingenious of Mary's formal arrangements is that
of her Psalm 55. It uses only three rhymes over the course of 72 lines
(a feat in English, which has fewer available rhymes than French or
Italian). Each stanza has twelve lines, with rhymes grouped in threes,
the arrangement of each triplet being reversed in the next triplet,
forming what critics have described as a kind of palindrome.[22] Thus
abc is followed by *cba*, and *acb* by *bca*. Each group of six is linked
to the next by the repetition of the last rhyme and the first, thus *a*
both ends the first sestet and begins the second. Furthermore, each
twelve-line stanza begins and ends with the same rhyme, and the
first–last rhymes of the six stanzas form another larger-scale palin-
drome: *abc/cba*. Finally, the rhyme scheme of the first six sestets is
repeated in the second six but in reverse order: another palindrome
(e.g. the first and last sestets of the poem are *abc/cba*, the second and

[20] See Derek Attridge, *Well-Weighed Syllables: Elizabethan Verse in Classical Metres*
(London: Cambridge University Press, 1974).

[21] Gavin Alexander, *Writing After Sidney: The Literary Response to Sir Philip Sidney
1586–1640* (Oxford and New York: Oxford University Press, 2006), 115–16.

[22] Gary Waller, *Mary Sidney, Countess of Pembroke: A Critical Study of Her Writings
and Literary Milieu* (Salzburg: University of Salzburg Press, 1979), 198; Alexander,
Writing After Sidney, 114–18.

fifth *acb/bca*). This level of formal intricacy is dizzying, more so even than Philip's famous double-sestina, 'Ye goatherd gods'. Still more remarkable is that the poem shows no signs of strained syntax or awkward diction in accommodating its tight formal constraints. In fact, Mary's language in this poem is full of rhetorical figures that match the palindromic rhymes, especially chiasmus (repeating words in reverse order), a favourite of hers. In line 12, for instance—'I fear, nay, shake, nay, quiv'ring quake with fear'—the pattern 'fear . . . shake' is reversed in 'quake . . . fear' (the inner words are linked by rhyme). Other examples occur in line 30, with the chiasmus, 'only he, he only', in line 15, with 'Stay . . . I' and 'I . . . stay', and in line 40, 'Whom unto me, me unto whom'.

The formal variety of the Sidney *Psalms* is not incidental 'showing off'. An ingenious formal design could certainly be delightful in itself, worthy of admiration like any feat of great skill. Yet in the best poems form reflects, contributes to, and is interwoven with content. In Psalm 55, for instance, the basic unit of the rhyme scheme is the number 3, the number of the Trinity, conventionally expressed as a palindrome ('three in one and one in three'). Furthermore, the total number of lines of the poem is 72, which according to cabbalistic mystical tradition is the number of letters in the name of God. In its arrangement on the page (in the indentation of the most authoritative manuscripts) each stanza resembles a pair of wings, visually embodying the desire expressed in verse 6, 'O that I had wings like a dove, for then I would fly away and be at rest' (BCP). Mary's use of stanza shape seems to have influenced George Herbert, in his most famous shape-poem, 'Easter-Wings'. Other examples of significant form in the Sidney *Psalms* include Psalm 51, in rhyme royal, an appropriate choice for the Psalm most closely associated with King David (the headnote links it to his remorse over Bathsheba and Uriah), and Psalm 140, with its complex leonine rhyme, a hidden 'net' of rhymes mirroring the 'net of foul mishap' laid for the Psalmist. The alphabetical organization of Psalm 119 (in the Hebrew as well as Mary's English version) reflected the universality of its subject, the Torah, or the Law of God, since the alphabet was believed to symbolize the sum of all knowledge. *Ottava rima* was associated with narrative verse in Italian (as well as English translations of Italian like Sir John Harington's *Orlando furioso*), and Mary uses it, not coincidentally, for Psalm 78, one of the most extended narratives in the Psalter.

Each of the Sidney Psalms merits close and repeated reading. Philip's Psalm 39, for instance, is written in seven stanzas of alternating iambic lines of pentameter and tetrameter, with a rhyme scheme of *aabbcc*. This stanza is not particularly intricate, but Philip conveys a remarkable impression of natural, direct speech by breaking up the syntax, especially by using punctuation (or its lack) to create pauses in the middle of lines, and to enjamb the line-ends:

> Thus did I think, 'I well will mark my way,
> Lest by my tongue I hap to stray.
> I muzzle will my mouth, while in the sight
> I do abide of wicked wight.'
> And so I nothing said, I muet stood,
> I silence kept, ev'n in the good.

Reading Philip's lines aloud will show how he works against the formal regularity of the stanza. The reader is thrust directly into the Psalmist's thought process and his struggle to remain silent under duress. The wordplay on 'well' and 'will' slows down the line, as the tongue (mentioned in the next line) and lips wrap themselves around the difficult consonants (a difficulty reflected in the inability of many non-English speakers to master the *w* and *l* sounds). The alliteration of *m*s ('muzzle', 'mouth', 'muet') and more *w*s ('wicked wight'), all requiring closed or nearly closed lips, imitates the mumbling or murmuring of the Psalmist in his forced silence, as do the four terse clauses, separated by silent pauses, of the last two lines. In the next stanza, as passion forces the Psalmist to speak, the alliteration again matches the poem's sense in the aspirates of 'my heart was hot in me' and the explosive fricatives of 'The fire took fire and forcibly outbrake'. Philip creates further intensity by means of rhetorical questions and repetition:

> Lo, thou a span's length, mad'st my living line.
> A span? Nay, nothing in thine eyne.
> What do we seek? The greatest state I see,
> At best is merely vanity.

> 'They are but shades, not true things where we live:
> Vain shades, and vain, in vain to grieve . . .'

The vanity—etymologically, 'emptiness'—is itself represented by the emptying out of significance over the multiple repetitions of 'vain', and the repetition also conveys the Psalmist's mood of disgust and contempt for the world, just as the assonance of the repeated 'aye' sounds in the final couplet sound like grieving sighs.

Such verbal repetition is a common device in the Sidney *Psalms*. Psalm 52's repetitions, heightened by its short lines, evokes a sense of angry urgency:

> Tyrant, why swell'st thou thus,
>   Of mischief vaunting?
> Since help from God to us,
>   Is never wanting?
>
> Lewd lies thy tongue contrives,
>   Loud lies it soundeth:
> Sharper than sharpest knives
>   With lies it woundeth.

The close sound of 'lewd' and 'loud' (spelled 'lowd' in the manuscript) adds to the aural effect, with thick alliteration on the *l*s of these words and the triply repeated 'lies'. The near-repetition of 'sharper' and 'sharpest' is another favourite device for the Sidneys, which Renaissance rhetoricians called polyptoton (repeating different forms of the words from the same root). The similarity of 'Lewd lies' and 'Loud lies' at the beginning of consecutive lines is almost anaphora, another rhetorical figure favoured in the Sidney *Psalms*, and one characteristic of Hebrew poetry, which uses many forms of repetition. A more perfect example of anaphora is in the opening stanza of Mary's Psalm 136:

> Oh, praise the Lord where goodness dwells,
>   For his kindness lasteth ever:
> Oh, praise the God all gods excels,
>   For his bounty endeth never.

The first and third and the second and fourth lines are linked by anaphora, and the second and third lines are repeated as double refrains throughout the rest of the Psalm. The Sidney Psalter truly is a 'School of English Versification', but one of the first lessons taught at this school is that the form of a poem both reflects and shapes its content.

Modern Reception

The Sidney Psalter was acknowledged in its own time as one of the masterpieces of English Renaissance poetry. Edmund Spenser,

John Donne, George Herbert, John Milton, and a host of lesser writers both praised it in print and also put their praise into practice by imitating the Sidney *Psalms* and borrowing from them in their own poems. Why then are these poems not better known today? Primarily, the answer is that the *Psalms* of Philip and Mary Sidney have resisted easy categorization according to conventional modern standards of literary appreciation. Even as the Sidney *Psalms* were rediscovered and reprinted in the latter part of the twentieth century, they have still been undervalued by the wider public. First, poems are expected to be original, and the Sidney *Psalms* are translations. Secondly, a secular age (as the late twentieth century was assumed to be) favours secular poetry, and the Sidney *Psalms* are not only religious but specifically biblical. Thirdly, a print culture is puzzled by a work that was never printed during the authors' lifetimes but yet was widely published. Finally, post-Romantic interest in the single, authoritative writer is troubled by a work not only written by two authors, but in which many poems are jointly authored (written by Philip, revised by Mary). That one of the authors, and the dominant one, was a woman, was perhaps for some a further obstacle.

The twenty-first century may bring to the Sidney Psalter the readers it deserves. Over many decades our notions of 'originality' have been productively challenged by masterful, and 'original', translations like Ezra Pound's from Chinese (helped by Ernest Fennelosa) and Provençal, Ted Hughes's *Tales from Ovid*, and Seamus Heaney's *Beowulf*, among others. Even accolades for the great, and less liberal, translations of Homer and Virgil by Richmond Lattimore, Robert Fitzgerald, Allen Mandelbaum, and Robert Fagles are directed as much toward the translators as the 'original' authors. For the most part, we English-speakers read non-English literature in translation. We should therefore recognize both the critical skill and creative power necessary to make a translation readable as an artistic work in its own right, as opposed to a lifeless crib of an ultimately unattainable 'original'. Renaissance readers already recognized this, and translations were among the most celebrated literary masterpieces of the age: the translations from Petrarch by Sir Thomas Wyatt and the Earl of Surrey, Thomas Norton's translation of Plutarch's Lives, Ovid's *Metamorphoses* as 'Englished' by Arthur Golding (one of Shakespeare's favourite sources) or George Sandys, and George Chapman's translations of the *Iliad* and *Odyssey* (so loved by John Keats). This was also the great age of English Bible translation, though we have now lived so long with the Bible in English (especially the 1611 Authorized or King James Version) that we sometimes forget it is not an 'original' work in our usual sense. Even Shakespeare, our model for authorial genius, was hardly an original writer, at least in the sense of spinning plotlines out of his own head. He appropriated—a kind of translation—from other writers: Arthur Brooke's *Romeus and Juliet*, Plutarch's Lives of Mark Antony and Julius Caesar, Thomas More's *History of King Richard III*, pre-existing plays of *Hamlet* and *King Leir*, and Italian novellas about moneylending Jews and Venetian Moors.

In the Renaissance it was not considered important to be 'original' in the sense of being without precedent; true originality involved making materials one's own by imitating, adapting, paraphrasing, and reinterpreting. In 'Tradition and the Individual Talent' (1919), T. S. Eliot argued that this process is fundamental to literature. Similarly, when Pound urged modern poets to 'make it new', the 'it' he referred to was the literary tradition inherited from the past, which explains why translation had so large a place in Pound's poetry. In this sense, the *Psalms* of Philip and Mary Sidney are among the greatest translations in Renaissance poetry, 'unoriginal' in that the 'original' material is biblical, but highly 'original' in the way they artfully turn the biblical Psalms into uniquely English poems.

Our attitudes to sacred versus secular literature have also undergone some changes recently. Most obviously, it is hard to claim any longer that we live in a post-religious world. For good or ill, religion is one of the shaping forces in the twenty-first-century world; leaders have returned to the language of the medieval crusades in describing international conflicts between Christians and Muslims, or Muslims and Jews, and in countries like Iraq, Israel, Pakistan, China, and the United States, religion is at the forefront of national political and social debates. This may be one reason that religious literature of the Renaissance is being restored to a more canonical position than it held for many years. The Holy Sonnets, divine poems, and even religious polemics of John Donne are now being read alongside his secular songs and sonnets, Renaissance Catholic poets have gained new readers, and studies have been published on Robert Southwell, Donne, Herbert, Milton, and even Shakespeare as religious writers, or writers interested in religious issues.

If joint or collaborative authorship was once difficult to reconcile with notions of individual creative genius, today's readers are more flexible. Film and television, not to mention the products of the internet, regularly require complex creative teamwork, and hypertext and videogames allow the reader or viewer to participate in the narrative process. Furthermore, critical understanding of Renaissance literary production has become more sophisticated, recognizing, for instance, the extent to which even a singular 'genius' like Shakespeare routinely collaborated in the writing of plays, both early and late in his career. Studies of early modern manuscript culture have also pointed out that popular poems were often transformed as they were passed and copied from one hand or commonplace book to another. In some cases, the 'original' authorial intention can be recovered, but in others not, and in many cases the authors themselves remain anonymous. The internet has reintroduced modern readers to additional aspects of manuscript culture, including the ways in which relatively less stable texts may be altered in the process of circulation and transmission, and the means by which a wide reputation and readership may be gained without the use of printed books.

Finally, feminist criticism, a general openness to previously non-canonical writers, and the increasing number of women active in scholarship, publishing, and the creative arts have led to a major reconsideration of Renaissance women writers. Sir Philip Sidney always had a place among the major English Renaissance poets, one of those whom C. S. Lewis labelled 'Golden', but Mary Sidney Herbert, Countess of Pembroke, is now being restored to the high literary position she had hitherto among her contemporaries, male and female. Barnabe Barnes described her as one 'in whom even Phoebus is most flourishing', while for Michael Drayton she was 'learning's famous Queen' and one who wears the poet's 'Laurel crown'. Lady Mary Wroth wrote Mary into her romance *Urania* as the 'Queen of Naples' and described her as 'perfect in Poetry, and all other Princely virtues as any woman that ever lived'.[23]

The *Psalms* of Philip and Mary Sidney have found new readers in recent decades, but they deserve more still. As in the sixteenth and

[23] C. S. Lewis, *English Literature in the Sixteenth Century* (Oxford: Oxford University Press, 1954); Barnabe Barnes, 'To the Most Vertuous Learned and bewtifull Lady Marie Countesse of Penbrooke', Michael Drayton, 'The sixth Eglog', in *Idea*, Lady Mary Wroth, *Urania*, all quoted in Pembroke, *Works*, i.17–18, 30.

seventeenth centuries, this Psalter will appeal to those who love the Psalms and who value their devotional intensity, but they will also appeal to anyone who appreciates poetry. The poems are a delight to the eye and ear but to the mind as well. As Donne remarked so accurately, they are truly 'the highest matter in the noblest form'.

NOTE ON THE TEXT

Eighteen manuscripts of the Sidney *Psalms* survive, one rediscovered as recently as 2000. The most important of these are known to textual scholars as *B*, *A*, and *J*. *B* (Bodleian, MS Rawlinson poet. 25) is a seventeenth-century copy by Samuel Woodford of Mary Sidney Herbert, Countess of Pembroke's own autograph copy, which he rescued from his brother, who was using it to hold ground coffee. The autograph disappeared, but Woodford's copy is important for showing Mary's practice of revision of her own Psalms as well as her brother's. Several of Philip Sidney's Psalms, for instance, ended with partial stanzas, which Mary normalized (the final stanza of Philip's original Psalm 1 is only four lines long; in Mary's revision, printed here, the stanza is complete). The texts of Psalms vary among the surviving manuscripts. Some of these (those in the *B* manuscript especially) are evidently early drafts which Mary later revised or rewrote. In two manuscripts, Mary's quantitative versions of Psalms 120–7 are replaced by more conventional accentual-syllabic versions, but the weakness of these particular variants suggests that they may not be authorial.[1] The Penshurst manuscript (*A*), still in the possession of the Sidney family, is the copy-text for the present edition, since it is the earliest and most authoritative manuscript. It is a late-sixteenth-century copy of Mary's autograph, commissioned by her from the celebrated scribe, writing master, and poet John Davies of Hereford. The first few leaves of this manuscript have disappeared, however, so for Psalms 1 to 3, as well as the dedication poems, this edition turns to the Tixall manuscript (*J*) as copy-text. Tixall is complete, and was copied from Penshurst (*A*) sometime before the early seventeenth century. One or other of these manuscripts is likely to have been prepared for presentation to Queen Elizabeth at a planned visit to Wilton in 1599. The queen ultimately did not make the trip.

[1] See *The Collected Works of Mary Sidney Herbert, Countess of Pembroke*, ed. Margaret P. Hannay, Noel J. Kinnamon, and Michael G. Brennan, 2 vols. (Oxford: Clarendon Press, 1998), ii. 355–6.

Editorial Procedures

The text has been modernized wherever possible, though we have tried to preserve distinctive features of the originals, including the Latin incipits (the opening phrase of the Vulgate translation) as they appear in some manuscripts. Mary's dedicatory poems appear as they do in Tixall, but we have added Donne's poem on the Sidney *Psalms*, thinking that it deserves such a place and may even have been intended for such by its author. To aid the reader, individual words are glossed on the page and fuller explanatory notes, signalled by a degree sign, can be found at the back of the book, together with more general comments on the content and structure of individual Psalms. In preparing the glosses, and in modernizing the text, the pioneering edition of J. C. A. Rathmell (New York: New York University Press, 1963) has been of great help. The following editorial principles have guided us.

1. We normally adopt modern British spelling for words included in standard dictionaries, and reference will be made, as required, to *The Oxford Dictionary for Writers and Editors* (1984 edn.). Otherwise, we emend the text when there is support in the manuscript tradition or in the sources. We similarly modernize quotations from other works of the period (except for the titles of Edmund Spenser's works), as well as titles except for those quoted in the titles of modern books and articles.

2. We retain common words or forms for which there is no exact modern English equivalent, but we standardize the spelling according to the *Oxford English Dictionary*. In cases where both older and modern forms occur, however, we normally adopt the modern form throughout (except when an older form is required by the rhyme). Special cases include 'sware[st]' for 'swore[st]' (as in 89. 121–2, 110. 18, etc.) and 'bare' for 'bore' (as in 35. 29, 131. 2, etc.); not only do the modern forms not appear at all in MS *A*, but the older forms are sometimes used as rhyme words. An example of a different sort is 'murder' *v.* 'murther', both of which occur in *A*: we adopt the former, except when the latter is required for rhyme, as in 44. 81. We retain common early verb forms throughout: 'waiteth' (1. 3), 'shalt' (2. 21), 'hast' (3. 27), 'art' (7. 1), 'dost' (7. 28), 'placest' (8. 21), 'bend'st' (i.e. bendest, 7. 34), etc.

3. We normally retain the apostrophe to indicate elision of vowels and syllables for the sake of the metre; we insert an apostrophe only in the frequently occurring cases of 'ev'n' for 'even', often on the authority of MS *J*, where the contracted form appears more frequently than in *A*, from which *J* was copied. In a few other isolated cases, we silently emend *A* from *J*, as in the substitution of 'heath'n' in the latter for 'heathen' in the former (9. 64, 33. 34), 'layèd' for 'laid' (21. 26), etc. When a syllable is silent in modern English, however, we expand the spelling and delete the apostrophe.

4. We indicate pronunciation of final inflectional syllables in some past-tense verbs and past participles with a grave accent, as in 'placèd', etc. The monosyllabic and disyllabic pronunciation of the preterite and participial forms of 'bless' are regularly indicated in *A* by the still current alternative spellings 'blest' and 'blessed' (as in the single line 37. 55). 'Prayer' is always disyllabic. At one point we print 'sayeth' (10. 23) for the disyllabic pronunciation of a form that is otherwise monosyllabic and thus spelled 'saith' (as in 10. 45). One frequently occurring instance is 'evil', which Philip Sidney treats as normally monosyllabic in his Psalms 1–43; the word is also monosyllabic in 49. 7 and 54. 15. Other instances of unusual pronunciations, not indicated in the text, include the following: monosyllabic ('layeth' 10. 42; 'never' 73. 41); disyllabic ('enemies' 9. 46, 38. 59; 'evilly' 18. 44; 'heavenly' 34. 57; 'flatterers' 36. 7; 'muet' for 'mute' 39. 5; 'honouring' 45. 34; 'covenant' 50. 42, 81. 27; 'uttering' 55. 5; 'atheists' 55. 53; 'ravening' 79. 12; 'flour' 81. 45; 'many a' 89. 125; 'seventy' 90. 37; 'hour' 90. 43; 'quivering' 104. 100; 'following' 109. 30; 'caprioled', 'capriole' 114. 9, 10, 15, 16; 'opening' 119R. 7; 'vehement' 130. 5); trisyllabic ('patient' 7. 31; 'valiant', 'motion' 76. 9, 15; 'millions' 78. 155; 'periods' 89. 8; 'continual' 119B. 20); tetrasyllabic ('devotion', 'motion', 'protection', 'affection' 76. 13, 15, 26, 28). In cases where varied pronunciations are possible even in modern English, we allow the reader to make the distinction: e.g. 'fire[s]' (12. 21, monosyllabic; 66. 37, disyllabic); 'devour' (27. 10, disyllabic; 14. 15, trisyllabic). Many names are special cases, sometimes varying according to metrical requirements: 'Israel' (14. 24, disyllabic; 22. 10, 50. 18, trisyllabic); 'Abraham' (47. 18, 105. 11, disyllabic; 105. 17, trisyllabic), 'Gilead' (60. 25, disyllabic), 'Zoan' (78. 40, disyllabic), 'Pharaoh' (89. 27, trisyllabic), 'Samuel' (99. 19, disyllabic); 'Canaan' (106. 95, trisyllabic), 'Canaanean' (105. 22, tetrasyllabic), 'Ephraim' (108. 26, trisyllabic). Occasionally,

the stress occurs on a syllable where some modern readers would not expect it: e.g. 'recòrd' as a noun (49. 24, 145. 5); 'edìcts' (119E. 2; 119N. 4, 22, etc.). In one case ('persever', 44. 88), we have altered normal modern spelling in order to guide the reader to preserve the rhyme.

5. We standardize the use of 'O' and 'oh': 'O' in vocative constructions; 'oh' in exclamations.

6. We modernize punctuation and occasionally emend it to clarify the sense of a passage. We add quotation marks to indicate direct discourse.

7. We adopt modern conventions for capitalization and the use of italics. We retain upper case for personifications.

8. Because we modernize the text, we list only verbal and selected punctuation emendations (where meaning is affected).

9. We use the title *Psalms* to distinguish the full collection of the Sidneys' metaphrases, or metrical Psalm paraphrases, from the biblical Psalms. Following convention we use a full stop for citing lines of metrical Psalms (e.g. Psalm 23. 2) and a colon for citing biblical verses (e.g. Psalm 139. 4). We use Roman numerals for some variant Psalms, as in the original.

10. In glossing, we use a comma between synonyms, and a semi-colon between words that represent varying uses of the same word (or words with similar spelling) in different senses.

11. Indentation requires special attention. In *A*, large gilded initial capitals often extend into the margin, thus obscuring the alignment of certain lines. We restore the alignment in Mary's psalms where the indentation is usually (though not invariably) functional, with rhyming lines aligned, even when they vary in length. The indentation of Philip's paraphrases is less systematic (even in MS *B*).

SELECT BIBLIOGRAPHY

Editions

The Collected Works of Mary Sidney Herbert, Countess of Pembroke, ed. Margaret P. Hannay, Noel J. Kinnamon, and Michael G. Brennan, 2 vols. (Oxford: Clarendon Press, 1998).

The Poems of Sir Philip Sidney, ed. William A. Ringler, Jr. (Oxford: Clarendon Press, 1962).

The Psalms of Sir Philip Sidney and the Countess of Pembroke, ed. J. C. A. Rathmell (Garden City, NJ: Anchor Books, 1963).

Sidney, Sir Philip, *A Defence of Poetry*, in *Miscellaneous Prose of Sir Philip Sidney*, ed. Katherine Duncan-Jones and Jan van Dorsten (Oxford: Clarendon Press, 1973).

Biography

Brennan, Michael G., and Kinnamon, Noel J., *A Sidney Chronology 1554–1654* (Basingstoke: Palgrave Macmillan, 2003).

Duncan-Jones, Katherine, *Sir Philip Sidney: Courtier Poet* (New Haven and London: Yale University Press, 1991).

Hannay, Margaret P., *Philip's Phoenix: Mary Sidney, Countess of Pembroke* (New York and Oxford: Oxford University Press, 1990).

Stewart, Alan, *Philip Sidney: A Double Life* (London: Chatto & Windus, 2000).

Criticism

Alexander, Gavin, *Writing After Sidney: The Literary Response to Sir Philip Sidney 1586–1640* (Oxford and New York: Oxford University Press, 2006).

Bloch, Chana, *Spelling the Word: George Herbert and the Bible* (Berkeley, Los Angeles, and London: University of California Press, 1985).

Brennan, Michael G., 'The Date of the Countess of Pembroke's Translation of the Psalms', *Review of English Studies*, 33 (1982), 434–6.

Demers, Patricia, '"Warpe" and "Webb" in the Sidney Psalms: The "Coupled Worke" of the Countess of Pembroke and Sir Philip Sidney', in Marjorie Stone and Judith Thompson (eds.), *Literary Couplings: Writing Couples, Collaborators, and the Construction of Authorship*. (Madison: University of Wisconsin Press, 2006), 41–58.

Fisken, Beth Wynne, '"The Art of Sacred Parody" in Mary Sidney's Psalmes', *Tulsa Studies in Women's Literature*, 8 (1989), 223–39.

Freer, Coburn, *Music for a King: George Herbert's Style and the Metrical Psalms* (Baltimore and London: Johns Hopkins University Press, 1972).

Greene, Roland, 'Sir Philip Sidney's Psalms, the Sixteenth-Century Psalter, and the Nature of Lyric', *Studies in English Literature*, 30 (1990), 19–40.

Hamlin, Hannibal, '"The Highest Matter in the Noblest Form": The Influence of the Sidney Psalms', *Sidney Journal*, 23 (2005), 133–57.

——*Psalm Culture and Early Modern English Literature* (Cambridge: Cambridge University Press, 2004).

Hannay, Margaret P., 'The Countess of Pembroke's Agency in Print and Scribal Culture', in George Justice and Nathan Tinker (eds.), *Women's Writing and the Circulation of Ideas: Manuscript Publication in England, 1550–1800* (Cambridge: Cambridge University Press, 2002), 17–49.

—— '"House-confined Maids": The Presentation of Woman's Role in the *Psalmes* of the Countess of Pembroke', *English Literary Renaissance*, 24 (1994), 44–71.

—— '"So may I with the Psalmist truly say": Early Modern Englishwomen's Psalm Discourse', in Barbara Smith and Ursula Appelt (eds.), *Write or Be Written: Early Modern Women Poets and Cultural Constraints* (Aldershot: Ashgate, 2001), 105–34.

Kinnamon, Noel J., 'The Sidney Psalms: The Penshurst and Tixall Manuscripts', *English Manuscript Studies*, 2 (1990), 139–61.

Prescott, Anne Lake, 'King David as "Right Poet": Sidney and the Psalmist', *English Literary Renaissance*, 19 (1989), 131–51.

Rienstra, Debra, and Kinnamon, Noel J., 'Circulating the Sidney-Pembroke Psalter', in George Justice and Nathan Tinker (eds.), *Women's Writing and the Circulation of Ideas: Manuscript Publication in England, 1550–1800* (Cambridge: Cambridge University Press, 2002), 50–72.

Smith, Hallett, 'English Metrical Psalms in the Sixteenth Century and Their Literary Significance', *Huntington Library Quarterly*, 9 (1946), 249–71.

Steinberg, Theodore, 'The Sidneys and the Psalms', *Studies in Philology*, 92 (1995), 1–17.

Todd, Richard, '"So well atyr'd abroad": A Background to the Sidney-Pembroke Psalter and its Implications for the Seventeenth-Century Religious Lyric', *Texas Studies in Literature and Language*, 29 (1987), 74–93.

Waller, Gary, *Mary Sidney, Countess of Pembroke: A Critical Study of Her Writings and Literary Milieu* (Salzburg: University of Salzburg Press, 1979).

Woods, Susanne, *Natural Emphasis: English Versification from Chaucer to Dryden* (San Marino, Calif.: The Huntington Library, 1984).

Zim, Rivkah, *English Metrical Psalms: Poetry as Praise and Prayer, 1535–1601* (Cambridge: Cambridge University Press, 1987).

Further Reading in Oxford World's Classics

The Bible: Authorized King James Version, ed. Robert Carroll and Stephen Prickett.

Sidney, Philip, *The Countess of Pembroke's Arcadia (The Old Arcadia)*, ed. Katherine Duncan-Jones.

——*The Major Works*, ed. Katherine Duncan-Jones.

A CHRONOLOGY OF THE SIDNEYS

1551 (29 Mar.) Henry Sidney marries Mary, daughter of John Dudley, Earl of Warwick. Major family dates are annotated into the calendar of a mid-fifteenth-century psalter, known as the 'Sidney Psalter' (now at Trinity College, Cambridge).

(11 Oct.) Henry Sidney is knighted and John Dudley is created Duke of Northumberland.

1552 (25 Apr.) King Edward VI grants Penshurst Place, Kent, to Sir Henry's father, William Sidney (d. 1554).

1553 Accession of Queen Mary.

1554 (30 Nov.) Birth of Philip Sidney, with Philip of Spain as godfather.

1556 (?) Birth of Margaret (Mary) Sidney (d. 1558), with Queen Mary as godmother.

1558 (17 Nov.) Accession of Queen Elizabeth.

1559 The Book of Common Prayer (first Elizabethan edition).

1560 The Bible and Holy Scriptures (Geneva Bible).

1560 Sir Henry Sidney, Lord President of the Council of Wales (to 1586).

1560 (? Oct.) Birth of Elizabeth Sidney (d. 1566), with Queen Elizabeth as godmother.

1561 (27 Oct.) Birth of Mary Sidney at Tickenhall near Bewdley, Worcestershire.

1562 *Pseaumes de David* (Marot–Beza Psalter) and *The Whole Book of Psalms* (Sternhold and Hopkins).

(late Oct.) Lady Mary Dudley Sidney catches smallpox while nursing the queen.

1563 (19 Nov.) Birth of Robert Sidney (d. 1626), with his uncle, Robert Dudley, as godfather.

1564 (17 Oct.) Philip enters Shrewsbury School with lifelong friend, Fulke Greville.

(?) Birth of Ambrosia Sidney (d. 1575).

1565 Sir Henry Sidney, Lord Deputy of Ireland (to 1571).

1567 *The Whole Psalter* (translated by Matthew Parker).

1567/8–71 Philip Sidney attends Oxford University and enrols at Gray's Inn on 2 February 1568.

1568 The Holy Bible (Bishops' Bible).

1569 (25 Mar.) Birth of Thomas Sidney (d. 1595).

1571 *The Psalms of David and others* (translated by Arthur Golding, with John Calvin's *Commentaries*).

1572 (May) Sir Henry Sidney declines a barony due to its related expenses.

(25 May) Queen Elizabeth grants Philip Sidney a licence to travel for two years on the Continent.

(24/25 Aug.) Philip Sidney present at Paris during the St Bartholomew's Day Massacre and escapes to Germany in September.

1573–4 Philip Sidney at Frankfurt, Vienna, Strasbourg, Bratislava, Venice, and Padua and then begins his journey homewards in August 1574 but does not arrive back in England until June 1575.

1575 Sir Henry Sidney, Lord Deputy of Ireland (to 1578).

(22 Feb.) Death of Ambrosia Sidney at Ludlow. Soon afterwards Queen Elizabeth invites Mary Sidney to court and she attends in July the entertainments for the queen held by her uncle, Robert Dudley, Earl of Leicester, at his Kenilworth estate.

1577 (Feb–June) Philip Sidney's embassy to Germany and the court of Emperor Rudolph II.

(21 Apr.) Mary Sidney marries Henry Herbert (d. 1601), 2nd Earl of Pembroke, with her brother Robert present.

(June) Returning to England, Philip Sidney meets Philippe Duplessis-Mornay whom he had first known in Paris in 1572.

(autumn) Philip Sidney drafts his 'Discourse on Irish Affairs', defending the actions of his father.

1578 (27 Oct.) Mary Sidney's seventeenth birthday, marked by a gathering of the Sidneys, Dudleys, and Herberts at Wilton House.

1578/9 (May) Philip Sidney's *The Lady of May* written for one of two of Queen Elizabeth's visits to the Earl of Leicester's house at Wanstead.

1579 (10 Apr.) E.K.'s prefatory epistle to Edmund Spenser's *The Shepheardes Calender*, is dedicated to 'PS' (Philip Sidney).

(autumn) Philip Sidney probably begins the first drafts of his *Arcadia* and is also drafting 'A Letter to Queen Elizabeth'.

1580 *Testamenti Veteris Biblia Sacra* (Latin Bible, translated by Franciscus Junius and Immanuel Tremellius).

(8 Apr.) Birth of William Herbert (d. 1630), later 3rd Earl of Pembroke, with Queen Elizabeth as his godmother.

Philip Sidney probably begins his *Defence of Poetry*, although it is only completed several years later.

1581 (15 Oct.) Birth of Katherine Herbert (d. 1584), with Sir Henry Sidney as godfather.

1583 (9 Mar.) Birth of Anne Herbert (d. 1606?). Philip Sidney knighted, and marries Frances Walsingham.

1584 (16 Oct.) Birth of Philip Herbert (d. 1650), later 4th Earl of Pembroke, with Mary Dudley Sidney and her two sons, Philip and Robert, as godparents. Philip Herbert's sister, Katherine, had died several hours earlier.

(?) Philip Sidney drafts 'A Discourse in Defence of the Earl of Leicester'.

1585 (late Aug.) Philip Sidney makes an unsuccessful attempt to join Sir Francis Drake's expedition at Plymouth.

(early Nov.?) Birth of Philip Sidney's only child, Elizabeth (d. 1612).

(9 Nov.) Philip Sidney appointed governor of Flushing and Rammekins.

1586 (1 or 5 May) Death of Sir Henry Sidney at Worcester.

(9 Aug.) Death of Lady Mary Dudley Sidney at London.

(23 Sept.) Philip Sidney is wounded in the left thigh during a skirmish at Zutphen.

(7 Oct.) Robert Sidney is knighted by the Earl of Leicester for valour at Zutphen.

(17 Oct.) Death of Philip Sidney from wounds received at Zutphen.

1587 (16 Feb.) Funeral of Philip Sidney at St Paul's cathedral, London.

Collections of elegies are published by Oxford, Cambridge, and Leiden universities.

1587(?) (18 Oct.) Birth of Mary Sidney (d. 1653), later Lady Mary Wroth.

1588 (Aug.) Mary Sidney Herbert at Wilton during the Spanish Armada crisis.

(23 Aug.) William Ponsonby is granted publication rights for the *Arcadia* and a translation of Du Bartas by Philip Sidney.

(4 Sept.) Death of Robert Dudley, Earl of Leicester.

(Nov.) Mary Sidney Herbert and her children return to London for Accession Day.

1589 Robert Sidney, Governor of Flushing (to 1616).

1590 Publication of *The Countess of Pembroke's Arcadia* and Books I–III of Edmund Spenser's *The Faerie Queene*.

1591 Publication of *Astrophil and Stella*.

1592 Publication of A *Discourse of Life and Death* and *Antonius*.

1593 Publication of *The Countess of Pembroke's Arcadia*, with Books I–III from 1590 edition and IV–V from manuscript.

Publication of 'The Doleful Lay of Clorinda' in Spenser's *Astrophel* (printed with his *Colin Clouts Come Home Againe*).

1595 Publication of *A Defence of Poetry*.

1598 Publication of *The Countess of Pembroke's Arcadia*, with *A Defence of Poetry* and *Astrophil and Stella*.

1599 Proposed royal visit to Wilton House for which 'A Dialogue' and the Tixall manuscript of the Psalms may have been prepared.

1600 Transcription of Mary Sidney Herbert's translation of Petrarch's *Triumph of Death*.

1601 (19 Jan.) Death of Henry Herbert, 2nd Earl of Pembroke.

1602 Publication of Mary Sidney Herbert's 'A Dialogue' in Francis Davison's *Poetical Rhapsody*.

1603 (24 Mar.) Death of Queen Elizabeth and accession of King James.

(13 May.) Sir Robert Sidney created Baron Sidney of Penshurst and appointed Chamberlain to Queen Anne.

(Aug.–Nov.) King James visits Wilton House.

1604 (27 Sept.) Mary Sidney marries Sir Robert Wroth at Penshurst.

(4 Nov.) William Herbert marries Mary Talbot at Wilton.

(27 Dec.) Philip Herbert marries Susan de Vere at London.

1605 (4 May.) Robert Sidney is created Viscount Lisle, and Philip Herbert is created Earl of Montgomery.

1608–13 Hiatus in biographical records for Mary Sidney Herbert.

1611 The Holy Bible (Authorized or King James Version).

1614 (June) Mary Sidney Herbert arrives at Flushing before sailing on to Antwerp. She remains on the Continent for about two years.

1618 Simon van de Passe's engraving of Mary Sidney Herbert's portrait.

(2 Aug.) Robert Sidney created Earl of Leicester.

1619 (13 May) Robert Sidney and Mary Sidney Herbert attend the funeral of Queen Anne, wife of James I.

1621 (21 July) King James visits Mary Sidney Herbert's Houghton House.

(25 Sept.) Mary Sidney Herbert dies from smallpox at her house in Aldergate Street, London. After her funeral at St Paul's she is taken to Wiltshire and buried at Salisbury cathedral.

THE SIDNEY PSALTER

Upon the Translation of the Psalms by Sir Philip Sidney, and the Countess of Pembroke His Sister

JOHN DONNE

Eternal God (for whom who ever dare
Seek new expressions, do the circle square,
And thrust into strait corners of poor wit
Thee, who art cornerless and infinite),
I would but bless thy name, not name thee now;   5
And thy gifts are as infinite as thou:
Fix we our praises therefore on this one,
That, as thy blessed Spirit fell upon
These Psalms' first author in a cloven tongue
(For 'twas a double power by which he sung   10
The highest matter in the noblest form),
So thou hast cleft that spirit, to perform
That work again, and shed it, here, upon
Two, by their bloods, and by thy Spirit one;
A brother and a sister, made by thee   15
The organ, where thou art the harmony.
Two that make one John Baptist's holy voice,
And who that Psalm 'Now let the Isles rejoice'
Have both translated, and applied it too,
Both told us what, and taught us how to do.   20
They show us islanders our joy, our King,
They tell us *why*, and teach us *how* to sing.
Make all this All, three choirs, heaven, earth, and spheres;
The first, heaven, hath a song, but no man hears,
The spheres have music, but they have no tongue,   25
Their harmony is rather danced than sung;
But our third choir, to which the first gives ear
(For, angels learn by what the church does hear),
This choir hath all. The organist is he
Who hath tuned God and man, the organ we: 30
The songs are these, which heaven's high holy muse
Whispered to David, David to the Jews:

And David's successors, in holy zeal,
In forms of joy and art do re-reveal
To us so sweetly and sincerely too,   35
That I must not rejoice as I would do
When I behold that these Psalms are become
So well attired abroad, so ill at home,
So well in chambers, in thy church so ill,
As I can scarce call that reformed, until   40
This be reformed. Would a whole state present
A lesser gift than some one man hath sent?
And shall our church, unto our Spouse and King
More hoarse, more harsh than any other, sing?
For *that* we pray, we praise thy name for *this*,   45
Which, by this Moses and this Miriam, is
Already done; and as those Psalms we call
(Though some have other authors) David's all:
So though some have, some may some Psalms translate,
We thy Sidneian Psalms shall celebrate,   50
And, till we come th'extemporal song to sing
(Learned the first hour that we see the King,
Who hath translated those translators) may
These their sweet learned labours, all the way
Be as our tuning, that, when hence we part   55
We may fall in with them, and sing our part.

Even now that care

MARY SIDNEY HERBERT

Even now that care which on thy crown attends
And with thy happy greatness daily grows
Tells me, thrice sacred Queen, my muse offends,
And of respect to thee the line outgoes.
One instant will, or willing can, she lose,   5
I say not reading, but receiving rhymes,
On whom in chief dependeth to dispose
What Europe acts in these most active times?

Yet dare I so, as humbleness may dare,
Cherish some hope they shall acceptance find,   10
Not weighing less thy state, lighter thy care,
But knowing more thy grace, abler thy mind.
What heav'nly pow'rs thee highest throne assigned,
Assigned thee goodness suiting that degree:
And by thy strength thy burden so defined,   15
To others toil, is exercise to thee.

Cares though still great, cannot be greatest still,
Business must ebb, though leisure never flow:
Then these, the posts of Duty and Goodwill,
Shall press to offer what their senders owe,   20
Which once in two, now in one subject go,
The poorer left, the richer reft away,
Who better might (oh, 'might': ah, word of woe!)
Have giv'n for me what I for him defray.

How can I name whom sighing sighs extend,   25
And not unstop my tears' eternal spring?
But he did warp, I weaved this web to end;
The stuff not ours, our work no curious thing,
Wherein yet well we thought the Psalmist King,
Now English denizened, though Hebrew born,   30

Would to thy music undispleasèd sing,
Oft having worse, without repining worn;

And I the cloth in both our names present,
A livery robe to be bestowed by thee:
Small parcel of that undischargèd rent,   35
From which nor pains nor payments can us free.
And yet enough to cause our neighbours see
We will our best, though scanted in our will:
And those nigh fields where sown thy favours be
Unwealthy do, not else unworthy, till.   40

For in our work what bring we but thine own?
What English is, by many names is thine.
There humble laurels in thy shadows grown
To garland others, would themselves repine.
Thy breast the cabinet, thy seat the shrine,   45
Where muses hang their vowèd memories:
Where wit, where art, where all that is divine
Conceivèd best and best defended lies,

Which if men did not (as they do) confess
And wronging worlds would otherwise consent,   50
Yet here who minds so meet a patroness
For author's state or writing's argument?
A king should only to a queen be sent:
God's lovèd choice unto his chosen love,
Devotion to devotion's president,   55
What all applaud, to her whom none reprove.

And who sees aught, but sees how justly square
His haughty ditties to thy glorious days,
How well beseeming thee his triumphs are,
His hope, his zeal, his prayer, plaint, and praise,   60
Needless thy person to their height to raise,
Less need to bend them down to thy degree:
These holy garments each good soul assays,
Some sorting all, all sort to none but thee.

For ev'n thy rule is painted in his reign: 65
Both clear in right, both nigh by wrong oppressed;
And each at length (man crossing God in vain)
Possessed of place, and each in peace possessed.
Proud Philistines did interrupt his rest,
The foes of heav'n no less have been thy foes: 70
He with great conquest, thou with greater blest;
Thou sure to win, and he secure to lose.

Thus hand in hand with him thy glories walk:
But who can trace them where alone they go?
Of thee two hemispheres on honour talk,   75
And lands and seas thy trophies jointly show.
The very winds did on thy party blow,
And rocks in arms thy foe men eft defy:
But soft, my muse, thy pitch is earthly low;
Forbear this heav'n, where only eagles fly.   80

Kings on a queen enforced their states to lay;
Mainlands for empire waiting on an isle;
Men drawn by worth a woman to obey;
One moving all, herself unmoved the while:
Truth's restitution, vanity's exile,   85
Wealth sprung of want, war held without annoy,
Let subject be of some inspirèd style,
Till then the object of her subjects' joy.

Thy utmost can but offer to her sight
Her handmaid's task, which most her will endears;   90
And pray unto thy pains, life from that light
Which lively lightsome court and kingdom cheers,
What wish she may (far past her living peers
And rival still to Judah's faithful King,
In more than he and more triumphant years)   95
Sing what God doth and do what men may sing.

To the Angel Spirit of the Most Excellent
Sir Philip Sidney

MARY SIDNEY HERBERT

To thee, pure sprite, to thee alone's addressed
    This coupled work, by double interest thine:
    First raised by thy blest hand, and what is mine
Inspired by thee, thy secret power impressed.
      So dared my Muse with thine itself combine,   5
      As mortal stuff with that which is divine;
Thy light'ning beams give lustre to the rest,

That heaven's king may deign his own, transformed
    In substance no, but superficial 'tire
    By thee put on, to praise—not to aspire   10
To—those high tones so in themselves adorned,
      Which angels sing in their celestial choir,
      And all of tongues with soul and voice admire
These sacred hymns the kingly prophet formed.

Oh, had that soul which honour brought to rest   15
    Too soon not left and reft the world of all
    What man could show, which we perfection call,
This half-maimed piece had sorted with the best.
      Deep wounds enlarged, long festered in their gall,
      Fresh bleeding smart; not eye—but heart—tears fall.   20
Ah, memory, what needs this new arrest?

Yet here behold (oh, wert thou to behold!)
    This finished now, thy matchless Muse begun,
    The rest but pieced, as left by thee undone.
Pardon (O blest soul) presumption too, too bold,   25
      If love and zeal such error ill become:
      'Tis zealous love, love which hath never done,
Nor can enough in world of words unfold.

And sith it hath no further scope to go,
 Nor other purpose but to honour thee,   30
 Thee in thy works where all the Graces be,
As little streams with all their all do flow
 To their great sea, due tribute's grateful fee,
 So press my thoughts, my burdened thoughts in me,
To pay the debt of infinites I owe   35

To thy great worth, exceeding Nature's store;
 Wonder of men, sole born perfection's kind,
 Phoenix thou wert, so rare thy fairest mind
Heav'nly adorned, Earth justly might adore,
 Where truthful praise in highest glory shined: 40
 For there alone was praise to truth confined;
And where but there, to live for evermore?

Oh, when to this account, this cast-up sum,
 This reckoning made, this audit of my woe,
 I call my thoughts, whence so strange passions flow, 45
How works my heart, my senses stricken dumb,
 That would thee more than ever heart could show,
 And all too short! Who knew thee best doth know
There lives no wit that may thy praise become.

Truth I invoke (who scorn elsewhere to move   50
 Or here in aught my blood should partialize),
 Truth, sacred truth, thee sole to solemnize
Those precious rites well known best minds approve:
 And who but doth, hath wisdom's open eyes
 (Not owlly blind the fairest light still flies),   55
Confirm no less? At least 'tis sealed above

Where thou art fixed among thy fellow lights:
 My day put out, my life in darkness cast,
 Thy angel's soul with highest angels placed
There blessed sings, enjoying heav'n-delights,   60
 Thy Maker's praise: as far from earthy taste
 As here thy works so worthily embraced
By all of worth, where never Envy bites.

As goodly buildings to some glorious end
   Cut off by Fate, before the Graces had   65
      Each wondrous part in all their beauties clad,
Yet so much done, as art could not amend;
      So thy rare works—to which no wit can add,
      In all men's eyes which are not blindly mad,
Beyond compare, above all praise extend—   70

Immortal monuments of thy fair fame,
      Though not complete, nor in the reach of thought,
      How on that passing piece time would have wrought
Had heav'n so spared the life of life to frame
      The rest. But ah, such loss! Hath this world aught   75
      Can equal it, or which like grievance brought?
Yet there will live thy ever praisèd name,

To which these dearest off'rings of my heart,
      Dissolved to ink while pen's impressions move
      The bleeding veins of never dying love,   80
I render here: these wounding lines of smart,
      Sad characters indeed of simple love,
      Not art nor skill which abler wits do prove,
Of my full soul receive the meanest part,

Receive these hymns, these obsequies receive;   85
      If any mark of thy sweet sprite appear,
      Well are they borne, no title else shall bear.
I can no more: Dear Soul, I take my leave;
      Sorrow still strives, would mount the highest sphere
      Presuming so just cause might meet thee there: 90
Oh happy change, could I so take my leave!

                  By the sister of that
                  incomparable Sidney

THE PSALMS OF DAVID

Psalm 1
Beatus vir

He blessed is who neither loosely treads
   The straying steps as wicked counsel leads,
Ne for bad mates in way of sinning waiteth,°
   Nor yet himself with idle scorners seateth:
But on God's law his heart's delight doth bind°   5
   Which night and day he calls to marking mind.

He shall be like a freshly planted tree
   To which sweet springs of waters neighbours be,°
Whose branches fail not timely fruit to nourish,
   Nor withered leaf shall make it fail to flourish.   10
So all the things whereto that man doth bend
   Shall prosper still with well-succeeding end.

Not so the wicked, but like chaff with wind°
   Scattered, shall neither stay in judgement find
Nor with the just, be in their meetings placèd: 15
   For good men's ways by God are known and gracèd.
But who from justice sinfully do stray,
   The way they go, shall be their ruin's way.

Psalm 2
Quare fremuerunt?

What ails this heath'nish rage? What do these people mean
   To mutter murmurs vain?°
Why do these earthly kings and lords such meetings make
   And counsel jointly take

---

1 loosely] immorally   6 marking] attentive   14 stay] suspension of legal proceedings

Against the Lord of Lords, the Lord of everything   5
    And his anointed king?°
'Come let us break their bonds,' say they, and fondly say
    And cast their yokes away.°
But he shall them deride, who by the heav'ns is borne,
    He shall laugh them to scorn   10
And after, speak to them with breath of wrathful fire,°
    And vex them in his ire,
And say, 'O kings, yet have I set my king upon
    My holy hill Zion.'
'And I will' (saith his king) 'the Lord's decree display   15
    And say that he did say:
"Thou art my son indeed, this day begot by me:
    Ask, I will give to thee
The heath'n for thy child's-right, and will thy realm extend
    Far as world's furthest end.   20
With iron sceptre bruise thou shalt and piecemeal break
    These men like potsherds weak."'
Therefore, O kings, be wise, O rulers, rule your mind,
    That knowledge you may find.
Serve God, serve him with fear, rejoice in him, but so   25
    That joy with trembling go.
With loving homage kiss that only son he hath,
    Lest you inflame his wrath,
Whereof if but a spark once kindled be, you all
    From your way perish shall.   30
And then, they that in him their only trust do rest,
    Oh, they be rightly blest!

Psalm 3

Domine, quid?

Lord, how do they increase
    That hateful never cease
    To breed my grievous trouble!

---

7 fondly] foolishly   14 hill Zion] the location of God's house   22 potsherds]
fragments of pottery

How many ones there be
   That all against poor me 5
   Their numbrous strength redouble!

Ev'n multitudes be they
   That to my soul do say,
   'No help for you remaineth

'In God on whom you build.' ° 10
   Yet, Lord, thou art my shield
   In thee my glory reigneth.

The Lord lifts up my head,
   To him my voice I spread,
   From holy hill he heard me. 15

I laid me down and slept,
   While he me safely kept,
   And safe from sleep I reared me.

I will not be afraid,
   Though legions round be laid 20
   Which all against me gather;

I say no more but this,
   'Up, Lord, now time it is:
   Help me, my God and father.

'For thou with cruel blows 25
   On jawbones of my foes
   My causeless wrongs hast wroken;

'Thou those men's teeth which bite
   Venomed with godless spite,
   Hast in their malice broken.' 30

6 numbrous] plentiful   18 reared] raised   27 wroken] wreaked, avenged

Salvation doth belong
   Unto the Lord most strong:
   He is he that defendeth,

And on those blessed same
   Which bear his people's name,   35
   His blessing he extendeth.

Psalm 4

Cum invocarem

Hear me, oh, hear me, when I call,
   O God, God of my equity:
   Thou sett'st me free when I was thrall,
   Have mercy therefore still on me,
   And hearken how I pray to thee.   5

O men, whose fathers were but men,
   Till when will ye my honour high
   Stain with your blasphemies? Till when
   Such pleasure take in vanity,
   And only hunt where lies do lie?   10

Yet know this too, that God did take
   When he chose me, a godly one:
   Such one, I say, that when I make
   My crying plaints to him alone,
   He will give good ear to my moan.   15

Oh, tremble then with awful will:°
   Sin from all rule in you depose,
   Talk with your hearts and yet be still:
   And when your chamber you do close,
   Yourselves yet to yourselves disclose.   20

---

3 thrall] captive   14 plaints] complaints   15 give good ear] hear, heed

The sacrifices sacrify
    Of just desires, on justice stayed°
    Trust in that Lord that cannot lie.
    Indeed full many folks have said,
    'From whence shall come to us such aid?'   25

But, Lord, lift thou upon our sight
    The shining clearness of thy face:
    Where I have found more heart's delight,
    Than they whose store in harvest's space
    Of grain and wine fills storing place.   30

So I in peace and peaceful bliss
    Will lay me down and take my rest:
    For it is thou, Lord, thou it is,
    By pow'r of whose own only breast
    I dwell, laid up in safest nest.°   35

Psalm 5

Verba mea auribus

Ponder the words, O Lord, that I do say,
    Consider what I meditate in me:
Oh, hearken to my voice which calls on thee,
    My king, my God, for I to thee will pray.
So shall my voice climb to thine ears betime: 5
    For unto thee I will my prayer send
With earliest entry of the morning prime,°
    And will my waiting eyes to thee-ward bend.°

For thou art that same God, far from delight
    In that which of foul wickedness doth smell: 10
No, nor with thee the naughty ones shall dwell,
    Nor glorious fools stand in thy awful sight.
Thou hatest all whose works in ill are placed.

21 sacrify] sacrifice   29 space] time
Psalm 5 5 betime] early   12 awful] full of awe

And shalt root out the tongues to lying bent:
   For thou, the Lord, in endless hatred hast   15
The murd'rous man and so the fraudulent.

But I myself will to thy house address
   With passport of thy graces manifold:
And in thy fear, knees of my heart will fold°
   Towards the temple of thy holiness.   20
Thou, Lord, thou, Lord, the saver of thine own,
   Guide me, oh, in thy justice be my guide:
   And make thy ways to me more plainly known,
For all I need, that with such foes do bide.

For in their mouth not one clear word is spent,   25
   Mischief their souls for inmost lining have:
Their throat it is an open swallowing grave,
   Whereto their tongue is flatt'ring instrument.
Give them their due unto their guiltiness,
   Let their vile thoughts the thinkers' ruin be:°   30
   With heapèd weights of their own sins oppress
These most ungrateful rebels unto thee.

So shall all they that trust on thee do bend,°
   And love the sweet sound of thy name, rejoice:
They ever shall send thee their praising voice,   35
   Since ever thou to them wilt succour send.
Thy work it is to bless, thou blessed'st them;
   The just in thee, on thee and justice build:
   Thy work it is such men safe in to hem
With kindest care, as with a certain shield.   40

---

24 bide] abide   36 wilt succour] will help   39 hem] enclose

Psalm 6

Domine, ne in furore

Lord, let not me, a worm, by thee be shent
    While thou art in the heat of thy displeasure:
    Ne let thy rage, of my due punishment
        Become the measure.
But mercy, Lord, let mercy thine descend,°   5
    For I am weak, and in my weakness languish:
    Lord, help, for ev'n my bones their marrow spend
        With cruel anguish.
Nay, ev'n my soul fell troubles do appal.
    Alas, how long, my God, wilt thou delay me?   10
    Turn thee, sweet Lord, and from this ugly fall,
        My dear God, stay me.
Mercy, oh, mercy, Lord, for mercy's sake,
    For death doth kill the witness of thy glory.
    Can of thy praise the tongues entombèd make   15
        A heav'nly story?°
Lo, I am tired while still I sigh and groan;
    My moistened bed proofs of my sorrow showeth:
    My bed (while I with black night mourn alone)
        With my tears floweth.   20
Woe, like a moth, my face's beauty eats,
    And age pulled on with pains all freshness fretteth;
    The while a swarm of foes with vexing feats
        My life besetteth.
Get hence, you evil, who in my ill rejoice,   25
    In all whose works vainness is ever reigning:
    For God hath heard the weeping, sobbing voice
        Of my complaining.
The Lord my suit did hear, and gently hear;
    They shall be shamed and vexed, that breed my crying: 30
    And turn their backs, and straight on backs appear
        Their shameful flying.

---

1 shent] shamed   3 Ne] nor   7 spend] consume   9 fell] terrible
appal] dismay   12 stay] support   22 fretteth] gnaws   23 feats] deeds

Psalm 7

Domine, Deus meus

O Lord, my God, thou art my trustful stay:°
    Oh, save me from this persecution's show'r;
    Deliver me in my endangered way

Lest lion-like, he do my soul devour,°
    And cruelly in many pieces tear,   5
    While I am void of any helping pow'r.

O Lord, my God, if I did not forbear
    Ever from deed of any such desert;
    If aught my hands of wickedness do bear;

If I have been unkind for friendly part;°   10
    Nay, if I wrought not for his freedom's sake,
    Who causeless now, yields me a hateful heart,

Then let my foe chase me, and chasing take:
    Then let his foot upon my neck be set:
    Then in the dust let him my honour rake.   15

Arise, O Lord, in wrath thyself up set°
    Against such rage of foes; awake for me
    To that high doom, which I by thee must get.

So shall all men with lauds environ thee;
    Therefore, O Lord, lift up thy throne on high   20
    That every folk thy wondrous acts may see.

Thou, Lord, the people shalt in judgement try:
    Then, Lord, my Lord, give sentence on my side
    After my clearness and my equity.

---

1 stay] protection   9 aught] anything   15 rake] bury   18 doom] judgement   19 lauds] praises   environ] encircle   24 clearness] purity

Oh, let their wickedness no longer bide 25
   From coming to the well-deservèd end:
   But still be thou to just men justest guide.

Thou righteous proofs to hearts and reins dost send:
   And all my help from none but thee is sent,
   Who dost thy saving-health to true men bend. 30

Thou righteous art, thou strong, thou patient,
   And each day art provoked, thine ire to show:
   And if this man will not learn to repent,

For him thou whett'st thy sword and bend'st thy bow,
   And hast thy deadly arms in order brought, 35
   And ready art to let thine arrows go.

Lo, he that first conceived a wretchèd thought,
   And great with child of mischief travailed long,
   Now brought abed, hath brought naught forth but naught.

A pit was digged by this man, vainly strong, 40
   But in the pit he ruined first did fall,
   Which fall he made, to do his neighbour wrong.

He against me doth throw, but down it shall
   Upon his pate; his pain employèd thus
   And his own ill, his own head shall appal. 45

I will give thanks unto the Lord of us
   According to his heav'nly equity,
   And will to highest name yield praises high.

Psalm 8

Domine, Dominus

O Lord, that rul'st our mortal line,
   How through the world thy name doth shine,°

---

28 reins] inmost self   38 travailed] laboured, as in childbirth   44 pate] head
45 appal] dismay

That hast of thine unmatchèd glory
Upon the heav'ns engrav'n the story.

From sucklings hath thy honour sprung,   5
  Thy force hath flowed from babies' tongue:°
  Whereby thou stopp'st thine en'mies' prating
  Bent to revenge and ever-hating.

When I upon the heav'ns do look,
  Which all from thee their essence took;   10
  When moon and stars, my thoughts beholdeth,
  Whose life no life, but of thee holdeth:°

Then think I: 'Ah, what is this man
  Whom that great God remember can?
  And what the race of him descended,   15
  It should be aught of God attended?

'For though in less than angels' state
  Thou planted hast this earthly mate:
  Yet hast thou made ev'n him an owner
  Of glorious crown, and crowning honour.   20

'Thou placest him upon all lands
  To rule the works of thine own hands:
  And so thou hast all things ordainèd,
  That ev'n his feet have on them reignèd.°

'Thou under his dominion placed   25
  Both sheep and oxen wholly hast:
  And all the beasts for ever breeding,
  Which in the fertile fields be feeding.

'The bird, free-burgess of the air,
  The fish, of sea the native heir,   30
  And what things else of waters traceth

---

7 prating] chattering   16 aught] anything   29 free-burgess] citizen

The unworn paths, his rule embraceth.°
　　O Lord, that rul'st our mortal line,
　　How through the world thy name doth shine!'

Psalm 9

Confitebor tibi

With all my heart, O Lord, I will praise thee,
　　My speeches all thy marvels shall descry:
　　In thee my joys and comforts ever be,
　　Yea, ev'n my songs thy name shall magnify,
　　　　O Lord most high,　　　　　　　　　　5

Because my foes to fly are now constrained,
　　And they are fall'n, nay, perished at thy sight:
　　For thou my cause, my right thou hast maintained,
　　Setting thyself in throne, which shinèd bright,
　　　　Of judging right.　　　　　　　　　　10

The Gentiles thou rebukèd sorely hast,
　　And wicked folks, from thee to wrack do wend:
　　And their renown, which seemed so like to last,
　　Thou dost put out, and quite consuming send
　　　　To endless end.　　　　　　　　　　15

O bragging foe, where is the endless waste
　　Of conquered states, whereby such fame you got?
　　What? Doth their memory no longer last?
　　Both ruins, ruiners, and ruined plot
　　　　Be quite forgot.　　　　　　　　　　20

But God shall sit in his eternal chair,
　　Which he prepared, to give his judgements high:
　　Thither the world for justice shall repair;
　　Thence he to all, his judgements shall apply
　　　　Perpetually.　　　　　　　　　　25

2 descry] declare　　12 wrack] ruin　　wend] turn　　23 repair] resort to

Thou, Lord, also th'oppressèd wilt defend,
　　That they to thee in troublous time may flee:
　　They that know thee, on thee their trust will bend,
　　For thou, Lord, found by them wilt ever be,
　　　　That seek to thee.　　　　　　　　　　　　30

Oh, praise the Lord, this Zion-dweller good,
　　Show forth his acts, and this as act most high:
　　That he enquiring, doth require just blood,
　　Which he forgetteth not, nor letteth die
　　　　Th'afflicted cry.　　　　　　　　　　　　35

'Have mercy, mercy, Lord,' I once did say,
　　'Ponder the pains which on me loaden be
　　By them whose minds on hateful thoughts do stay:
　　Thou, Lord, that from death-gates hast lifted me,
　　　　I call to thee.　　　　　　　　　　　　40

'That I within the ports most beautiful
　　Of Zion's daughter may sound forth thy praise:°
　　That I, ev'n I, of heav'nly comfort full
　　May only joy in all thy saving ways
　　　　Throughout my days.'　　　　　　　　　45

No sooner said, but, lo, mine enemies sink
　　Down in the pit which they themselves had wrought:
　　And in that net which they well hidden think,
　　Is their own foot, led by their own ill thought,
　　　　Most surely caught.　　　　　　　　　　50

For then the Lord in judgement shows to reign,°
　　When godless men be snared in their own snares:
　　When wicked souls be turned to hellish pain,°
　　And that forgetful sort which never cares
　　　　What God prepares.　　　　　　　　　　55

31 Zion-dweller] inhabitant of God's house

But on the other side, the poor in sprite
   Shall not be scraped from out of heavn'ly score:
   Nor meek abiding of the patient wight
   Yet perish shall (although his pain be sore)
      For evermore.   60

Up, Lord, and judge the Gentiles in thy right,
   And let not man have upper hand of thee:
   With terrors great, O Lord, do thou them fright,
   That by sharp proofs the heath'n themselves may see
      But men to be.   65

Psalm 10

Ut quid, Domine?

Why standest thou so far,
   O God, our only star,
   In time most fit for thee
   To help who vexèd be?
For, lo, with pride the wicked man   5
   Still plagues the poor the most he can:
   Oh, let proud him be throughly caught
   In craft of his own crafty thought.

For he himself doth praise
   When he his lust doth ease,   10
   Extolling rav'nous gain,
   But doth God's self disdain.
Nay, so proud is his puffèd thought,
   That after God he never sought,
   But rather much he fancies this: 15
   The name of God a fable is.°

For while his ways do prove,
   On them he sets his love:

---

56 sprite] spirit   57 scraped] erased   score] tally, list   58 wight] person
64 proofs] reproofs
Psalm 10 7 throughly] thoroughly   10 lust] desire

Thy judgements are too high,
  He can them not espy.   20
Therefore he doth defy all those,
  That dare themselves to him oppose:
  And sayeth in his bragging heart,
  This gotten bliss shall never part.

Nor he removèd be,   25
  Nor danger ever see,
    Yet from his mouth doth spring
    Cursing and cozening;
Under his tongue do harboured lie
  Both mischief and iniquity.   30
  For proof, oft lain in wait he is
  In secret by-way villages,

In such a place unknown
  To slay the hurtless one,
    With winking eyes aye bent   35
    Against the innocent.
Like lurking lion in his den,
  He waits to spoil the simple men:
  Whom to their loss he still doth get,
  When once he draw'th his wily net.   40

Oh, with how simple look,
  He oft layeth out his hook!
    And with how humble shows
    To trap poor souls he goes!
Thus freely saith he in his sprite: 45
  'God sleeps, or hath forgotten quite,
  His far-off sight now hoodwinked is,
  He leisure wants to mark all this.'

---

20 espy] spy, see   28 cozening] deception   32 by-way] secluded
34 hurtless] harmless   35 aye] ever   38 spoil] destroy   simple] unsuspecting
45 sprite] spirit   47 hoodwinked] blindfolded

Then rise and come abroad,
   O Lord, our only God: 50
   Lift up thy heav'nly hand
   And by the silly stand.
Why should the evil, so evil despise
   The pow'r of thy through-seeing eyes?
   And why should he in heart so hard   55
   Say, 'Thou dost not thine own regard'?

But nak'd before thine eyes
   All wrong and mischief lies:
   For of them in thy hands
   The balance ev'nly stands.   60
But who aright poor-minded be
   Commit their cause, themselves to thee,
   The succour of the succourless
   The father of the fatherless.

Break thou the wicked arm,   65
   Whose fury bends to harm:
   Search them, and wicked he
   Will straightway nothing be.
O Lord, we shall thy title sing,
   Ever and ever, to be king   70
   Who hast the heath'ny folk destroyed
   From out thy land by them annoyed.

Thou op'nest heav'nly door
   To prayers of the poor:
   Thou first prepared'st their mind,   75
   Then ear to them inclined.
Oh, be thou still the orphan's aid,
   That poor from ruin may be stayed:
   Lest we should ever fear the lust
   Of earthly man, a lord of dust.   80

---

52 silly] helpless   54 through-seeing] penetrating   61 poor-minded] humble
63 succour] help   71 heath'ny] heathen   72 annoyed] harmed   78 stayed]
prevented

Psalm 11

In Domino confido

Since I do trust Jehovah still,
  Your fearful words why do you spill
  That like a bird to some strong hill
    I now should fall a-flying?

Behold the evil have bent their bow,   5
  And set their arrows in a row,
  To give unwares a mortal blow
    To hearts that hate all lying.

But that in building they begun,
  With ground-plot's fall, shall be undone:°   10
  For what, alas, have just men done?
    In them no cause is growing.

God in his holy temple is:
  The throne of heav'n is only his,
  Naught his all-seeing sight can miss;   15
    His eyelids peise our going.

The Lord doth search the just man's reins,
  But hates, abhors, the wicked brains,
  On them storms, brimstone, coals he rains:
    That is their share assignèd.   20

But so of happy other side
  His lovely face on them doth bide
  In race of life their feet to guide
    Who be to God inclinèd.°

2 spill] waste, squander   7 unwares] unaware   15 Naught] nothing
16 peise] judge   17 reins] inmost self

Psalm 12

Salvum me fac

Lord, help, it is high time for me to call,
   No men are left that charity do love:
   Nay, ev'n the race of good men are decayed.

Of things vain with vain mates they babble all,
   Their abject lips, no breath, but flatt'ry move,   5
   Sent from false heart on double meaning stayed.

But thou (O Lord) give them a thorough fall:
   Those lying lips, from cozening head remove,
   In falsehood wrapped, but in their pride displayed.

'Our tongues', say they, 'beyond them all shall go: 10
   We both have pow'r and will our tales to tell:
   For what lord rules our brave emboldened breast?'°

'Ah, now ev'n for their sakes, that taste of woe,
   Whom troubles toss, whose natures need doth quell,
   Ev'n for the sighs, true sighs of man distressed: 15

'I will get up,' saith God, 'and my help show
   Against all them, that against him do swell;
   Maugre his foes, I will him set at rest.'

These are God's words, God's words are ever pure:
   Pure, purer than the silver throughly tried,   20
   When fire sev'n times hath spent his earthy parts.°

Then thou (O Lord) shalt keep the good still sure;
   By thee preserved, in thee they shall abide:
   Yea, in no age, thy bliss from them departs.

---

2 charity] *caritas*, divine love   5 abject] despicable   6 stayed] relied
8 cozening] deceitful   18 Maugre] despite   20 throughly] thoroughly

Thou seest each side the walking doth endure°   25
  Of these bad folks, more lifted up with pride,
  Which if it last, woe to all simple hearts!

Psalm 13

Usquequo, Domine?

How long (O Lord) shall I forgotten be?°
    What? Ever?
How long wilt thou thy hidden face from me
    Dissever?
How long shall I consult with careful sprite   5
    In anguish?
How long shall I with foes' triumphant might
    Thus languish?
Behold me, Lord, let to thy hearing creep
    My crying.   10
Nay, give me eyes, and light, lest that I sleep
    In dying.
Lest my foe brag, that in my ruin he
    Prevailèd:
And at my fall they joy that, troublous, me   15
    Assailèd.
No, no, I trust on thee, and joy in thy
    Great pity:
Still therefore of thy graces shall be my
    Song's ditty.   20

Psalm 14

Dixit insipiens

The foolish man by flesh and fancy led,°
  His guilty heart with this fond thought hath fed:
    'There is no God that reigneth.'

---

27 simple] unsuspecting
Psalm 13 4 Dissever] separate   5 sprite] spirit   15 troublous] troubled
20 ditty] lyric

And so thereafter he, and all his mates
  Do works, which earth corrupt, and heaven hates: 5
    Not one that good remaineth.

Ev'n God himself sent down his piercing eye,
  If of this clayey race he could espy°
    One, that his wisdom learneth.

And, lo, he finds that all a-straying went: 10
  All plunged in stinking filth, not one well bent,
    Not one that God discerneth.

Oh, madness of these folks, thus loosely led!
  These cannibals, who as if they were bread,°
    God's people do devour,   15

Nor ever call on God: but they shall quake
  More than they now do brag, when he shall take
    The just into his power.

Indeed the poor, oppressed by you, you mock;
  Their counsels are your common jesting stock: 20
    But God is their recomfort.

Ah, when from Zion, shall the saver come
  That Jacob freed by thee, may glad become
    And Israel full of comfort?

Psalm 15

Domine, quis habitabit?

In tabernacle thine, O Lord, who shall remain?
  Lord, of thy holy hill, who shall the rest obtain?
  Ev'n he that leads of life an uncorrupted train,

---

8 clayey] of mortal clay   21 recomfort] consolation   22 Zion] house of the
God of Israel   saver] saviour

Psalm 15 3 train] course of action

Whose deeds of righteous heart, whose hearty words be plain;
 Who with deceitful tongue, hath never used to feign, 5
  Nor neighbour hurts by deed, nor doth with slander stain;
 Whose eyes a person vile, doth hold in vile disdain,
  But doth with honour great, the godly entertain;
 Who oath and promise given, doth faithfully maintain,
  Although some worldly loss thereby he may sustain; 10
From biting usury who ever doth refrain;°
  Who sells not guiltless cause for filthy love of gain;
Who thus proceeds for aye in sacred mount shall reign.

Psalm 16

Conserva me

Save me, Lord, for why thou art
  All the hope of all my heart:
  Witness thou my soul with me,
  That to God, my God, I say:
  'Thou, my Lord, thou art my stay, 5
  Though my works reach not to thee.'

This is all the best I prove:
  Good and godly men, I love,
  And foresee their wretched pain,
  Who to other gods do run; 10
  Their blood off'rings I do shun,
  Nay, to name their names disdain.

God my only portion is,
  And of my child's part the bliss:
  He then shall maintain my lot. 15
  Say then, is not my lot found
  In a goodly pleasant ground?
  Have not I fair partage got?°

5 feign] dissemble   13 for aye] for ever
 Psalm 16 1 for why] because   5 stay] support   7 prove] experience
18 partage] portion

Ever, Lord, I will bless thee,
 Who dost ever counsel me,   20
 Ev'n when night with his black wing
 Sleepy darkness doth o'ercast,
 In my inward reins I taste
 Of my faults and chastening.

My eyes still my God regard,   25
 And he my right hand doth guard;
 So can I not be oppressed,
 So my heart is fully glad,
 So in joy my glory clad,
 Yea, my flesh in hope shall rest.   30

For I know the deadly grave
 On my soul no pow'r shall have;
 For I know thou wilt defend
 Ev'n the body of thine own
 Dear belovèd holy one,   35
 From a foul corrupting end.

Thou life's path wilt make me know
 In whose view doth plenty grow
 All delights that souls can crave,
 And whose bodies placèd stand   40
 On thy blessed-making hand
 They all joys like-endless have.

Psalm 17
Exaudi, Domine, justitiam

My suit is just, just Lord, to my suit hark.
 I plain: sweet Lord, my plaint for pity mark.
 And since my lips feign not to thee,
 Thine ears vouchsafe to bend to me.

23 reins] inmost self

Psalm 17 2 plain] complain 3 feign . . . to] pretend, lie to 4 vouchsafe]
graciously agree

Oh, let my sentence pass from thine own face: 5
 Show that thine eyes respect a faithful case,
  Thou that by proof acquainted art
  With inward secrets of my heart.

Where silent night might seem all faults to hide,
 Then was I, by thy searching insight tried: 10
  And then by thee, was guiltless found
  From ill word and ill meaning sound.

Not weighing aught how fleshly fancies run,
 Led by thy word, the rav'ners' steps I shun,
  And pray that still thou guide my way,   15
  Lest yet I slip or go astray.

I say again that I have called on thee,
 And boldly say thou wilt give ear to me:
  Then let my words, my cries ascend
  Which to thyself my soul will send.   20

Show then, O Lord, thy wondrous kindness show.
 Make us in marvels of thy mercy know,
  That thou by faithful men wilt stand,
  And save them from rebellious hand.

Then keep me as the apple of an eye,   25
 In thy wings' shade then let me hidden lie,°
  From my destroying wicked foes
  Who for my death do me enclose.

Their eyes do swim, their face doth shine in fat,
 And cruel words their swelling tongues do chat   30
  And yet their high hearts look so low
  As how to watch our overthrow.

Now like a lion, gaping to make preys
 Now like his whelp, in den, that lurking stays:

7 proof] experience 13 aught] at all 14 rav'ners'] robbers'
18 give ear] listen

Up, Lord, prevent those gaping jaws,   35
And bring to naught those watching paws.°

Save me from them, thou usest as thy blade,
From men, I say, and from men's worldly trade,
Whose life doth seem most greatly blest
And count this life their portion best,   40

Whose bellies so with dainties thou dost fill,
And so with hidden treasures grant their will,
That they in riches flourish do,
And children have to leave it to.

What would they more? And I would not their case: 45
My joy shall be pure, to enjoy thy face,
When waking of this sleep of mine
I shall see thee in likeness thine.°

Psalm 18

Diligam te

Thee will I love, O Lord, with all my heart's delight,
My strength, my strongest rock which my defence hast borne,°
My God, and helping God, my might, and trustful might,
My never-piercèd shield, my ever-saving horn,°
My refuge, refuge then, when most I am forlorn: 5
Whom then shall I invoke, but thee, most worthy praise,
On whom (against my foes) my only safety stays?

On me the pains of death already gan to prey;
The floods of wickedness on me did horrors throw;
Like in a winding sheet, wretch, I already lay,°   10
Already, ready to my snaring grave to go.
This my distress to God, with wailful cries I show:
My cries climbed up, and he bent down from sacred throne,
His eyes unto my case, his ears unto my moan.

36 naught] nothing
Psalm 18 7 stays] relies   8 gan] began   11 snaring] entrapping

And so the earth did fall to tremble and to quake;°   15
   The mountains proudly high, and their foundations bent
   With motion of his rage, did to the bottom shake.
   He came, but came with smoke, from out his nostrils sent;
   Flames issued from his mouth, and burning coals out went;
   He bowed the heav'ns, and from the bowed heav'ns did
      descend   20
   With hugy darkness, which about his feet did wend.

The cherubims their backs, the winds did yield their wings°
   To bear his sacred flight; in secret place then closed,
   About which he dim clouds, like a pavilion brings,
   Clouds ev'n of waters dark, and thickest air composed.   25
   But straight his shining eyes this misty mass disclosed,
   Then hail, then fi'ry coals, then thundered heav'nly sire,
   Then spake he his loud voice, then hailstones, coals, and fire.

Then out his arrows fly; and straight they scattered been:
   Lightning on lightning he did for their wrack augment;   30
   The gulfs of waters then were through their channels seen;
   The world's foundations then lay bare; because he shent
   With blasting breath, O Lord, that in thy chiding went.
   Then sent he from above, and took me from below,
   Ev'n from the waters' depth, my God preserved me so.   35

So did he save me, from my mighty furious foe,
   So did he save me, from their then prevailing hate:
   For they had caught me up, when I was weak in woe.
   But he, staff of my age, he stayed my stumbling state.
   This much: yet more, when I by him this freedom gat,   40
   By him because I did find in his eyesight grace
   He lifted me unto a largely noble place.

My justice, my just hands thus did the Lord reward,
   Because I walked his ways, nor gainst him evilly went,

21 hugy] huge   30 wrack] ruin   32 shent] shamed, ruined
39 stayed] supported   40 gat] obtained   44 gainst] against

Still to his judgements looked, still for his statutes cared: 45
Sound and upright with him, to wickedness not bent.
Therefore I say again, this goodness he me sent,
As he before his eyes, did see my justice stand,
According as he saw the pureness of my hand.

Meek to the meek thou art, the good thy goodness taste;   50
  Pure, to the pure, thou deal'st with crooked crookedly:
  Up then thou lift'st the poor, and down the proud wilt cast;
  Up, thou dost light my light, and clear my darkened eye.
  I hosts o'ercome by thee; by thee o'er walls I fly;
  Thy way is soundly sure, thy word is purely tried;   55
  To them that trust in thee, a shield thou dost abide.

For who is God besides this great Jehovah ours?
  And so besides our God, who is endued with might?
  This God then girded me in his almighty pow'rs,
  He made my cumbrous way, to me most plainly right: 60
  To match with light-foot stags, he made my foot so light,
  That I climbed highest hill; he me war-points did show,
  Strength'ning mine arms, that they could break an iron bow.°

Thou gav'st me saving shield; thy right hand was my stay,
  Me in increasing still, thy kindness did maintain;   65
  Unto my strengthened steps, thou didst enlarge the way,
  My heels, and plants, thou didst from stumbling slip sustain:
  What foes I did pursue, my force did them attain
  That I, ere I returned, destroyed them utterly,
  With such brave wounds, as they under my feet did lie.   70

For why? My fighting strength, by thy strength, strengthened was:
  Not I, but thou throw'st down those, who gainst me do rise,
  Thou gavest me their necks, on them thou mad'st me pass.
  Behold they cry, but who to them his help applies?
  Nay, unto thee they cried, but thou heard'st not their cries: 75

---

60 cumbrous] troublesome   62 war-points] war advice   67 plants] footsteps
71 For why?] for what reason?   73 mad'st] made

I beat those folks as small as dust, which wind doth raise,
I beat them as the clay is beat in beaten ways.

Thus freed from mutine men, thou makest me to reign;
　Yea, thou dost make me served by folks I never knew;
　My name their ears, their ears their hearts to me enchain;　80
Ev'n fear makes strangers show much love, though much untrue.
But they do fail, and in their mazèd corners rue:
Then live Jehovah still, my rock still blessed be;
Let him be lifted up, that hath preservèd me.

He that is my revenge, in whom I realms subdue,　　　　85
　Who freed me from my foes, from rebels guarded me,
　And rid me from the wrongs which cruel wits did brew.
Among the Gentiles then I (Lord) yield thanks to thee,
I to thy name will sing, and this my song shall be:
He nobly saves his king, and kindness keeps in store,　　90
For David his anoint and his seed evermore.

Psalm 19
Coeli enarrant

　The heav'nly frame sets forth the fame
　　Of him that only thunders;
　The firmament so strangely bent
　　Shows his hand-working wonders.

　Day unto day, it doth display,　　　　　　　5
　　Their course doth it acknowledge:
　And night to night succeeding right
　　In darkness teach clear knowledge.

　There is no speech, nor language, which
　　Is so of skill bereavèd:　　　　　　　　10

78 mutine] mutinous　　　82 mazèd] amazed　　　rue] regret　　　91 anoint]
anointed one
　Psalm 19 3 firmament so strangely bent] vault of heaven so wonderfully bowed

But of the skies the teaching cries
    They have heard and conceivèd.

There be no eyne, but read the line
    From so fair book proceeding:°
Their words be set in letters great   15
    For everybody's reading.

Is not he blind that doth not find
    The tabernacle builded
There, by his grace, for sun's fair face
    In beams of beauty gilded?   20

Who forth doth come, like a bridegroom
    From out his veiling places:
As glad is he, as giants be
    To run their mighty races.

His race is ev'n from ends of heav'n,   25
    About that vault he goeth:
There be no rea'ms hid from his beams,
    His heat to all he throweth.

Oh, law of his, how perfect 'tis
    The very soul amending;   30
God's witness sure for aye doth dure
    To simplest, wisdom lending.

God's dooms be right and cheer the sprite:
    All his commandments being
So purely wise, as give the eyes   35
    Both light and force of seeing.

Of him the fear doth cleanness bear
    And so endures for ever:°

---

12 conceivèd] understood   13 eyne] eyes   27 rea'ms] realms   31 for
aye] for ever   dure] endure   33 dooms] judgements   sprite] spirit

His judgements be self verity
   They are unrighteous never.   40

Then what man would so soon seek gold
   Or glitt'ring golden money?
By them is past, in sweetest taste,
   Honey, or comb of honey.

By them is made thy servant's trade   45
   Most circumspectly guarded:
And who doth frame to keep the same
   Shall fully be rewarded.

Who is the man that ever can
   His faults know and acknowledge?   50
O Lord, cleanse me from faults that be
   Most secret from all knowledge.

Thy servant keep, lest in him creep
   Presumptuous sin's offences:
Let them not have me for their slave,   55
   Nor reign upon my senses.

So shall my sprite be still upright
   In thought and conversation;
So shall I bide, well purified
   From much abomination.   60

So let words sprung from my weak tongue
   And my heart's meditation,
My saving might, Lord, in thy sight
   Receive good acceptation.

---

47 frame] prepare   59 bide] abide   60 abomination] sinful or shameful
behaviour

Psalm 20

Exaudiat te Dominus

Let God, the Lord, hear thee,
    Ev'n in the day, when most thy troubles be;
    Let name of Jacob's God,
    When thou on it dost cry,
    Defend thee still from all thy foes abroad.   5

From sanctuary high
    Let him come down, and help to thee apply
    From Zion's holy top;
    Thence let him undertake
    With heav'nly strength, thy earthly strength to prop.   10

Let him notorious make,
    That in good part, he did thy off'rings take.
    Let fire for trial burn
    (Yea, fire from himself sent)
    Thy off'rings, so that they to ashes turn.   15

And so let him consent
    To grant thy will, and perfect thy intent
    That in thy saving we
    May joy, and banners raise
    Up to our God, when thy suits granted be.   20

Now in me knowledge says,
    That God from fall his own anointed stays.°
    From heav'nly holy land
    I know that he hears thee:
    Yea, hears with pow'rs, and helps of helpful hand.   25

Let trust of some men be
    In chariots armed, others in chivalry:°
    But let all our conceit

---

8 Zion's holy top] location of God's house   22 stays] protects

Upon God's holy name,
Who is our Lord, with due remembrance wait.   30

Behold their broken shame!
  We stand upright, while they their fall did frame.
  Assist us, Saviour dear;
  Let that king deign to hear,
  When as to him our prayers do appear.   35

Psalm 21

Domine, in virtute

New joy, new joy unto our king,
    Lord, from thy strength is growing:
Lord, what delight to him doth bring
    His safety, from thee flowing!

Thou hast giv'n what his heart would have,   5
    Nay, soon as he but movèd
His lips to crave what he would crave,
    He had as him behovèd.

Yea, thou prevent'st ere ask he could,
    With many lib'ral blessing: 10
Crown of his head with crown of gold
    Of purest metal dressing.

He did but ask a life of thee,
    Thou him a long life gavest:
Lo, ev'n unto eternity   15
    The life of him thou savest.

We may well call his glory great,
    That springs from thy salvation:
Thou, thou it is, that hast him set
    In so high estimation.   20

32 frame] cause
  Psalm 21 8 behovèd] required   9 prevent'st] anticipates   ere] before
10 lib'ral] liberal

Like storehouse thou of blessings mad'st
   This man of everlasting:
Unspeakably his heart thou gladd'st
   On him thy count'nance casting.

And why all this? Because our king   25
   In heav'n, his trust hath layèd:
He only leans on highest thing,
   So from base slip is stayèd.

Thy hand thy foes shall overtake,
   That thee so evil have hated: 30
Thou as in fiery ov'n shalt make
   These mates to be amated.

The Lord on them with causeful ire
   Shall use destroying power:
And flames of never-quenchèd fire   35
   Shall these bad wights devour.

Their fruit shalt thou from earthly face
   Send unto desolation:
And from among the human race
   Root out their generation.   40

For they to overthrow thy will
   Full wilily intended:
But all their bad mischievous skill
   Shall fruitlessly be ended.

For like a mark thou shalt a-row   45
   Set them in pointed places:
And ready make thy vengeful bow
   Against their guilty faces.

21 mad'st] made   23 gladd'st] made glad   28 stayèd] protected   31 ov'n] oven   32 amated] cast down, dismayed   33 causeful] justified   36 wights] persons   42 wilily] slyly   45 a-row] in a row   46 pointed] appointed

Lord, in thy strength, Lord, in thy might,
    Thy honour high be raisèd,   50
And so shall in our songs' delight,
    Thy power still be praisèd.

Psalm 22

Deus, Deus meus

My God, my God, why hast thou me forsaken?
    Woe me, from me, why is thy presence taken?
    So far from seeing, mine unhealthful eyes:
    So far from hearing to my roaring cries.

O God, my God, I cry while day appeareth: 5
    But, God, thy ear, my crying never heareth.
    O God, the night is privy to my plaint
    Yet to my plaint, thou hast no audience lent.

But thou art holy, and dost hold thy dwelling
    Where Israel thy lauds is ever telling: 10
    Our fathers still to thee their trust did bear;°
    They trusted, and by thee delivered were.

They were set free, when they upon thee callèd,
    They hoped on thee, and they were not appallèd.
    But I a worm, not I of mankind am,°   15
    Nay, shame of men, the people's scorning game.

The lookers now at me, poor wretch, be mocking;
    With mows, and nods, they stand about me flocking.
    'Let God help him' (say they) 'whom he did trust:
    Let God save him in whom was all his lust.'   20

And yet even from the womb thyself didst take me:
    At mother's breast, thou didst good hope betake me.

---

7 plaint] complaint   10 lauds] praises   14 appallèd] dismayed
18 mows] grimaces   flocking] gathering   20 lust] delight

No sooner my child eyes could look abroad,
Than I was giv'n to thee, thou wert my God.

Oh, be not far, since pain so nearly presseth, 25
  And since there is not one, who it redresseth.
  I am enclosed with young bulls' madded rout,
  Nay, Basan's mighty bulls close me about.

With gaping mouths, these folks, on me have chargèd,
  Like lions fierce, with roaring jaws enlargèd.° 30
  On me all this, who do like water slide,
  Whose loosèd bones quite out of joint be wried,

Whose heart, with these huge flames, like wax o'erheated
  Doth melt away, though it be inmost seated:
  My moist'ning strength is like a potsherd dried, 35
  My cleaving tongue, close to my roof doth bide:

And now am brought, alas, brought by thy power
  Unto the dust of my death's running hour:°
  For bawling dogs have compassed me about,
  Yea, worse than dogs, a naughty, wicked rout. 40

My humble hands, my fainting feet they piercèd:
  They look, they gaze, my bones might be rehearsèd.
  Of my poor weeds, they do partition make,
  And do cast lots, who should my vesture take.

But be not far, O Lord, my strength, my comfort, 45
  Hasten to help me, in this deep discomfort.
  Ah, from the sword, yet save my vital sprite,
  My desolated life from doggèd might.°

From lion's mouth, oh, help, and show to hear me
  By aiding, when fierce unicorns come near me. 50

32 wried] twisted   35 potsherd] fragment of pottery   40 rout] pack
42 rehearsèd] discerned, counted   43 weeds] clothes   47 sprite] spirit
48 doggèd] spiteful

To brethren, then, I will declare thy fame,
And with these words, when they meet, praise thy name:

'Who fear the Lord, all praise and glory bear him,
You Israel's seed, you come of Jacob, fear him.
For he hath not abhorred, nor yet disdained   55
The silly wretch, with foul affliction stained,

'Nor hid from him his face's fair appearing.°
But when he called, this Lord did give him hearing.'
In congregation great, I will praise thee:
Who fear thee shall my vows performèd see.   60

Th'afflicted then shall eat, and be well pleasèd:°
And God shall be, by those his seekers praisèd.
Indeed, O you: you that be such of mind,
You shall the life, that ever-liveth find.

But what? I say, from earth's remotest border   65
Unto due thoughts, mankind his thoughts shall order,
And turn to God, and all the nations be
Made worshippers, before almighty thee.

And reason, since the crown to God pertaineth,
And that by right upon all realms he reigneth.   70
They that be made ev'n fat, with earth's fat good
Shall feed, and laud the giver of their food.

To him shall kneel ev'n who to dust be stricken,
Ev'n he whose life, no help of man can quicken,
His service shall from child to child descend,   75
His dooms one age shall to another send.

56 silly] pitiable   74 quicken] revive   76 dooms] judgements

Psalm 23

Dominus regit me

The Lord, the Lord my shepherd is,
  And so can never I
    Taste misery.
He rests me in green pasture his:°
  By waters still, and sweet°   5
    He guides my feet.

He me revives: leads me the way,
  Which righteousness doth take,
    For his name's sake.
Yea, though I should through valleys stray,   10
  Of death's dark shade, I will
    No whit fear ill.

For thou, dear Lord, thou me besett'st:
  Thy rod, and thy staff be
    To comfort me;   15
Before me thou a table sett'st,
  Ev'n when foe's envious eye
    Doth it espy.

Thou oil'st my head, thou fill'st my cup:°
  Nay, more, thou endless good,   20
    Shalt give me food.
To thee, I say, ascended up,
  Where thou, the Lord of all,
    Dost hold thy hall.

Psalm 24

Domini est terra

The earth is God's, and what the globe of earth containeth,
  And all who in that globe do dwell:

---

12 No whit] not at all   13 besett'st] establishes   18 espy] spy, see

For by his pow'r, the land upon the ocean reigneth,
    Through him the floods to their beds fell.

Who shall climb to the hill which God's own hill is namèd?   5
    Who shall stand in his holy place?
He that hath hurtless hands, whose inward heart is framèd°
    All pureness ever to embrace;

Who shunning vanity and works of vainness leaving
    Vainly doth not puff up his mind,   10
Who never doth deceive, and much less his deceiving
    With perjury doth falsely bind.

A blessing from the Lord, from God of his salvation
    Sweet righteousness shall he receive.
Jacob, this is thy seed, God-seeking generation,   15
    Who search of God's face never leave.

Lift up your heads, you gates and you doors ever biding:°
    In comes the king of glory bright.
Who is this glorious king in might and power riding?
    The Lord, whose strength makes battle's fight.   20

Lift up your heads, you gates and you doors ever biding:
    In comes the king of glory bright.
Who is this glorious king? The Lord of armies guiding
    Ev'n he, the king of glory hight.

Psalm 25

Ad te, Domine

To thee, O Lord most just,
    I lift my inward sight.
My God, in thee I trust,
    Let me not ruin quite:

7 hurtless] innocent   24 hight] named
Psalm 25 4 quite] entirely

Let not those foes that me annoy   5
On my complaint build up their joy.

Sure, sure, who hope in thee,
   Shall never suffer shame:
Let them confounded be
   That causeless wrongs do frame.   10
      Yea, Lord, to me thy ways do show;
      Teach me, thus vexed, what path to go.

Guide me as thy truth guides;
   Teach me; for why thou art
The God in whom abides   15
   The saving me from smart.
      For never day such changing wrought,
      That I from trust in thee was brought.

Remember, only king,
   Thy mercy's tenderness: 20
To thy remembrance bring
   Thy kindness, lovingness.
      Let those things thy remembrance grave,
      Since they eternal essence have.

But Lord, remember not   25
   Sins brewed in youthful glass:°
Nor my rebellions' blot,
   Since youth, and they, do pass.
      But in thy kindness me record
      Ev'n for thy mercy's sake, O Lord.   30

Of grace and righteousness
   The Lord such plenty hath
That he deigns to express
   To sinning men his path.
      The meek he doth in judgement lead,   35
      And teach the humble how to tread.

---

10 frame] contrive   14 for why] because   16 smart] pain
23 grave] engrave   33 deigns] condescends

And what, think you, may be
　　The paths of my great God?
Ev'n spotless verity,
　　And mercy spread abroad,　　　　　　　　　　40
　　　　To such as keep his covenant
　　　　And on his testimonies plant.

O Lord, for thy name's sake,
　　Let my iniquity
Of thee some mercy take,　　　　　　　　　　45
　　Though it be great in me:
　　　　Oh, is there one with his fear fraught?
　　　　He shall be, by best teacher taught.

Lo, how his blessing buds
　　Inward, an inward rest;　　　　　　　　　　50
Outward, all outward goods
　　By his seed eke possessed.
　　　　For such he makes his secret know,
　　　　To such he doth his cov'nant show.

Where then should my eyes be,　　　　　　　　　　55
　　But still on this Lord set?
Who doth and will set free
　　My feet from tangling net.
　　　　Oh, look, oh, help, let mercy fall,
　　　　For I am poor and least of all.°　　　　　　　　　　60

My woes are still increased:
　　Shield me from these assaults;
See how I am oppressed,
　　And pardon all my faults.
　　　　Behold my foes, what store they be,　　　　　　　　　　65
　　　　Who hate, yea, hate me cruelly.

---

39 verity] truth　　　42 plant] rely　　　52 eke] also

My soul which thou didst make,
    Now made, O Lord, maintain:
And me from these ills take,
    Lest I rebuke sustain.   70
        For thou, the Lord, thou only art
        Of whom the trust lives in my heart.

Let my uprightness gain
    Some safety unto me:
I say, and say again,   75
    My hope is all in thee.
        In fine, deliver Israel,
        O Lord, from all his troubles fell.

Psalm 26

Judica me, Domine

Lord, judge me and my case,
    For I have made my race
Within the bounds of innocence to bide:
    And setting thee for scope
    Of all my trustful hope,   5
I held for sure, that I should never slide.

Prove me, O Lord most high,
    Me with thy touchstone try:
Yea, sound my reins, and inmost of my heart.
    For so thy loving hand   10
    Before my eyes did stand,
That from thy truth will not depart.°

I did not them frequent,
    Who be to vainness bent,
Nor kept with base dissemblers company.   15

77 fine] conclusion   78 fell] terrible
Psalm 26 3 bide] abide   4 scope] target   8 touchstone] criterion
9 reins] inmost self

Nay, I did ev'n detest
    Of wicked wights the nest,
And from the haunts of such bad folks did fly.

In th'innocence of me
    My hands shall washèd be;°   20
And with those hands, about thy altar wait,
    That I may still express
    With voice of thankfulness
The works performed by thee, most wondrous great.

Lord, I have lovèd well   25
    The house where thou dost dwell,
Ev'n where thou mak'st thy honour's biding place.
    Sweet Lord, write not my soul,
    Within the sinners' roll:
Nor my life's cause, match with blood-seekers' case,°   30

With hands of wicked shifts,
    With right hands stained with gifts.
But while I walk in my unspotted ways
    Redeem and show me grace
    So I in public place   35
Set on plain ground will thee, Jehovah, praise.

Psalm 27

Dominus illuminatio

The shining Lord he is my light:
    The strong God my salvation is:
    Who shall be able me to fright?
    This Lord with strength my life doth bliss:
        And shall I then   5
        Fear might of men?

17 wights] persons   31 shifts] stratagems

When wicked folk, ev'n they that be
  My foes, to utmost of their pow'r
  With raging jaws environ me,
  My very flesh for to devour:°   10
      They stumble so,
      That down they go.

Then though against me armies were,
  My courage should not be dismayed:
  Though battle's brunt, I needs must bear,   15
  While battle's brunt, on me were laid,
      In this I would
      My trust still hold.°

One thing indeed I did, and will
  For ever crave: that dwell I may   20
  In house of high Jehovah still
  On beauty his mine eyes to stay,
      And look into
      His temple too.

For when great griefs to me be meant,   25
  In tabernacle his he will
  Hide me, ev'n closely in his tent:
  Yea, noble height of rocky hill,
      He makes to be
      A seat for me.   30

Now, now, shall he lift up my head
  On my besieging enemies:
  So shall I sacrifices spread,
  Off'rings of joy in temple his,
      And song accord   35
      To praise the Lord.

Hear, Lord, when I my voice display,
  Hear, to have mercy eke of me.

9 environ] surround   15 brunt] chief assault   38 eke] also

'Seek ye my face,' when thou didst say,°
  In truth of heart I answered thee,   40
        'O Lord, I will
        Seek thy face still.'

Hide not therefore from me that face,
  Since all my aid in thee I got:
  In rage, thy servant do not chase;   45
  Forsake not me, oh, leave me not,
        O God of my
        Salvation, hie.

Though father's care and mother's love
  Abandoned me, yet my decay   50
  Should be restored by him above,
  Teach, Lord, Lord, lead me thy right way,
        Because of those
        That be my foes,

Unto whose ever-hating lust,   55
  Oh, give me not; for there are sprung
  Against me witnesses unjust,
  Ev'n such, I say, whose lying tongue
        Fiercely affords
        Most cruel words.   60

What had I been, except I had
  Believed God's goodness for to see,
  In land with living creatures clad?
  Hope, trust in God, be strong, and he
        Unto thy heart   65
        Shall joy impart.

---

48 hie] hasten   55 lust] desire   59 affords] performs, speaks

Psalm 28

Ad te, Domine

To thee, Lord, my cry I send;
   O my strength, stop not thine ear:
   Lest if answer thou forbear,
   I be like them that descend
   To the pit, where flesh doth end.   5

Therefore while that I may cry,
   While I that way hold my hands
   Where thy sanctuary stands:°
   To thyself those words apply,
   Which from suing voice do fly.   10

Link not me in selfsame chain,°
   With the wicked-working folk:
   Who their spotted thoughts to cloak,
   Neighbours friendly entertain,
   When in hearts they malice mean.   15

Spare not them, give them reward,
   As their deeds have purchased it,
   As deserves their wicked wit;
   Fare they, as their hands have fared:
   Ev'n so be their guerdon shared.   20

To thy works they give no eye:
   Let them be thrown down by thee;
   Let them not restorèd be.
   But let me give praises high°
   To the Lord, that hears my cry.   25

That God is my strength, my shield:
   All my trust on him was set,

3 forbear] withhold   10 suing] making suit, petitioning   20 guerdon] reward

And so I did safety get.
So shall I with joy be filled,
So my songs his lauds shall yield.   30

God on them his strength doth lay,
  Who his anointed helpèd have.
  Lord, then still thy people save;
  Bless thine heritage, I say,
  Feed and lift them up for aye.   35

Psalm 29

Afferte Domino

Ascribe unto the Lord of light,
  Ye men of pow'r ev'n by birth-right,
  Ascribe all glory and all might.

Ascribe due glory to his name;
  And in his ever-glorious frame   5
  Of sanctuary do the same.

His voice is on the waters found,°
  His voice doth threat'ning thunders sound,
  Yea, through the waters doth resound.

The voice of that Lord ruling us   10
  Is strong, though he be gracious,
  And ever, ever glorious.

By voice of high Jehovah we
  The highest cedars broken see,
  Ev'n cedars which on Leban be;   15

Nay, like young calves, in leaps are born;
  And Leban's self with nature's scorn;
  And Shirion, like young unicorn.°

---

30 lauds] praises   35 for aye] for ever
Psalm 29 5 frame] structure   15 Leban] Lebanon   18 Shirion] Mount Hermon

His voice doth flashing flames divide:
    His voice have trembling deserts tried,°   20
    Ev'n deserts where the Arabs bide.°

His voice makes hinds their calves to cast;
    His voice makes bald the forest waste:
    But in his church his fame is placed.

He sits on seas, he endless reigns,°   25
    His strength his people's strength maintains,
    Which blest by him in peace remains.

Psalm 30

Exaltabo te, Domine

O Lord, thou hast exalted me
    And saved me from foes' laughing scorn:
    I owe thee praise, I will praise thee.

For when my heart with woes was torn,°
    In cries to thee, I showed my cause: 5
    And was from ill, by thee upborne.

Yea, from the grave's most hungry jaws
    Thou wouldst not set me on their score,
    Whom Death to his cold bosom draws.

Praise, praise this Lord then evermore,   10
    Ye saints of his, rememb'ring still
    With thanks his holiness therefore.

For quickly ends his wrathful will
    But his dear favour where it lies,
    From age to age life joys doth fill.   15

---

22 hinds] deer   cast] give birth to   23 bald] treeless
Psalm 30 8 score] list   15 life joys] life's joys

Well may the evening clothe the eyes
　　In clouds of tears, but soon as sun
　　Doth rise again, new joys shall rise.

For proof, while I my race did run
　　Full of success, fond I did say,　　　　　　　　20
　　That I should never be undone.

For then my hill good God did stay:
　　But, ah, he straight his face did hide,
　　And what was I but wretched clay?

Then thus to thee I praying cried,　　　　　　　　25
　　'What serves, alas, the blood of me
　　When I within the pit do bide?

'Shall ever earth give thanks to thee?°
　　Or shall thy truth on mankind laid
　　In deadly dust declarèd be?　　　　　　　　　　30

'Lord, hear, let mercy thine be stayed
　　On me, from me help this annoy.'
　　This much I said, this being said,

Lo, I that wailed, now dance for joy:
　　Thou didst ungird my doleful sack,　　　　　　　35
　　And mad'st me gladsome weeds enjoy.

Therefore my tongue shall never lack
　　Thy endless praise: O God, my king,
　　I will thee thanks for ever sing.

22 stay] protect　　　27 bide] abide　　　31 stayed] continued　　　32 annoy]
annoyance　　35 ungird] take off　　doleful] sorrowful　　sack] sackcloth, worn for
mourning　　36 weeds] clothes

Psalm 31

In te, Domine, speravi

All, all my trust, Lord, I have put in thee.
  Never therefore, let me confounded be,
    But save me, save me in thy righteousness.
Bow down thine ear, to hear how much I need:
  Deliver me, deliver me in speed;   5
    Be my strong rock, be thou my forteress.

Indeed thou art my rock, my forteress:°
  Then since my tongue delights that name to bless,
    Direct me how to go, and guide me right.
Preserve me from the wily wrapping net,   10
  Which they for me, with privy craft have set:
    For still I say, 'Thou art my only might.'

Into thy hands, I do commend my sprite:°
  For it is thou, that hast restored my light,
    O Lord, that art the God of verity.   15
I hated have those men, whose thoughts do cleave
To vanities, which most trust, most deceive:
    For all my hope fixed upon God doth lie.

Thy mercy shall fill me with jollity,
  For my annoys have come before thine eye: 20
    Thou well hast known what plunge my soul was in.
And thou hast not for aye enclosèd me
Within the hand of hateful enmity:
    But hast enlarged my feet from mortal gin.

O Lord, of thee, let me still mercy win;   25
  For troubles, of all sides, have me within:
    My eye, my guts, yea, my soul, grief doth waste.
    My life with heaviness, my years with moan

---

11 privy] secret   13 sprite] spirit   15 verity] truth   16 cleave] cling
20 annoys] annoyances   21 plunge] depths   22 for aye] for ever
24 enlarged] released   gin] snare

Do pine; my strength with pain is wholly gone;
   And ev'n my bones consume, where they be placed.   30

All my fierce foes reproach on me did cast;
   Yea, neighbours, more, my mates, were so aghast,
      That in the streets from sight of me they fled:
   Now I, now I myself forgotten find,
   Ev'n like a dead man, dreamèd out of mind,   35
      Or like a broken pot, in mire tread.°

I understand what railing great men spread;
   Fear was each where, while they their councils led
      All to this point, how my poor life to take:
   But I did trust in thee, Lord, I did say,   40
   'Thou art my God, my time on thee doth stay:
      Save me from foes, who seek my bane to bake.

'Thy face to shine upon thy servant make,
   And save me in, and for, thy mercy's sake;
      Let me not taste of shame, O Lord most high,   45
   For I have called on thee. Let wicked folk
   Confounded be and pass away like smoke;
      Let them in bed of endless silence die.

'Let those lips be made dumb, which love to lie:
   Which full of spite, of pride, and cruelty   50
      Do throw their words against the most upright.
   Oh, of thy grace what endless pleasure flows
   To whom fear thee! What thou hast done for those
      That trust in thee, ev'n in most open sight!

'And when need were, from pride, in privy plight   55
   Thou hast hid them, yet leaving them thy light
      From strife of tongues, in thy pavilions placed.'°

---

36 tread] trodden   37 railing] ranting   38 each where] everywhere
41 stay] wait   42 bane to bake] cause my destruction   55 plight] pleat, fold

Then praise, then praise I do the Lord of us
Who was to me more than most gracious,
   Far, far more sure, than walls most firmly fast.   60

Yet I confess in that tempestuous haste,
  I said that I from out thy sight was cast:
    But thou didst hear, when I to thee did moan.
Then love the Lord all ye that feel his grace,
Who pares the proud, preserves the faithful race: 65
    Be strong in hope, his strength shall you supply.

Psalm 32

Beati quorum

Blessed is he whose filthy stain
    The Lord with pardon doth make clean,
      Whose fault well hidden lieth.
    Blessed indeed to whom the Lord
    Imputes not sins to be abhorred,   5
      Whose spirit falsehood flieth.

Thus I, pressed down with weight of pain,
    Whether I silent did remain,
      Or roared, my bones still wasted.
    For so both day and night did stand   10
    On wretched me, thy heavy hand;
      My life hot torments tasted,

Till myself did my faults confess,
    And opened mine own wickedness,
      Whereto my heart did give me: 15
    So I myself accused to God,

62 out] out of   65 pares] prunes
Psalm 32 9 roared] cried out

And his sweet grace straight eased the rod,
   And did due pain forgive me.

Therefore shall every godly one
   In fit time make to thee his moan,   20
      When thou wilt deign to hear him.
   Sure, sure, the flood of straying streams,°
   However they put in their claims,
      Shall never dare come near him.

Thou art my safe and secret place,   25
   Who savest me from troublous case,
      To songs and joyful biding.
   But whoso will instructed be,
   Come, come the way I will teach thee,
      Guide thee by my eyes' guiding.   30

Oh, be not like a horse or mule
   Wholly devoid of reason's rule;
      Whose mouths thyself dost bridle:
   Knowing full well, that beasts they be,
   And therefore soon would mischief thee,   35
      If thou remained'st idle.

Woes, woes shall come to wicked folks.
   But who on God, his trust invokes,
      All mercies shall be swarmèd.
   Be glad you good, in God have joy,   40
   Joy be to you, who do enjoy
      Your hearts with clearness armèd.

21 deign] condescend   35 mischief] cause mischief to   42 clearness] purity

Psalm 33

Exultate, justi

Rejoice in God, O ye
    That righteous be:
  For cheerful thankfulness,
  It is a comely part
    In them whose heart   5
  Doth cherish rightfulness.

Oh, praise with harp the Lord,
    Oh, now accord
  Viols with singing voice:
  Let ten-stringed instrument,   10
    Oh, now be bent
  To witness you rejoice.°

A new, sing a new song
    To him most strong,
  Sing loud and merrily: 15
  Because that word of his
    Most righteous is
  And his deeds faithful be.

He righteousness approves
    And judgement loves: 20
  God's goodness fills all lands.
  His word made heav'nly coast,
    And all that host°
  By breath of his mouth stands.

The waters of the seas   25
    In heaps he lays,
  And depths in treasure his:
  Let all the earth fear God,
    And who abroad
  Of world a dweller is.   30

8 accord] tune

For he spake not more soon,
    Than it was done:
  He bade, and it did stand.
  He doth heath'n council break,
    And maketh weak   35
  The might of people's hand.

But ever, ever shall
    His counsels all
  Throughout all ages last.
  The thinkings of that mind   40
    No end shall find
  When time's times shall be past.

That realm indeed hath bliss,
    Whose God he is,
  Who him for their Lord take: 45
  Ev'n people that, ev'n those,
    Whom this Lord chose
  His heritage to make.

The Lord looks from the sky:
    Full well his eye   50
  Beholds our mortal race.
  Ev'n where he dwelleth, he
    Throughout doth see
  Who dwell in dusty place.

Since he their hearts doth frame,   55
    He knows the same:
  Their works he understands.
  Hosts do the king not save;
    Nor strong men have
  Their help from mighty hands.   60

Of quick strength is a horse
    And yet his force
  Is but a succour vain:

55 frame] create   63 succour] help

Who trusts him, sooner shall
    Catch harmful fall
Than true deliverance gain.

But, lo, Jehovah's sight
    On them doth light
Who him do truly fear:
And them who do the scope
    Of all their hope
Upon his mercy bear.

His sight is them to save
    Ev'n from the grave,
And keep from famine's pain.
Then on that Lord most kind
    Fix we our mind,
Whose shield shall us maintain.

Our hearts sure shall enjoy
    In him much joy
Who hope on his name just.
Oh, let thy mercy great
    On us be set,
We have no plea, but trust.

Psalm 34

Benedicam Domino

I, ev'n I will always
    Give hearty thanks to him on high,
    And in my mouth continually
Inhabit shall his praise.
    My soul shall glory still
    In that dear Lord with true delight:
    That hearing it the hearts contrite
May learn their joys to fill.

Come then and join with me,
    Somewhat to speak of his due praise: 10
    Strive we, that in some worthy phrase
    His name may honoured be.
       Thus I begin: I sought
    This Lord, and he did hear my cry:
    Yea, and from dreadful misery 15
    He me, he only brought.

This shall men's fancies frame
    To look and run to him for aid,
    Whose faces on his comfort stayed
    Shall never blush for shame. 20
       For, lo, this wretch did call,
    And, lo, his call, the skies did climb:
    And God freed him in his worst time
    From out his troubles all.

His angels' armies round 25
    About them pitch, who him do fear:
    And watch and ward for such do bear,
    To keep them safe and sound.
       I say but taste and see,
    How sweet, how gracious is his grace: 30
    Lord, he is in thrice blessed case
    Whose trust is all on thee.

Fear God, ye saints of his,
    For nothing they can ever want
    Who faithful fears in him do plant: 35
    They have, and shall have bliss.
       The lions oft lack food,
    Those raveners' whelps oft starvèd be:
    But who seek God with constancy
    Shall need naught that is good. 40

17 frame] make   19 stayed] relied   27 watch and ward] guard and protect
40 naught] nothing

Come, children, lend your ear°
   To me, and mark, what I do say:
   For I will teach to you the way
   How this our Lord to fear.
     Among you, who is here,   45
   That life and length of life requires
   And blessing such, with length desires,
   As life may good appear?

Keep well thy lips and tongue,
   Lest inward ills do them defile: 50
   Or that by words, enwrapped in guile
   Another man be stung.
     Do good, from faults decline,
   Seek peace, and follow after it:
   For God's own eyes on good men sit,   55
   And ears to them incline.

So his high heavenly face
   Is bent, but bent against those same
   That wicked be, their very name
   From earth quite to displace.   60
     The just when harms approach,
   Do cry, their cry of him is heard:
   And by his care from them is barred
   All trouble, all reproach.

To humble, broken minds,   65
   This Lord is ever, ever near:
   And will save whom his true sight clear
   In sprite afflicted finds.
     Indeed the very best
   Most great and grievous pains doth bear: 70
   But God shall him to safety rear,
   When most he seems oppressed.

68 sprite] spirit   71 rear] raise

His bones he keepeth all,
 So that not one of them is broke:
 But malice shall the wicked choke,   75
Who hate the good shall fall.
 God doth all souls redeem
Who wear his blessed livery:
 None, I say still, shall ruined be,
Who him their trust esteem.   80

Psalm 35
Judica, Domine

Speak thou for me, against wrong-speaking foes:
 Thy force, O Lord, against their force oppose.
Take up thy shield and for my succour stand,
 Yea, take thy lance and stop the way of those
That seek my bane; oh, make me understand   5
 In sprite, that I shall have thy helping hand.

Confound those folks, thrust them in shameful hole
 That hunt so poor a prey, as is my soul.
Rebuke and wrack on those wrong-doers throw
 Who for my hurt, each way their thoughts did roll,   10
And as vile chaff, away the wind doth blow,
 Let angel thine a-scatt'ring make them go.

Let angel thine pursue them as they fly
 But let their flight be dark and slippery,
For causeless they, both pit and net did set;   15
 For causeless they did seek to make me die:
Let their sly wits unwares destruction get,
 Fall in self pit, be caught in their own net.

Then shall I joy in thee, then saved by thee
 I both in mind and bones shall gladded be.   20

3 succour] help   5 bane] destruction   6 sprite] spirit
9 wrack] ruin   18 self pit] their own pit

Ev'n bones shall say, 'O God, who is thy peer,
    Who poor and weak, from rich, and strong dost free,
Who helpest those whose ruin was so near,
    From him whose force did in their spoils appear?

'Who did me wrong, against me witness bear,   25
    Laying such things, as never in me were:
So my good deeds they pay, with evil share,
    With cruel minds, my very soul to tear.
And whose? Ev'n his, who when they sickness bare,
    With inward woe, an outward sackcloth ware.'   30

I did pull down myself, fasting for such,
    I prayed, with prayers, which my breast did touch:
In sum I showed, that I to them was bent
    As brothers, or as friends belovèd much.
Still, still, for them I humbly mourning went,   35
    Like one that should his mother's death lament.

But, lo, soon as they did me stagg'ring see,
    Who joy but they, when they assembled be?
Then abjects, while I was unwitting quite
    Against me swarm, ceaseless to rail at me   40
With scoffers false, I was their feast's delight,
    Ev'n gnashing teeth, to witness more their spite.

Lord, wilt thou see, and wilt thou suffer it?
    Oh, on my soul, let not these tumults hit.
Save me, distressed, from lion's cruel kind.   45
    I will thank thee, where congregations sit,
Ev'n where I do most store of people find,
    Most to thy lauds will I my speeches bind.

Then, then let not my foes unjustly joy;
    Let them not fleer, who me would causeless stroy;   50
Who never word of peace yet utter would,

---

29 bare] bore   30 sackcloth] mourning clothes   ware] wore   39 abjects]
wicked people   unwitting] unknowing   48 lauds] praises   50 fleer] mock
stroy] destroy

But hunt with craft the quiet man's annoy,
And said to me, wide mowing, as they could:
'Aha! Sir, now we see you where we should.'

This thou hast seen: and wilt thou silent be?   55
O Lord, do not absent thyself from me:
But rise, but wake, that I may judgement get.
My Lord, my God, ev'n to my equity,
Judge, Lord, judge, God, ev'n in thy justice great:
Let not their joy upon my woes be set.   60

Let them not, Lord, within their hearts thus say:
'O soul, rejoice, we made this wretch our prey.'
But throw them down, put them to endless blame,
Who make a cause to joy of my decay.
Let them be clothed with most confounding shame,   65
That lift themselves my ruin for to frame.

But make such glad and full of joyfulness
That yet bear love unto my righteousness:
Yet, let them say, 'Laud be to God always,
Who loves with good his servants' good to bless.'   70
As for my tongue, while I have any days,
Thy justice witness shall, and speak thy praise.

Psalm 36

Dixit injustus

Me thinks amid my heart I hear
What guilty wickedness doth say,
Which wicked folks do hold so dear:
Ev'n thus itself, it doth display,
No fear of God, doth once appear,   5
Before his eyes that so doth stray.

---

52 annoy] annoyance   53 mowing] grimacing   66 frame] contrive
69 Laud] praise
Psalm 36 4 it] i.e. wickedness

For those same eyes, his flatterers be,
    Till his known ill do hatred get;°
His words, deceit; iniquity,
    His deeds: yea, thoughts all good forget.   10
Abed on mischief, museth he,
    Abroad his steps be wrongly set.

Lord, how the heav'ns thy mercy fills!
    Thy truth above the clouds most high,
Thy righteousness like hugest hills,   15
    Thy judgements like the deeps do lie.
Thy grace with safety man fulfils,
    Yea, beasts, made safe, thy goodness try.

O Lord, how excellent a thing
    Thy mercy is, which makes mankind   20
Trust in the shadow of thy wing,°
    Who shall in thy house fatness find,
And drink from out thy pleasures' spring
    Of pleasures past the reach of mind.

For why? The well of life thou art   25
    And in thy light, we shall see light.
Oh, then extend thy loving heart
    To them that know thee and thy might:
Oh, then, thy righteousness impart
    To them that be in souls upright.   30

Let not proud feet make me their thrall;
    Let not ill hands, discomfit me:
Lo, there, I now foresee their fall,
    Who do ill works. Lo, I do see
They are cast down and never shall   35
    Have pow'r again to raisèd be.

11 museth] thinks   16 deeps] oceans   22 fatness] abundance
25 For why?] for what reason?   31 thrall] captive   32 discomfit] overthrow

Psalm 37

Noli aemulari

Fret not thyself, if thou do see
  That wicked men do seem to flourish:
  Nor envy in thy bosom nourish
 Though ill deeds well succeeding be.

They soon shall be cut down like grass   5
  And wither like green herb or flower:°
  Do well, and trust on heav'nly power,
 Thou shalt have both good food and place.

Delight in God, and he shall breed
  The fullness of thy own heart's lusting: 10
  Guide thee by him, lay all thy trusting
On him, and he will make it speed.

For like the light he shall display
  Thy justice, in most shining lustre:
  And of thy judgement make a muster   15
 Like to the glory of noonday.

Wait on the Lord with patient hope;
  Chafe not at some man's great good fortune:
  Though all his plots without misfortune,
 Attain unto their wishèd scope.   20

Fume not, rage not, fret not, I say,
  Lest such things sin in thyself cherish:
  For those bad folks, at last shall perish,
Who stay for God, in bliss shall stay.

Watch but a while, and thou shalt see   25
  The wicked by his own pride banished:
  Look after him, he shall be vanished,
 And never found again shall be.

10 lusting] desiring 15 muster] display 24 stay . . . stay] wait . . . remain

But meek men shall the earth possess,°
   In quiet home they shall be planted: 30
   And this delight to them is granted,
They shall have peace in plenteousness.

Evil men, work ill to utmost right,
   Gnashing their teeth full of disdaining:
   But God shall scorn their moody meaning,   35
For their short time is in his sight.

The evil bent bows, and swords they drew,
   To have their hate on good souls wroken:
   But, lo, their bows, they shall be broken,
Their swords shall their own hearts imbrue.   40

Small goods in good men better is,
   Than of bad folks the wealthy wonder:
   For wicked arms shall break asunder,
But God upholds the just in bliss.

God keeps account of good men's days,   45
   Their heritage shall last for ever:
   In peril they shall perish never,
Nor want in dearth, their want to ease.

Bad folks shall fall, and fall for aye;
   Who to make war, with God presumèd,   50
   Like fat of lambs shall be consumèd,
Ev'n with the smoke shall waste away.

The naughty borrows, paying not;
   The good is kind, and freely giveth.
   Lo, whom God blest, he blessed liveth: 55
Whom he doth curse, to naught shall rot.

---

35 moody] sullen   38 wroken] wreaked   40 imbrue] stain with blood
48 dearth] famine   49 for aye] for ever   53 naughty] wicked person
56 naught] nothing

The man whom God directs, doth stand
    Firm on his way, his way God loveth;
    Though he doth fall, no wrack he proveth:
He is upheld by heav'nly hand.   60

I have been young, now old I am,
    Yet I the man that was betaken
    To justice, never saw forsaken:
Nor that his seed a-begging came.

He lends, he gives, more he doth spend,   65
    The more his seed in blessing flourish:
    Then fly all ill, and goodness nourish,
And thy good state, shall never end.

God loving right doth not forsake
    His holy ones; they are preservèd   70
    From time to time, but who be swervèd
To ill, both they and theirs shall wrack.

I say, I say the righteous minds
    Shall have the land in their possessing,
    Shall dwell thereon, and this their blessing   75
No time within his limits binds.°

The good mouth will in wisdom bide,
    His tongue of heav'nly judgements telleth,
    For God's high law in his heart dwelleth:
What comes thereof? He shall not slide.   80

The wicked watch the righteous much,
    And seek of life for to bereave him:
    But in their hand God will not leave him,
Nor let him be condemned by such.

Wait thou on God, and keep his way,   85
    He will exalt thee unto honour:

59 wrack] ruin   62 betaken] committed

And of the earth make thee an owner,
Yea, thou shalt see the evil decay.

I have the wicked seen full sound,
    Like laurel fresh himself outspreading: 90
    Lo, he was gone; print of his treading,
Though I did seek, I never found.

Mark the upright, the just attend:
    His end shall be in peace enjoyèd.
    But strayers vile, shall be destroyèd,   95
And quite cut off with helpless end.

Still, still the godly shall be stayed
    By God's most sure, and sweet salvation:
    In time of greatest tribulation
He shall be their true strength and aid.   100

He shall be their true strength and aid,
    He shall save them from all the fetches
    Against them used, by wicked wretches:
Because on him their trust is laid.

Psalm 38

Domine, ne in furore

Lord, while that thy rage doth bide,
    Do not chide:
    Nor in anger chastise me.
For thy shafts have pierced me sore;
    And yet more,   5
Still thy hands upon me be.

No sound part caused by thy wrath,
    My flesh hath:
    Nor my sins let my bones rest.

91 treading] footsteps   102 fetches] tricks
Psalm 38 1 bide] abide   4 shafts] arrows

For my faults are highly spread 10
    On my head,
Whose foul weights have me oppressed.

My wounds putrefy and stink
    In the sink
Of my filthy folly laid: 15
Earthly I do bow and crook,
    With a look
Still in mourning cheer arrayed.

In my reins hot torments reigns,
    There remains 20
Nothing in my body sound.
I am weak and broken sore,
    Yea, I roar,
In my heart such grief is found.

Lord, before thee I do lay 25
    What I pray:
My sighs are not hid from thee.
My heart pants, gone is my might,
    Ev'n the light
Of mine eyes abandons me. 30

From my plague, kin, neighbour, friend,
    Far off wend:
But who for my life do wait,
They lay snares, they nimble be,
    Who hunt me, 35
Speaking evil, thinking deceit.

But I like a man become
    Deaf and dumb,
Little hearing, speaking less,

14 sink] cesspool   16 crook] kneel (Rathmell)   18 cheer] countenance
19 reins] inmost feelings   23 roar] cry out   32 wend] depart

I ev'n as such kind of wight, 40
  Senseless quite,
Word with word do not repress.

For on thee, Lord, without end
  I attend:
My God, thou wilt hear my voice 45
For I said, 'Hear, lest they be
  Glad on me,
Whom my fall doth make rejoice.'

Sure I do but halting go,
  And my woe 50
Still my o'erthwart neighbour is.
Lo, I now to mourn begin
  For my sin,
Telling mine iniquities.

But the while, they live and grow 55
  In great show,
Many, mighty, wrongful foes,
Who do evil for good, to me
  Enemies be:
Why? Because I virtue chose. 60

Do not, Lord, then me forsake,
  Do not take
Thy dear presence far from me.
Haste, O Lord, that I be stayed
  By thy aid, 65
My salvation is in thee.

40 wight] person   49 halting] limping   51 o'erthwart] hostile
56 show] display   64 stayed] sustained

Psalm 39

Dixi, custodiam

Thus did I think, 'I well will mark my way,
    Lest by my tongue I hap to stray.
I muzzle will my mouth, while in the sight
    I do abide of wicked wight.'
And so I nothing said, I muet stood,   5
    I silence kept, ev'n in the good.

But still the more that I did hold my peace,
    The more my sorrow did increase.
The more me thought, my heart was hot in me,
    And as I mused such world to see,   10
The fire took fire and forcibly out-brake;
    My tongue would needs and thus I spake:

'Lord, unto me my time's just measure give,
    Show me how long I have to live:
Lo, thou a span's length, mad'st my living line.°   15
    A span? Nay, nothing in thine eyne.
What do we seek? The greatest state I see,
    At best is merely vanity.

'They are but shades, not true things where we live:
    Vain shades, and vain, in vain to grieve.   20
Look but on this: man still doth riches heap,
    And knows not, who the fruit shall reap.
This being thus, for what, O Lord, wait I?
    I wait on thee, with hopeful eye.

'Oh, help, oh, help me; this far yet I crave,   25
    From my transgressions me to save.
Let me not be thrown down to so base shame,
    That fools of me may make their game.

---

2 Lest] unless   hap] happen   4 wight] person   5 muet] mute
11 out-brake] broke out   12 would needs] was compelled to   16 eyne] eyes

But I do hush, why do I say thus much,
    Since it is thou that mak'st one such? 30

'Ah! Yet from me let thy plagues be displaced,
    For with thy handy strokes I waste.°
I know that man's foul sin doth cause thy wrath,
    For when his sin thy scourging hath,
Thou moth-like mak'st his beauty fading be: 35
    So what is man, but vanity?

'Hear, Lord, my suits, and cries; stop not thine ears
    At these my words all clothed in tears:
For I with thee, on earth a stranger am,
    But baiting, as my fathers came. 40
Stay then thy wrath, that I may strength receive
    Ere I my earthly being leave.'

Psalm 40

Expectans expectavi

While long I did with patient constancy,
    The pleasure of my God attend,
    He did himself to me-ward bend,
And hearkened how and why that I did cry.
      And me from pit bemirèd, 5
      From dungeon he retirèd,
      Where I, in horrors lay:
      Setting my feet upon
      A steadfast rocky stone
      And my weak steps did stay. 10

So in my mouth he did a song afford,
    New song unto our God of praise:°
    Which many seeing hearts shall raise

32 handy] of thy hand   40 baiting] pausing on journey   41 Stay] cease
42 Ere] before

Psalm 40 3 to me-ward] towards me   5 bemirèd] stuck in mud
6 retirèd] removed   10 stay] support   11 afford] supply

To fear with trust, and trust with fear the Lord.
    Oh, he indeed is blessed   15
    Whose trust is so addressèd:
    Who bends not wand'ring eyes
    To great men's peacock pride,
    Nor ever turns aside
    To follow after lies.   20

My God, thy wondrous works how manifold!
    What man thy thoughts can count to thee?
    I fain of them would speaking be,
But they are more than can by me be told.
    Thou sacrifice nor off'ring,   25
    Burnt off'ring nor sin off'ring
    Didst like, much less didst crave:°
    But thou didst pierce my ear,
    Which should thy lessons bear,
    And witness me thy slave.   30

Thus bound, I said, 'Lo, Lord, I am at hand
    For in thy book's roll, I am writ
    And sought with deeds, thy will to hit,
Yea, Lord, thy law within my heart doth stand:
    I to great congregation,   35
    Thou know'st, made declaration
    Of this sweet righteousness;
    My lips shall still reveal,
    My heart shall not conceal
    Thy truth, health, graciousness.   40

'Then, Lord, from me, draw not thy tender grace:
    Me still in truth, and mercy save.
    For endless woes, me compassed have,
So pressed with sins, I cannot see my case.
    But trial well doth teach me,   45
    Foul faults' sore pains do reach me,
    More than my head hath hairs.

23 fain . . . would] would gladly   44 pressed] oppressed   44 case] situation

So that my surest part,
My life-maintaining heart,
Fails me, with ugly fears.   50

'Vouchsafe me help, O Lord, and help with haste:
  Let them have shame, yea, blush for shame
  Who jointly sought, my bale to frame;
Let them be curst away that would me waste.
        Let them with shame be cloyèd,   55
        Yea, let them be destroyèd,
        For guerdon of their shame,
        Who so unpiteous be
        As now to say to me,
        "Aha! This is good game."   60

'But fill their hearts with joy who bend their ways,
  To seek thy beauty past conceit,
  Let them that love thy saving seat,
Still gladly say, "Unto our God be praise!"
        Though I in want be shrinking,   65
        Yet God on me is thinking.
        Thou art my help for aye,
        Thou only, thou art he,
        That dost deliver me:
        My God, oh, make no stay.'°   70

Psalm 41

Beatus qui intelligit

He blessed is who with wise temper can
  Judge of th'afflicted man.
For God shall him deliver in the time,
  When most his troubles climb.
The Lord will keep his life yet safe and sound,   5

---

53 bale] misery   frame] contrive   55 cloyèd] pierced   57 guerdon] reward
62 conceit] thought   67 for aye] for ever   70 stay] delay
Psalm 41 1 temper] temperament

With blessings of the ground,
And will not him unto the will expose,
  Of them that be his foes.

When bed from rest becomes his seat of woe,
  In God his strength shall grow: 10
And turn his couch, where sick he couchèd late,°
  To well-recovered state.
Therefore I said in most infirmity,
  'Have mercy, Lord, on me:
Oh, heal my soul, let there thy cure begin,   15
  Where gainst thee lay my sin.'

My foes' evil words, their hate of me display,
  While thus, alas, they say:
'When, when will death o'ertake this wretched wight,
  And his name perish quite?'   20
Their courteous visitings, are courting lies,
  They inward evils disguise
Ev'n heaps of wicked thoughts, which straight they show
  As soon as out they go.

For then their hateful heads, close whisp'ring be,   25
  With hurtful thoughts to me:
'Now he is wracked,' say they. 'Lo, there he lies,
  Who never more must rise.'
Oh, yea, my friend, to whom I did impart
  The secrets of my heart.   30
My friend, I say, who at my table sat,
  Did kick against my state.°

Therefore, O Lord, abandoned thus of all,
  On me let mercy fall,
And raise me up, that I may once have might,   35
  Their merits to requite:

11 couchèd] lay down   16 gainst] against   19 wight] person

But what? This doth already well appear
    That I to thee am dear:
Since foes, nor have, nor shall have cause to be
    Triumphing over me.   40

But triumph well may I, whom thou dost stay
    In my sound rightful way:
Whom thou (O place of places all) dost place
    For aye before thy face.
So then be blest now, then, at home, abroad,   45
    Of Israel the God:
World without end, let this his blessing flow,
    Oh, so, oh, be it so.

Psalm 42

Quemadmodum

As the chafèd hart which brayeth,
    Seeking some refreshing brook,
So my soul in panting playeth,
    Thirsting on my God to look.
      My soul thirsts indeed in me   5
    After ever-living thee.
    Ah! When comes my blessed being,
    Of that face to have a seeing?

Day and night my tears out-flowing
    Have been my ill-feeding food,   10
With their daily questions throwing:
    'Where is now, thy God so good?'
      My heart melts rememb'ring so,
    How in troops I wont to go:
    Leading them, his praises singing,   15
    Holy dance to God's house bringing.

41 stay] support   44 For aye] for ever.
Psalm 41 1 chafèd hart . . . brayeth] heated deer cries out   14 wont] am
accustomed to

Why art thou, my soul, so sorry,
   And in me so much dismayed?
   Wait on God, for yet his glory
   In my song shall be displayed.   20
      When but with one look of his
   He shall me restore to bliss:
   Ah! My soul itself appalleth,
   In such longing thoughts it falleth.

For my mind on my God bideth,°   25
   Ev'n from Hermon's dwelling led,°
   From the grounds where Jordan slideth,
   And from Mizar's hilly head.°
      One deep with noise of his fall,°
   Other deeps of woes doth call: 30
   While my God, with wasting wonders°
   On me, wretch, his tempest thunders.

All thy floods on me abounded,
   Over me all thy waves went:
   Yet thus still my hope is grounded,   35
   That thy anger being spent,
      I by day thy love shall taste;
   I by night shall singing last,
   Praying, prayers still bequeathing
   To my God, that gave me breathing.   40

I will say, 'O Lord, my tower,
   Why am I forgot by thee?
   Why should grief my heart devour
   While the foe oppresseth me?
      Those vile scoffs of naughty ones°   45
   Wound and rent me to the bones:°
   When foes ask with foul deriding,
   "Where is now your God abiding?"'

---

25 bideth] abideth   29 deep] abyss   31 wasting] devastating
45 naughty] wicked   46 rent] rend

Why art thou, my soul, so sorry,
    And in me so much dismayed? 50
Wait on God, for yet his glory
In my song shall be displayed.
    To him my thanks shall be said,
Who is still my present aid:
And in fine my soul be raisèd, 55
God is my God, by me praisèd.

Psalm 43

Judica me, Deus

Judge of all, judge me
    And protector be
Of my cause, oppressèd
    By most cruel sprites;
Save me from bad wights, 5
In false colours dressèd.

For, my God, thy sight
    Giveth me my might,
Why then hast thou left me?
    Why walk I in woes, 10
While prevailing foes
Have of joys bereft me?

Send thy truth and light,°
    Let them guide me right
From the paths of folly, 15
    Bringing me to thy
Tabernacle high,°
In thy hill most holy.

55 in fine] at last

Psalm 43 4 sprites] spirits   5 wights] people   6 colours] heraldic insignia
(Rathmell)

To God's altars tho
    Will I boldly go,   20
Shaking off all sadness,
    To that God that is
God of all my bliss,
God of all my gladness.

Then, lo, then I will   25
    With sweet music's skill
Grateful meaning show thee:
    Then, God, yea, my God,
I will sing abroad
What great thanks I owe thee.   30

Why art thou, my soul,
    Cast down in such dole?
What ails thy discomfort?
    Wait on God, for still
Thank my God, I will,   35
Sure aid, present comfort.

Psalm 44

Deus, auribus

Lord, our fathers' true relation
    Often made, hath made us know
How thy pow'r in each occasion
    Thou of old for them didst show;
    How thy hand the pagan foe   5
        Rooting hence, thy folk implanting,
Leafless made that branch to grow,
        This to spring, no verdure wanting.°

Never could their sword procure them
    Conquest of the promised land;   10

19 tho] then   32 dole] sorrow
Psalm 44 1 relation] report   6 Rooting] uprooting

Never could their force assure them
   When they did in danger stand.
   No, it was thy arm, thy hand,
      No, it was thy favour's treasure
Spent upon thy lovèd band: 15
      Lovèd, why? For thy wise pleasure.

Unto thee stand I subjected,°
   I that did of Jacob spring:
Bid then that I be protected,
   Thou that art my God, my king.   20
   By that succour thou didst bring,
      We their pride that us assailèd,
   Down did tread, and back did fling,
      In thy name confused and quailèd.

For my trust was not reposèd   25
   In my own, though strongest, bow,
Nor my scabbard held enclosèd
   That, whence should my safety flow.°
   Thou, O God, from every foe
      Didst us shield, our haters shaming: 30
   Thence thy daily praise we show,
      Still thy name with honour naming.

But aloof thou now dost hover,
   Grieving us with all disgrace,
Hast resigned and given over   35
   In our camp thy captain's place.
   Back we turn, that turnèd face,°
      Flying them, that erst we foilèd:
   Lo, our goods (oh, changèd case!)
      Spoiled by them that late we spoilèd.   40

Right as sheep to be devourèd,
   Helpless here we lie alone;
Scatt'ringly by thee out-pourèd,

11 force] strength   24 quailèd] cowered   38 erst] once, earlier

Slaves to dwell with lords unknown.
Sold we are, but silver none   45
    Told for us: by thee so prizèd,
As for naught to be forgone,
     Graceless, worthless, vile, despisèd.

By them all that dwell about us,
    Tossed we fly as balls of scorn;°   50
All our neighbours laugh, and flout us,
    Men by thee in shame forlorn.
    Proverb-like our name is worn,
     Oh, how fast in foreign places!
What head-shakings are forborne,   55
     Wordless taunts and dumb disgraces!

So rebuke before me goeth,
    As myself do daily go;
So confusion on me groweth,
    That my face I blush to show.°   60
    By reviling sland'ring foe
     Inly wounded, thus I languish:
Wreakful spite with outward blow
     Anguish adds to inward anguish.

All, this all on us hath lighted,   65
    Yet to thee our love doth last;
As we were, we are delighted
    Still to hold thy cov'nant fast.
    Unto none our hearts have passed;
     Unto none our feet have slidden;   70
Though us down to dragons cast,
     Thou in deadly shade hast hidden.

If our God we had forsaken,
    Or forgot what he assigned,
If ourselves we had betaken   75

---

46 Told] counted out, paid   47 naught] nothing   forgone] neglected
54 fast] quickly firmly   63 Wreakful] vengeful   70 slidden] slid
75 ourselves . . . betaken] gone

Gods to serve of other kind,
Should not he our doubling find,°
    Though concealed and closely lurking,
Since his eye of deepest mind
    Deeper sinks than deepest working?   80

Surely, Lord, this daily murther
    For thy sake we thus sustain;
For thy sake esteemed no further
    Than as sheep, that must be slain.
    Up, O Lord, up once again,   85
        Sleep not ever, slack not ever.
Why dost thou forget our pain?
    Why to hide thy face persever?

Heavy grief our soul abaseth;
    Prostrate it on dust doth lie.   90
Earth our body fast embraceth;
    Nothing can the clasp untie.
    Rise, and us with help supply;
        Lord, in mercy so esteem us,
That we may thy mercy try,   95
        Mercy may from thrall redeem us.

Psalm 45

Eructavit cor meum

My heart indites an argument of worth,
    The praise of him that doth the sceptre sway:
My tongue the pen to paint his praises forth,
    Shall write as swift as swiftest writer may.
    Then to the king these are the words I say: 5
        'Fairer art thou than sons of mortal race:
Because high God hath blessed thee for aye,
    Thy lips, as springs, do flow with speaking grace.

77 doubling] duplicity   81 murther] murder   91 fast] closely
95 try] experience
Psalm 45 1 indites] proclaims   7 for aye] for ever   8 speaking] eloquent.

'Thy honour's sword gird to thy mighty side,
    O thou that dost all things in might excel: 10
With glory prosper, on with triumph ride,
    Since justice, truth, and meekness with thee dwell.
So that right hand of thine shall teaching tell°
        Such things to thee as well may terror bring,
And terror such as never erst befell   15
        To mortal minds at sight of mortal king.

'Sharp are thy shafts to cleave their hearts in twain
    Whose heads do cast thy conquests to withstand:
Good cause to make the meaner people fain
    With willing hearts to undergo thy hand.°   20
Thy throne, O God, doth never-falling stand;
        Thy sceptre, ensign of thy kingly might,
To righteousness is linked with such a band,
        That righteous hand still holds thy sceptre right.

'Justice in love, in hate thou holdest wrong,   25
    This makes that God, who so doth hate and love,
Glad-making oil, that oil on thee hath flung,
    Which thee exalts thine equals far above.
The fragrant riches of Sabean grove
        Myrrh, aloes, cassia, all thy robes do smell: 30
When thou from ivory palace dost remove,
        Thy breathing odours all thy train excel.

'Daughters of kings among thy courtly band,
    By honouring thee, of thee do honour hold;
On thy right side thy dearest queen doth stand   35
    Richly arrayed in cloth of Ophir gold.°
O daughter, hear what now to thee is told;
        Mark what thou hear'st, and what thou mark'st obey:

---

15 erst] before   17 shafts] arrows   18 cast] plan   19 meaner] of lower
social class   fain] glad   26 makes] causes 27 flung] anointed   29 Sabean]
Arabian   30 Myrrh, aloes] fragrant resins cassia] cinnamon   33 courtly band]
maids of honour

Forget to keep in memory enrolled
    The house and folk where first thou saw'st the day.   40

'So in the king, thy king, a dear delight
    Thy beauty shall both breed, and bred maintain:°
For only he on thee hath lordly right,
    Him only thou with awe must entertain.
    Then unto thee both Tyrus shall be fain   45
        Presents present, and richest nations mo,°
    With humble suit thy royal grace to gain,
        To thee shall do such homage as they owe.

'This queen that can a king her father call,
    Doth only she in upper garment shine?   50
Nay, underclothes, and what she weareth all,
    Gold is the stuff, the fashion art divine;
    Brought to the king in robe embroidered fine,
        Her maids of honour shall on her attend
    With such, to whom more favour shall assign   55
        In nearer place their happy days to spend,°

'Brought shall they be with mirth and marriage joy,
    And enter so the palace of the king:
Then let no grief thy mind, O queen, annoy,
    Nor parents left thy sad remembrance sting.°   60
    Instead of parents, children thou shalt bring,
        Of partaged earth the kings and lords to be:
    Myself thy name in lasting verse will sing,
        The world shall make no end of thanks to thee.'

Psalm 46

Deus noster refugium

God gives us strength, and keeps us sound,
    A present help when dangers call;

---

46 mo] more   52 stuff] fabric   62 partaged] divided into portions

Then fear not we, let quake the ground,
　　And into seas let mountains fall,
　　　Yea, so let seas withal,　　　　　　　　　5
　　　　In wat'ry hills arise,
　　As may the earthly hills appal,
　　　With dread and dashing cries.

For, lo, a river streaming joy
　　With purling murmur safely slides,　　　　10
That city washing from annoy,
　　In holy shrine where God resides.
　　God in her centre bides:
　　　What can this city shake?
　　God early aids and ever guides:　　　　　15
　　　Who can this city take?

When nations go against her bent,
　　And kings with siege her walls enround:°
The void of air his voice doth rent,
　　Earth fails their feet with melting ground.　20
　　To strength and keep us sound,
　　　The God of armies arms:
　　Our rock on Jacob's God we found,
　　　Above the reach of harms.

Oh, come with me, oh, come and view　　　　25
　　The trophies of Jehovah's hand:
What wracks from him our foes pursue,
　　How clearly he hath purged our land.
　　By him wars silent stand:
　　　He brake the archer's bow,　　　　　　30
　　Made chariot's wheel a fi'ry brand,
　　　And spear to shivers go.

'Be still,' saith he; 'know, God am I:
　　Know I will be with conquest crowned,

---

7 appal] dismay　　　10 purling] rippling, gurgling　　　11 annoy] annoyance
18 enround] encircle　　　19 rent] rend, tear　　　27 wracks] ruins
31 fi'ry] fiery　　　32 shivers] splinters

Above all nations raisèd high,   35
      High raised above this earthy round.'
    To strength and keep us sound,
       The God of armies arms:
    Our rock on Jacob's God we found,
      Above the reach of harms.   40

Psalm 47

Omnes gentes, plaudite

All people to Jehovah bring
      A glad applause of clapping hands:
To God a song of triumph sing,
      Who high, and highly fearèd stands,
Of all the earth sole-ruling king,   5

From whose almighty grace it grows
      That nations by our power oppressed,°
Our foot on humbled countries goes:
      Who Jacob's honour lovèd best,
A heritage for us hath chose.   10

There passed he by: hark how did ring,
      Harmonious air with trumpet's sound!
Praise, praise our God; praise, praise our king,
      King of the world, you judgements sound,°
With skilful song his praises sing.   15

On sacred throne, not knowing end,
      For God the king of kingdoms reigns,
The folk of Abraham's God to friend
      He, greatest prince, great princes gains,°
Princes, the shields that earth defend.   20

The Sidney Psalter

Psalm 48

Magnus Dominus

He that hath eternal being
    Glorious is, and glorious shows
    In the city he hath chose,
        Where stands his holy hill.
Hill Zion, hill of fairest seeing,   5
    City of the king most great,
    Seated in a northly seat,
        All climes with joy doth fill;
    In each palace she containeth
    God a well-known rock remaineth.   10

One day kings, a day appointed
    There with joinèd force to be.
    See they it? The things they see,°
        Amaze their mated minds.
Flying, trembling, disappointed,   15
    So they fear, and so they fare,
    As the wife, whose woeful care
        The pangs of childbed finds,
    Right as ships from Tarshish going,°
    Crushed with blasts of Eurus' blowing.   20

Now our sight hath matched our hearing
    In what state God's city stands,
    How supported by his hands
        God ever holds the same.
In thy temple's midst appearing   25
    We thy favour, Lord, attend:
    Righteous Lord both free from end,°
        Thy fame doth match thy name.
    Thy just hand brings Zion gladness,
    Turns to mirth all Judah's sadness.   30

---

5 Hill Zion] location of God's house   14 mated] confounded, amazed
20 Eurus'] east wind's   27 free from end] everlasting

Compass Zion in her standing,
   Tell her towers, mark her forts:
   Note with care the stately ports
     Her royal houses bear.
For that age's understanding,   35
   Which shall come, when we shall go,
   Glad in former time to know,
     How many, what they were.
For God is our God for ever,
Us till death forsaking never.   40

Psalm 49

Audite haec, omnes

World-dwellers all, give heed to what I say,
   To all I speak, to rich, poor, high, and low:
   Knowledge the subject is my heart conceives,
   Wisdom the words shall from my mouth proceed,
   Which I will measure by melodious ear   5
   And riddled speech to tunèd harp accord.

The times of evil why should they me dismay,
   When mischief shall my footsteps overflow?
   And first from him whom fickle wealth deceives,
   Which his though great, vain confidence doth breed   10
   Since no man can his brother's life out-bear
   Nor yield for him his ransom to the Lord.

For dear the price that for a soul must pay:
   And death his prisoner never will forgo.
   Nay, tell me whom but longer time he leaves°   15
   Respited from the tomb for treasure's meed?°
   Sure at his summons, wise and fools appear,
   And others spend the riches they did hoard.

6 riddled] allegorical (Rathmell)   11 out-bear] preserve   16 meed] bribery

A second thinks his house shall not decay,
    Nor time his glorious buildings overthrow,   20
    Named proudly of his name: where folly reaves
    Exalted men of sense, and they indeed
    A brutish life and death, as beasts they were,
    Do live and die of whom is no record.

Yea, these, whose race approves their peevish way,   25
    Death in the pit his carrion food doth stow,°
    And, lo, the first succeeding light perceives
    The just installèd in the great man's stead;
    Nay, far his prince: when once that lovely cheer°
    Lovely in house, in tomb becomes abhorred.   30

But God, my God, to intercept the prey
    Of my life from the grave will not forslow,
    For he, it is he only me receives.
    Then though one rich do grow, though glory's seed
    Spring with increase: yet stand thou free from fear,   35
    Of all his pomp death shall him naught afford.

Please they themselves, and think at happiest stay
    Who please themselves, yet to their fathers go
    Must they to endless dark: for folly reaves
    Exalted men of sense, and they indeed   40
    A brutish life and death, as beasts they were,
    Do live and die of whom is no record.

Psalm 50

Deus Deorum

The mighty God, the ever-living Lord,
    All nations from earth's uttermost confines
    Summoneth by his pursuivant, his word,°
    And out of beauty's beauty, Zion shines.°

21 reaves] robs   25 peevish] foolish   32 forslow] be slow.
36 naught] nothing   37 stay] condition
Psalm 50 3 pursuivant] courtly messenger   4 Zion] house of God of Israel

God comes, he comes, with ear and tongue restored;° 5
    His guard huge storms, hot flames his ushers go:
And callèd their appearance to record,
    Heav'n hasteth from above, earth from below.

He sits his people's judge, and thus commands:
    'Gather me hither that belovèd line 10
Whom solemn sacrifice's holy bands
    Did in eternal league with me combine.
Then when the heav'ns subsignèd with their hands,°
    That God in justice eminently reigns:
Controlling so, as nothing countermands 15
    What once decreed, his highest doom contains.

'You then my folk, to me your God attend;
    Hark, Israel, and hear thy people's blame:
Not want of sacrifice doth me offend,
    Nor do I miss thy altar's daily flame. 20
To me thy stall no fatted bull shall send:
    Should I exact one he-goat from thy fold?
I, that as far as hills, woods, fields extend,
    All birds and beasts in known possession hold.

'Suppose me hungry; yet to beg thy meat, 25
    I would not tell thee that I hungry were:
Myself may take, what needs me then entreat,
    Since earth is mine, and all that earth doth bear?
But do I long the brawny flesh to eat
    Of that dull beast that serves the ploughman's need? 30
Or do I thirst, to quench my thirsty heat,
    In what the throats of bearded cattle bleed?

'Oh, no: bring God of praise a sacrifice;°
    Thy vowèd debts unto the highest pay.
Invoke my name, to me erect thy cries, 35
    Thy praying plaints, when sorrow stops thy way;

7 appearance] legal witness   15 countermands] revokes, counteracts
32 bearded cattle] goats (Rathmell)

I will undo the knot that anguish ties,
    And thou at peace shalt glorify my name.'
Mildly the good, God schooleth in this wise,
    But this sharp check doth to the godless frame: 40

'How fits it thee my statutes to report,
    And of my covenant in thy talk to prate
Hating to live in right reformèd sort,
    And leaving in neglect what I relate?
Seest thou a thief? Thou grow'st of his consort,   45
    Dost with adult'rers to adult'ry go:
Thy mouth is slander's ever-open port,
    And from thy tongue doth naught, but treason, flow.

'Nay, ev'n thy brother thy rebukes disgrace,
    And thou in spite defam'st thy mother's son.   50
And for I wink a while, thy thoughts embrace:
    "God is like me, and doth as I have done."
But, lo, thou seest I march another pace,
    And come with truth thy falsehood to disclose:
Thy sin revived, upbraids thy blushing face,   55
    Which thou long dead in silence didst suppose.

'Oh, lay up this in marking memory,
    You that are wont God's judgements to forget:
In vain to others for release you fly,
    If once on you I gripping fingers set.   60
And know the rest: my dearest worship I
    In sweet perfume of offered praise do place,
And who directs his goings orderly,
    By my conduct shall see God's saving grace.'

40 frame] make   42 prate] chatter   48 naught] nothing
51 wink] ignore   58 wont] accustomed

Psalm 51

Miserere mei, Deus

O Lord, whose grace no limits comprehend;
  Sweet Lord, whose mercies stand from measure free;
To me that grace, to me that mercy send,
  And wipe, O Lord, my sins from sinful me.
    Oh, cleanse, oh, wash, my foul iniquity;   5
      Cleanse still my spots, still wash away my stainings,
      Till stains and spots in me leave no remainings.

For I, alas, acknowledging do know
  My filthy fault, my faulty filthiness
To my soul's eye incessantly doth show,   10
  Which done to thee, to thee I do confess,
  Just judge, true witness, that for righteousness
      Thy doom may pass against my guilt awarded,
      Thy evidence for truth may be regarded.°

My mother, lo, when I began to be,   15
  Conceiving me, with me did sin conceive:
And as with living heat she cherished me,°
  Corruption did like cherishing receive.
  But, lo, thy love to purest good doth cleave,
      And inward truth: which, hardly else discernèd,   20
      My truant soul in thy hid school hath learnèd.

Then as thyself to lepers hast assigned,
  With hyssop, Lord, thy hyssop, purge me so:°
And that shall cleanse the lepry of my mind.
  Make over me thy mercy's streams to flow,   25
  So shall my whiteness scorn the whitest snow.
      To ear and heart send sounds and thoughts of gladness,
      That bruisèd bones may dance away their sadness.

---

1 comprehend] contain, restrict   10 show] appear
13 doom] judgement   19 cleave] cling   24 lepry] leprosy

Thy ill-pleased eye from my misdeeds avert;
   Cancel the registers my sins contain: 30
Create in me a pure, clean, spotless heart;
   Inspire a sprite where love of right may reign.
     Ah, cast me not from thee; take not again
        Thy breathing grace; again thy comfort send me,
        And let the guard of thy free sprite attend me.   35

So I to them a guiding hand will be,
   Whose faulty feet have wandered from thy way,
And turned from sin will make return to thee,
   Whom turned from thee sin erst had led astray.
     O God, God of my health, oh, do away   40
        My bloody crime: so shall my tongue be raisèd
        To praise thy truth, enough cannot be praisèd.

Unlock my lips, shut up with sinful shame:
   Then shall my mouth, O Lord, thy honour sing.
For bleeding fuel for thy altar's flame,   45
   To gain thy grace what boots it me to bring?
     Burnt-off'rings are to thee no pleasant thing.
        The sacrifice that God will hold respected,
        Is the heart-broken soul, the sprite dejected.

Lastly, O Lord, how so I stand or fall,   50
   Leave not thy lovèd Zion to embrace:
But with thy favour build up Salem's wall,°
   And still in peace, maintain that peaceful place.
     Then shalt thou turn a well-accepting face
        To sacred fires with offered gifts perfumèd: 55
        Till ev'n whole calves on altars be consumèd.°

---

30 registers] records (containing sins)　　32 sprite] spirit　　34 breathing grace]
Holy Spirit　　39 erst] formerly　　45 bleeding fuel] animal sacrifices
46 boots] avails　　51 Leave] leave off, neglect　　Zion] house of the God of Israel
52 Salem's] Jerusalem's

Psalm 52
Quid gloriaris?

Tyrant, why swell'st thou thus,°
    Of mischief vaunting?
Since help from God to us,
    Is never wanting?

Lewd lies thy tongue contrives,   5
    Loud lies it soundeth:
Sharper than sharpest knives
    With lies it woundeth.

Falsehood thy wit approves,
    All truth rejected: 10
Thy will all vices loves,
    Virtue neglected.

Not words from cursèd thee,
    But gulfs are pourèd.
Gulfs wherein daily be   15
    Good men devourèd.

Think'st thou to bear it so?
    God shall displace thee;
God shall thee overthrow,
    Crush thee, deface thee.   20

The just shall fearing see
    These fearful chances:
And laughing shoot at thee
    With scornful glances.

Lo, lo, the wretched wight,   25
    Who God disdaining,

2 vaunting] boasting   25 wight] person

His mischief made his might,
  His guard his gaining.

I as an olive tree,
  Still green shall flourish: 30
God's house the soil shall be
  My roots to nourish.°

My trust on his true love
  Truly attending,
Shall never thence remove,   35
  Never see ending.

Thee will I honour still,
  Lord, for this justice:
There fix my hopes I will,
  Where thy saints' trust is.   40

Thy saints trust in thy name,
  Therein they joy them:
Protected by the same
  Naught can annoy them.

Psalm 53
Dixit insipiens

'There is no god,' the fool doth say,
  If not in word, in thought and will:
This fancy rotten deeds bewray,
  And studies fixed on loathsome ill.°
  Not one doth good: from heav'nly hill   5
   Jehovah's eye one wiser mind
Could not discern, that held the way
  To understand and God to find.

44 Naught] nothing annoy] harm
Psalm 53 3 bewray] reveal

'They all have strayed, are cankered all:
   Not one, I say, not one doth good.   10
But senselessness, what should I call
   Such carriage of this cursèd brood?
   My people are their bread, their food,
    Upon my name they scorn to cry,
Whom vain affright doth yet appal,   15
   Where no just ground of fear doth lie.'

But on their bones shall wreakèd be
   All thy invaders' force and guile,
In vile confusion cast by thee,
   For God himself shall make them vile.   20
   Ah, why delays that happy while
    When Zion shall our saver bring?
The Lord his folk will one day free:
   Then Jacob's house shall dance and sing.

Psalm 54

Deus, in nomine

Lord, let thy name my saving succour be:
 Defend my wrongèd cause by thy just might.
Lord, let my crying voice be heard of thee,
 Let not my heavy words be counted light.°
For strangers I against me risen see,   5
 Who hunt me hard, and sore my soul affright:
Possessed with fear of God in no degree.
 But, God, thou art my helper in my right,
Thou succour send'st to such as succour me.
 Then pay them home, who thus against me fight,   10
And let thy truth cut down their treachery.
 So I with off'rings shall thy altars dight,

9 cankered] corrupt 11 But] except 12 carriage] behaviour
15 affright] fear appal] dismay 17 wreakèd] avenged 21 while] time
22 Zion] house of the God of Israel 22 saver] saviour 24 Jacob's house]
Israel, God's people

Psalm 54 1 succour] help 10 pay them home] give deserved punishment
12 dight] adorn

Praising thy name which thus hast set me free,
    Giving me scope to soar with happy flight
Above my evils: and on my enemy°   15
    Making me see, what I to see delight.

Psalm 55
Exaudi, Deus

My God, most glad to look, most prone to hear,
    An open ear, oh, let my prayer find,
        And from my plaint turn not thy face away.
        Behold my gestures, hearken what I say,
    While uttering moans with most tormented mind,   5
My body I no less torment and tear.°
For, lo, their fearful threat'nings wound mine ear,
    Who griefs on griefs on me still heaping lay,
        A mark to wrath and hate and wrong assigned;
        Therefore, my heart hath all his force resigned   10
    To trembling pants; death's terrors on me prey;
I fear, nay, shake, nay, quiv'ring quake with fear.

Then say I, oh, might I but cut the wind,
    Borne on the wing the fearful dove doth bear:
        Stay would I not, till I in rest might stay.   15
        Far hence, oh, far, then would I take my way
Unto the desert, and repose me there,
These storms of woe, these tempests left behind.
But swallow them, O Lord, in darkness blind,
    Confound their counsels, lead their tongues astray,   20
        That what they mean by words may not appear.
        For mother Wrong within their town each where,
    And daughter Strife their ensigns so display,
As if they only thither were confined.

These walk their city walls both night and day;   25
    Oppressions, tumults, guiles of every kind

9 mark] target   10 force] strength   15 Stay . . . stay] stop . . . remain
22 each where] each place

Are burgesses and dwell the middle near;
　　About their streets his masking robes doth wear
　　Mischief clothed in deceit, with treason lined,
Where only he, he only bears the sway.°　　　　　　　30
But not my foe with me this prank did play,
　　For then I would have borne with patient cheer
　　An unkind part from whom I know unkind,
　　Nor he whose forehead Envy's mark had signed,
　　His trophies on my ruins sought to rear,　　　　　35
From whom to fly I might have made assay.

But this to thee, to thee impute I may,
　　My fellow, my companion, held most dear,
　　My soul, my other self, my inward friend:
　　Whom unto me, me unto whom did bind　　　　　40
　　Exchangèd secrets, who together were
God's temple wont to visit, there to pray.
Oh, let a sudden death work their decay,
　　Who speaking fair such cankered malice mind,
　　Let them be buried breathing in their bier.°　　　45
　　But purple morn, black ev'n, and midday clear
　　Shall see my praying voice to God inclined,
Rousing him up, and naught shall me dismay.

He ransomed me; he for my safety fined
　　In fight where many sought my soul to slay;　　　50
　　He, still himself to no succeeding heir
　　Leaving his empire shall no more forbear
But at my motion, all these atheists pay,
By whom, still one, such mischiefs are designed.
Who but such caitiffs would have undermined,　　55
　　Nay, overthrown, from whom but kindness mere°
　　They never found? Who would such trust betray?
　　What buttered words! Yet war their hearts bewray.

27 burgesses] citizens　　36 made assay] tried　　42 wont] accustomed
44 cankered] corrupt　　48 naught] nothing　　49 fined] paid a penalty or ransom
53 But] except　　motion] urging or bidding　　54 still one] always the same
55 caitiffs] base persons　　56 but kindness mere] anything but kindness
58 bewray] reveal

Their speech more sharp than sharpest sword or spear
Yet softer flows than balm from wounded rind.°   60

But my o'erloaden soul, thyself upcheer,
    Cast on God's shoulders what thee down doth weigh
        Long borne by thee with bearing pained and pined:
        To care for thee he shall be ever kind;
    By him the just in safety held alway   65
Changeless shall enter, live, and leave the year:
But, Lord, how long shall these men tarry here?
    Fling them in pit of death where never shined
        The light of life, and while I make my stay
        On thee, let who their thirst with blood allay   70
    Have their life-holding thread so weakly twined
That it, half-spun, death may in sunder shear.°

Psalm 56

Miserere mei, Deus

Fountain of pity, now with pity flow:
These monsters on me daily gaping go.
        Daily me devour these spies;°
        Swarms of foes against me rise,
O God that art more high than I am low.   5

Still when I fear, yet will I trust in thee:
Thy word, O God, my boast shall ever be;
        God shall be my hopeful stay;
        Fear shall not that hope dismay,
For what can feeble flesh do unto me?   10

I as I can, think, speak, and do the best:
They to the worst my thoughts, words, doings wrest.
        All their hearts with one consent

---

60 rind] tree bark   63 pined] tormented or troubled   69 make my stay] rely
70 allay] satisfy

Psalm 56 2 gaping] shouting, biting   6 Still] yet   8 stay] support

Are to work my ruin bent,
From plotting which they give their heads no rest.   15

To that intent they secret meetings make,
They press me near my soul in snare to take,
          Thinking sleight shall keep them safe.
          But thou, Lord, in wrathful chafe
Their league so surely linked in sunder shake.   20

Thou didst, O Lord, with careful counting look
On every journey I, poor exile, took:
          Every tear from my sad eyes
          Savèd in thy bottle lies;
These matters are all entered in thy book.   25

Then whensoever my distressèd sprite
Crying to thee brings these unto thy sight,°
          What remaineth for my foes?
          Blames and shames and overthrows,
For God himself I know for me will fight.   30

God's never-falsèd word my boast shall be,
My boast shall be his word to set me free.
          God shall be my hopeful stay,
          Fear shall not that hope dismay,
For what can mortal man do unto me?   35

For this to thee how deeply stand I bound,
Lord, that my soul dost save, my foes confound?°
          Ah, I can no payment make,
          But if thou for payment take
The vows I pay, thy praises I resound: 40

Thy praises who from death hast set me free,
Whither my feet did headlong carry me,
          Making me of thy free grace
          There again to take my place,
Where light of life with living men I see.°   45

17 press] oppress   19 chafe] rage, fury   20 in sunder] apart
26 sprite] spirit   42 headlong] impulsively

Psalm 57

Miserere mei, Deus

Thy mercy, Lord, Lord, now thy mercy show:
      On thee I lie;
      To thee I fly.
    Hide me, hive me, as thine own,°
    Till these blasts be overblown,   5
Which now do fiercely blow.

To highest God I will erect my cry,
      Who quickly shall
      Dispatch this all.
    He shall down from heaven send   10
    From disgrace me to defend
His love and verity.°

My soul encagèd lies with lions' brood,
      Villains whose hands°
      Are fi'ry brands,   15
    Teeth more sharp than shaft or spear,
    Tongues far better edge do bear
Than swords to shed my blood.

As high as highest heav'n can give thee place,
      O Lord, ascend,   20
      And thence extend
    With most bright, most glorious show
    Over all the earth below,
The sunbeams of thy face.

Me to entangle every way I go   25
      Their trap and net
      Is ready set.
    Holes they dig but their own holes
    Pitfalls make for their own souls:
So, Lord, oh, serve them so.   30

4 hive] shelter as in a hive

My heart prepared, prepar\`ed is my heart
      To spread thy praise
      With tun\`ed lays:
    Wake my tongue, my lute awake,
    Thou my harp the consort make,°   35
Myself will bear a part.°

Myself when first the morning shall appear,
      With voice and string
      So will thee sing:
    That this earthly globe, and all   40
    Treading on this earthly ball,
My praising notes shall hear.

For God, my only God, thy gracious love
      Is mounted far
      Above each star,°   45
    Thy unchang\`ed verity
    Heav'nly wings do lift as high
As clouds have room to move.

As high as highest heav'n can give thee place,
      O Lord, ascend   50
      And thence extend
    With most bright, most glorious show
    Over all the earth below,
The sunbeams of thy face.°

Psalm 58
Si vere utique

And call ye this to utter what is just,
    You that of justice hold the sov'reign throne?
And call ye this to yield, O sons of dust,°
    To wrong\`ed brethren every man his own?
      Oh, no: it is your long-malicious will°   5

35 consort] harmony

Now to the world to make by practice known
    With whose oppression you the balance fill,
Just to yourselves, indiff'rent else to none.°

But what could they, who ev'n in birth declined°
    From truth and right to lies and injuries?   10
To show the venom of their cankered mind
    The adder's image scarcely can suffice.
       Nay, scarce the aspic may with them contend,
    On whom the charmer all in vain applies
       His skilfull'st spells: aye missing of his end,°   15
While she self-deaf and unaffected lies.°

Lord, crack their teeth; Lord, crush these lions' jaws;
    So let them sink as water in the sand:
When deadly bow their aiming fury draws,
    Shiver the shaft ere past the shooter's hand.°   20
       So make them melt as the dishousèd snail
    Or as the embryo, whose vital band°
       Breaks ere it holds, and formless eyes do fail
To see the sun, though brought to lightful land.

Oh, let their brood, a brood of springing thorns,   25
    Be by untimely rooting overthrown
Ere bushes waxed, they push with pricking horns,
    As fruits yet green are off by tempest blown:°
       The good with gladness this revenge shall see,
    And bathe his feet in blood of wicked one,   30
       While all shall say, 'The just rewarded be:
There is a God that carves to each his own.'°

---

6 practice] trickery   8 indiff'rent] impartial   11 cankered] corrupt
13 aspic] asp, snake   15 aye] always   20 Shiver] shatter   shaft] arrow
ere] before   21 dishousèd] expelled from its shell   27 waxed] grown
pricking] tormenting

Psalm 59

Eripe me de inimicis

Save me from such as me assail;
    Let not my foes,
O God, against my life prevail:
    Save me from those,
      Who make a trade of cursèd wrong 5
      And bred in blood, for blood do long.°

Of these one sort do seek by sleight
    My overthrow:
The stronger part with open might
    Against me go 10
      And yet (thou, God, my witness be)
      From all offence my soul is free.

But what if I from fault am free?°
    Yet they are bent,
To band and stand against poor me, 15
    Poor innocent.
      Rise, God, and see how these things go:
      And rescue me from instant woe.

Rise, God of armies, mighty God
    Of Israel: 20
Look on them all who spread abroad
    On earth do dwell.
      And let thy hand no longer spare
      Such as of malice wicked are.

When golden sun in west doth set 25
    Returned again,°
As hounds that howl their food to get
    They run amain

---

5 trade] habit   14 bent] inclined   18 instant] urgent
28 amain] at full speed

The city through from street to street
With hungry maw some prey to meet.   30

Night elder grown, their fittest day,
       They babbling prate
How my lost life extinguish may
       Their deadly hate.
    They prate and babble void of fear,   35
    For, 'Tush,' say they, 'who now can hear?'

Ev'n thou canst hear, and hearing, scorn
       All that they say,
For them (if not by thee upborne)
       What props do stay?   40
    Then will I, as they wait for me,
    O God my fortress, wait on thee.°

Thou ever me with thy free grace
       Prevented hast:°
With thee my prayer shall take place   45
       Ere from me passed.
    And I shall see who me do hate
    Beyond my wish in woeful state.

For fear my people it forget,
       Slay not outright   50
But scatter them and so them set
       In open sight
    That by thy might they may be known
    Disgraced, debased and overthrown.

No witness of their wickedness   55
       I need produce
But their own lips, fit to express
       Each vile abuse:
    In cursing proud, proud when they lie,
    Oh, let them dear such pride aby.   60

---

30 maw] jaws   32 prate] chatter   40 stay] support   60 aby] purchase

At length in rage consume them so
  That naught remain:
Let them all being quite forgo,
  And make it plain,
   That God who Jacob's rule upholds 65
   Rules all, all-bearing earth enfolds.

Now thus they fare: when sun doth set,
  Returned again,
As hounds that howl their food to get
  They run amain 70
   The city through from street to street
   With hungry maws some prey to meet.

Abroad they range and hunt apace
  Now that, now this,
As famine trails a hungry trace, 75
  And though they miss
   Yet will they not to kennel hie
   But all the night at bay will lie.°

But I will of thy goodness sing
  And of thy might 80
When early sun again shall bring
  His cheerful light,
   For thou my refuge and my fort
   In all distress dost me support.

My strength doth of thy strength depend; 85
  To thee I sing;
Thou art my fort, me to defend,
  My God, my king,
   To thee I owe and thy free grace
   That free I rest in fearless place. 90

---

62 naught] nothing 70 amain] at full speed 73 apace] swiftly
75 trails] marks trace] path 77 hie] hasten

Psalm 60

Deus, repulisti nos

Thy anger erst in field
    Our scattered squadrons brake:
O God be reconciled,
    Our leading now retake.
    This land at thee did quake,   5
        It chinked and gaping lay:
    Oh, sound her ruptures make,
        Her quaking bring to stay.

Worse haps no heart could think,
    Than did thy wrath ensue: 10
Dull horror was our drink,
    We drinking giddy grew.
    But now an ensign new
        Recheering all dismays
    To guide thy fearers' view   15
        Thy truth, our chief, doth raise.

Then set thy lovèd free,
    Preserve me when I pray:°
'Hark, hark, so shall it be,'
    God from his house doth say.   20
    Then make a merry stay:
        And share we Sichem's fields;
    The land in parcels lay,
        That Succoth's valley yields.

Mine Gilead, lo, by this,   25
    Manasses, lo, mine own:
My soldier Ephraim is,
    My law by Judah shown.

---

1 erst] once   6 chinked] cracked   8 stay] cease
14 Recheering] encouraging   21 stay] abode   23 parcels] pieces of land

My wash-pot Moab grown
    My shoe at Edom flung!   30
Philistia overthrown,
    Sing now thy triumph song.

But whom shall I attend,
    Till I these conquests make?
On whose conduct depend   35
    Till Edom's forts I take?
    Oh, thine to whom we spake,
        But spake before in vain:
    Thine, God, that didst forsake
        Our troops for war to train.°   40

Against distressing foes
    Let us thy succour find:
Who trust in man repose,
    Do trust repose in wind.
    In God let hand and mind   45
        Their force and valour show:
    He, he, in abject kind
        Shall lay our haters low.

Psalm 61

Exaudi, Deus

To thee I cry,
    My crying hear.
To thee my praying voice doth fly:
    Lord, lend my voice a list'ning ear.
        From country banishèd,°   5
        All comfort vanishèd,
To thee I run when storms are nigh.

Up to thy hill,
    Lord, make me climb;

42 succour] help

Which else to scale exceeds my skill: 10
    For in my most distressèd time
        Thy eye attended me,
        Thy hand defended me,
Against my foe my fortress still.

Then where a tent   15
    For thee is made,
To harbour still is my intent:
    And to thy wings' protecting shade
        Myself I carry will,
        And there I tarry will,   20
Safe from all shot against me bent.

What first I crave
    First granting me,
That I the royal rule may have
    Of such as fear and honour thee: 25
        Let years as manifold,
        As can be any told,
Thy king, O God, keep from the grave.

Before thy face
    Grant ever he   30
May sit, and let thy truth and grace
    His endless guard appointed be.
        Then singing pleasantly,
        Praising incessantly,
I daily vows will pay to thee.   35

Psalm 62

Nonne Deo

Yet shall my soul in silence still
    On God, my help, attentive stay:

2 stay] remain

Yet he my fort, my health, my hill,
    Remove I may not, move I may.
How long then shall your fruitless will 5
    An enemy so far from fall
With weak endeavour strive to kill,
    You rotten hedge, you broken wall?

Forsooth that he no more may rise
    Advancèd eft to throne and crown: 10
To headlong him their thoughts devise,
    And past relief to tread him down.
Their love is only love of lies:
    Their words, and deeds, dissenting so,
When from their lips most blessing flies, 15
    Then deepest curse in heart doth grow.

Yet shall my soul in silence still
    On God my hope attentive stay:
Yet he my fort, my health, my hill,
    Remove? Oh, no: not move I may.° 20
My God doth me with glory fill,
    Not only shield me safe from harm:
To shun distress, to conquer ill
    To him I climb, in him I arm.

Oh, then on God our certain stay, 25
    All people in all times rely:
Your hearts before him naked lay.
    To Adam's sons is vain to fly
So vain, so false, so frail are they,
    Ev'n he that seemeth most of might 30
With lightness self if him you weigh,
    Than lightness self will weigh more light.°

In fraud and force no trust repose:
    Such idle hopes from thoughts expel
And take good heed, when riches grows° 35

6 fall] falling   10 eft] again   11 headlong] throw down   25 stay] support

Let not your heart on riches dwell.
All pow'r is God's, his own word shows,
    Once said by him, twice heard by me:
Yet from thee, Lord, all mercy flows,
    And each man's work is paid by thee.   40

Psalm 63

Deus, Deus meus

O God, the God where all my forces lie,
    How do I hunt for thee with early haste!
How is for thee my spirit thirsty dry!
    How gasps my flesh for thy refreshing taste!
    Witness this waterless, this weary waste:°   5
        Whence, oh, that I again transferred might be,
        Thy glorious might in sacred place to see.

Then on thy praise would I my lips employ,
    With whose kind mercies nothing may contend:
No, not this life itself, whose care and joy   10
    In praying voice, and lifted hands should end.
    This to my soul should such a banquet send,
        That sweetly fed my mouth should sing thy name
        In gladdest notes contented mirth could frame.

And, lo, ev'n here I mind thee in my bed,°   15
    And interrupt my sleeps with nightly thought,
How thou hast been the target of my head,
    How thy wings' shadow hath my safety wrought.
    And though my body from thy view be brought,
        Yet fixed on thee my loving soul remains,   20
        Whose right right hand from falling me retains.°

But such as seek my life to ruinate,
    Them shall the earth in deepest gulf receive.
First murd'ring blade shall end their living date,

14 frame] compose   17 target] shield

And then their flesh to teeth of foxes leave,   25
As for the king, the king shall then conceive
    High joy in God, and all that God adore,°
    When lying mouths, shall, stoppèd, lie no more.

Psalm 64

Exaudi, Deus

With gracious hearing entertain°
    This voice the agent of my woe:
And let my life, O God, remain
    Safe in thy guard from fearèd foe.
    Hide me where none may know,   5
        That hateful plots contrive;
    And right to overthrow
        With tumult wrongly strive.

For tongues they bear, not tongues, but swords,
    So piercing sharp they have them ground;   10
And words deliver, shafts, not words,
    With bitter dint so deep they wound,
    Whose shot against the sound
        And harmless they direct:
    In safe and fearless ground   15
        Ambushed without suspect.

Nay, obstinate to ill they are,
    And meeting, all their talk apply
Who can most closely couch his snare:
    'And who', say they, 'shall us descry?'   20
    No guile so low doth lie,
        Nor in so hidden part,
    But these will sound and try,°
        Ev'n out of deepest heart.

11 shafts] arrows   12 dint] strike   19 closely couch] secretly hide

But thou, O God, from sudden bow   25
    Death striking them a shaft shalt send:
And their own tongues to their own woe
    Shall all their wounding sharpness bend.
    Thus wounded shall they end,
        Thus ending shall they make   30
    Each mortal eye attend,
        Each eye attending quake.

Not one, I say, but shall behold
    This work of God which he again
Shall as he can in words unfold,   35
    If yet his fear he entertain.°
    In who doth timeless reign
        The just shall joy and hope:°
    The hearts uprightly plain
        Shall have their vaunting scope.   40

Psalm 65

Te decet hymnus

Zion it is where thou art praisèd,
    Zion, O God, where vows they pay thee:
There all men's prayers to thee raisèd
    Return possessed of what they pray thee.
There thou my sins prevailing to my shame   5
Dost turn to smoke of sacrificing flame.°

Oh, he of bliss is not deceivèd,
    Whom chosen thou unto thee takest:
And whom into thy court receivèd
    Thou of thy check-roll number makest.°   10
The dainty viands of thy sacred store
Shall feed him so, he shall not hunger more.

---

37 who] him who   39 plain] complain   40 vaunting scope] vainglorious ambition

Psalm 65 1 Zion] house of the God of Israel   10 check-roll] payroll
11 viands] food

From thence it is thy threat'ning thunder,
    Lest we by wrong should be disgracèd,
Doth strike our foes with fear and wonder: 15
    O thou on whom their hopes are placèd,
Whom either earth doth steadfastly sustain,
Or cradle rocks of restless wavy plain.°

Thy virtue stays the mighty mountains,
    Girded with pow'r, with strength abounding: 20
The roaring dam of wat'ry fountains
    Thy beck doth make surcease her sounding.
When stormy uproars toss the people's brain
That civil sea to calm thou bring'st again.°

Where earth doth end with endless ending, 25
    All such as dwell, thy signs affright them:
And in thy praise their voices spending
    Both houses of the sun delight them;°
Both whence he comes, when early he awakes,
And where he goes, when evening rest he takes. 30

Thy eye from heav'n this land beholdeth,
    Such fruitful dews down on it raining,
That storehouse-like her lap enfoldeth,
    Assurèd hope of ploughman's gaining.
Thy flowing streams her drought doth temper so, 35
That buried seed through yielding grave doth grow.°

Drunk is each ridge of thy cup drinking;
    Each clod relenteth at thy dressing:
Thy cloud-born waters inly sinking,
    Fair spring sprouts forth blest with thy blessing. 40
The fertile year is with thy bounty crowned:
And where thou go'st, thy goings fat the ground.

Plenty bedews the desert places;
    A hedge of mirth the hills encloseth;°

19 stays] supports   22 beck] summons   surcease] stop   42 fat] enrich

The fields with flocks have hid their faces;   45
    A robe of corn the valleys clotheth.°
Deserts, and hills, and fields, and valleys all,
Rejoice, shout, sing, and on thy name do call.

Psalm 66

Jubilate Deo

All lands, the limbs of earthy round,
With triumph tunes God's honour sound:
    Sing of his name the praiseful glory,
    And glorious make his praise's story.
Tell God: 'O God, what frightful wonder   5
    Thy works do witness, whose great might,
Thy enemies so bringeth under,
    Though frown in heart, they fawn in sight!'

All earth and every land therefore
Sing to this God, this God adore!   10
    All earth, I say, and all earth dwellers,
    Be of his worth the singing tellers.
Oh, come, behold, oh, note beholding,
    What dreadful wonders from him flow:
More height, more weight, more force enfolding,   15
    Than Adam's earthy brood can show.

The sea up-drièd by his hand,
Became a field of dusty sand:
    Through Jordan's streams we dry-shod waded,°
    The joy whereof not yet is faded.   20
His throne of strength unmovèd standeth;
    His eye on every coast is cast:
The rebel who against him bandeth,
    Of ruin's cup shall quickly taste.

---

7 bringeth under] defeat   8 fawn] grovel   22 coast] seaside, but also border,
region, district

You folk, his flock, come then, employ   25
In lauding him, your songs of joy,
  On God, our God, your voices spending,
  Still praying, praising, never ending.
For he our life hath us re-given,
  Nor would he let our goings slide: 30
Though for our trial nearly driven,
  Yea, silver-like in furnace tried.

For God, thou didst our feet innet,
And pinching saddles on us set.
  Nay (which is worse to be abidden),   35
  Ev'n on our heads a man hath ridden.
He rode us through where fires flashèd;
  Where swelling streams did rudely roar:°
Yet scorchèd thus, yet we thus washèd,
  Were set by thee, on plenty's shore.   40

I therefore to thy house will go,
To pay and offer what I owe:
  To pay my vows my lips then vowèd,
  When under grief my body bowèd;°
To offer whole burnt sacrifices,   45
  The fat of rams with sweet perfume:
Nay, goats, nay, bulls, of greater sizes,
  And greater prices to consume.

Oh, come, all ye that God do fear,
Oh, come, and lend attentive ear;   50
  While by my tongue shall be expressèd,
  How blessed he my soul hath blessed.
I cried to him, my cry procurèd
  My free discharge from all my bands:
His ear had not my voice endurèd,   55
  But that my heart unstainèd stands.

33 innet] ensnare 35 abidden] endured, borne

Now as my heart was innocent,
God heard the hearty sighs I spent:
    What I to prayers recommended
    Was graciously by him attended.   60
Praise, praise him then, for what is left me,°
    But praise to him: who what I prayed,
Rejected not, nor hath bereft me
    My hopeful help, his mercies' aid.

Psalm 67

Deus misereatur

God, on us thy mercy show,
Make on us thy blessings flow;
    Thy face's beams
    From heav'n upon us show'r
      In shining streams: 5
      That all may see
      The way of thee,
And know thy saving pow'r.

God, the nations praise thee shall,
Thee, shall praise the nations all;   10
    To mirth and joy
    All such as earth possess
      Shall them employ:
      For thou their guide
      Go'st never wide   15
From truth and righteousness.

God, the nations praise thee shall,
Thee, shall praise the nations all;
    Then every field,
    As far as earth hath end,   20
      Rich fruits shall yield:
      And God, our God,

13 them] themselves   15 wide] apart or astray

With bliss shall load
Who of his bliss depend.°

God, I say, with plenteous bliss   25
To enrich us shall not miss:
            And from the place
            The father of the year°
            Begins his race,
            To Zephyr's nest,   30
            His race's rest,
All lands his force shall fear.

Psalm 68

Exurgat Deus

Let God but rise, his very face shall cast
        On all his haters flight and disarray:
As smoke in wind, as wax at fire doth waste,
        At God's aspect th'unjust shall flit away.
            The just meanwhile shall in Jehovah's presence   5
        Play, sing, and dance. Then unto him, I say,°
            Unto our God, named of eternal essence,°
        Present yourselves with song, and dance, and play.

Prepare his path, who thronèd on delights,
        Doth sit a father to the orphan son,   10
And in her cause the wrongèd widow rights:
        God in his holy house late here begun.
            With families he empty houses filleth,
        The prisoner's chains are by his hands undone:
            But barren sand their fruitless labour tilleth,   15
        Who crossing him rebelliously do run.

O God, when thou in desert didst appear,
        What time thy folk that uncouth journey took,

24 bliss] joy   30 Zephyr's] west wind's

Psalm 68 4 aspect] appearance   11 rights] redresses   12 late] recently
18 What time] when   uncouth] unfamiliar, strange

Heav'n at the sight did sweat with melting fear;
    Earth bowed her trembling knee; mount Sinai shook.   20
        The land bedewed, all wants by thee restorèd,
    That well thy people might the country brook,
        As to a fold with sheep in plenty storèd,
    So to their state thy shepherd's care did look.

There taught by thee in this triumphant song   25
    A virgin army did their voices try:
'Fled are these kings, fled are these armies strong:
    We share the spoils that weak in house did lie.'°
        Though late the chimney made your beauties loathèd,
    Now shine you shall, and shine more gracefully,   30
        Than lovely dove in clear gold-silver clothèd,
    That glides with feathered oar through wavy sky.°

For when God had (that this may not seem strange)°
    Expelled the kings with utter overthrow,
The very ground her mourning clouds did change   35
    To weather clear, as clear as Salmon snow.°
        Bashan, huge Bashan, that so proudly standest,°
    Scorning the highest hills as basely low,
        And with thy top so many tops commandest,
    Both thou, and they, what makes ye brave it so?   40

This mountainet, not you, doth God desire;°
    Here he intends his lodging's plot to lay:
Hither Jehovah will himself retire
    To endless rest and unremovèd stay.
        Here twice ten thousands, doubled twice he holdeth,   45
    Of hookèd chariots, clad in war's array:
        And hence more might, more majesty unfoldeth,
    Than erst he did from Sinai mount display.

Ascended high, immortal God thou art,
    And captives' store thou hast led up with thee   50

21 bedewed] covered with dew   22 brook] possess   44 stay] residence
48 erst] formerly

Whose gathered spoils to men thou wilt impart:
    Nay, late thy rebels, now thy tenants be.
      Blest be the Lord, by whom our bliss increaseth,
    The God of might by whom we safety see:
      God, our strong God, who us each way releaseth,   55
    And ev'n through gates of death conducts us free.°

God of his enemies the head shall wound
    And those proud looks that stiff in mischief go.
'From Bashan safe, and from the deep undrowned,
    I brought thee once, and oft I will do so.'   60
      This said by him, thy foot in blood was stainèd,
    Thy dogs' tongues dyed in blood of slaughtered foe:
      And God, my king, men saw thee entertainèd
    In sacred house with this triumphant show.

In vanguard marched who did with voices sing;   65
    The rearward loud on instruments did play
The battle maids and did with timbrels ring,°
    And all in sweet consort did jointly say:
      'Praise God, the Lord, of Jacob you descended,
    Praise him upon each solemn meeting day: 70
      Benjamin, little, but with rule attended,°
    Judah's brave lords, and troops in fair array,

'Stout Naphtali with noble Zebulun:
    And sith our might thy bidding word did make,
Confirm, O God, what thou in us hast done,   75
    From out thy house, and that for Salem's sake.
      So kings bring gifts, so in thy check their ending
    These furious, wanton bulls and calves shall take,°
      These arrow-armèd bands, which us offending,
    Are now so ready war to undertake.   80

'They shall bring silver stooping humbly low,
    Egypt's great peers with homage shall attend:

66 rearward] rear guard   68 consort] musical harmony   74 sith] since
76 Salem's] Jerusalem's   79 offending] assailing

And Ethiop with them shall not forslow°
    To God with speed like service to commend.
        Then kingdoms all to God present your praises,   85
    And on the Lord your singing gladness spend:
        Above the heav'n of heav'ns his throne he raises,
    And thence his voice, a voice of strength doth send.

'Then of all strength acknowledge God the well,°
    With brave magnificence and glory bright,   90
Shining no less on lovèd Israel
    Than showing in the clouds his thund'ring might.
        Thou from the shrine where Jacob thee adoreth,
    All folk, O God, with terror dost affright:
        He (praised be he) with strength his people storeth,   95
    His force it is, in which their forces fight.'

Psalm 69

Salvum me fac

Troublous seas my soul surround:
    Save, O God, my sinking soul,
Sinking, where it feels no ground,
    In this gulf, this whirling hole.
        Waiting aid, with earnest eyeing;   5
        Calling God with bootless crying:
Dim and dry in me are found
Eye to see, and throat to sound.

Wrongly set to work my woe
    Haters have I, more than hairs: 10
Force in my afflicting foe
    Bett'ring still, in me impairs.
        Thus to pay and leese constrainèd
        What I never ought or gainèd,

83 forslow] delay   89 well] source   96 force] strength
Psalm 69 5 Waiting] awaiting   6 bootless] useless   13 leese] lose
14 ought] owed

Yet say I: 'Thou, God, dost know   15
How my faults and follies go.'

Mighty Lord, let not my case
    Blank the rest that hope on thee:
Let not Jacob's God deface
    All his friends in blush of me.   20
        Thine it is, thine only quarrel
        Dights me thus in shame's apparel:
Note, nor spot, nor least disgrace,
But for thee, could taint my face.

To my kin a stranger quite,   25
    Quite an alien am I grown:
In my very brethren's sight
    Most uncared for, most unknown.
        With thy temple's zeal out-eaten,
        With thy slanders' scourges beaten,   30
While the shot of piercing spite
Bent at thee, on me doth light.

If I weep, and weeping fast,
    If in sackcloth sad I mourn,
In my teeth the first they cast,   35
    All to jest the last they turn.
        Now in streets with public prating
        Pouring out their inward hating:
Private now at banquets placed,
Singing songs of winy taste.°   40

As for me to thee I pray,
    Lord, in time of grace assigned:
Gracious God, my kindest stay,
    In my aid be truly kind.
        Keep me safe from such, and mirèd,°   45

---

18 Blank] frustrate   22 Dights] clothes   23 Note] mark of disgrace
24 taint] stain   29 out-eaten] eaten away   37 prating] chattering   43 stay]
support

Safe from flowing foes retirèd:
Calm these waves, these waters bay,
Leave me not this whirlpool's prey.

In the goodness of thy grace,
    Lord, make answer to my moan: 50
Eye my ill, and rue my case
    In those mercies told by none.°
        Let not by thy absence languish
        Thy true server drowned in anguish.
Haste, and hear, come, come apace,   55
Free my soul from foemen's chase.

Unto thee what needs be told
    My reproach, my blot, my blame?
Sith both these thou didst behold,
    And canst all my haters name.   60
        Whiles afflicted, whiles heart-broken,
        Waiting yet some friendship's token,
Some I looked would me uphold,
Looked: but found all comfort cold.

Comfort? Nay (not seen before),°   65
    Needing food they set me gall:
Vinegar they filled me store,
    When for drink my thirst did call.
        Oh, then snare them in their pleasures,
        Make them, trapped ev'n in their treasures,   70
Gladly sad, and richly poor,
Sightless most, yet mightless more.

Down upon them fury rain
    Lighten indignation down:
Turn to waste, and desert plain,   75
    House, and palace, field and town.
        Let not one be left abiding
        Where such rancour had residing

47 bay] obstruct, dam   51 rue] pity   55 apace] swiftly   59 Sith] since
67 me] my   74 Lighten] hurl like lightning

Whom thou painest, more they pain:
Hurt by thee, by them is slain.   80

Causing sin on sin to grow,
   Add still ciphers to their sum.
Righter let them never go,
     Never to thy justice come.
       But from out the book be crossèd,   85
        Where the good men live engrossèd:
While my God, me poor and low
High shall mount from need and woe.

Then by me his name with praise,
   Gladsome praise, shall be upborne.   90
That, shall more Jehovah please,
     Than the beast with hoof and horn.°
       With what joy, ye godly grievèd
        Shall your hearts be then relievèd?
When Jehovah takes such ways   95
Bound to loose, and fall'n to raise.

Laud him then, O heav'nly skies,
   Earth with thine, and seas with yours:°
For by him shall Zion rise,
     He shall build up Judah's tow'rs.   100
       There his servants, and their races,
        Shall in fee possess their places:
There his name who love and prize,
Stable stay shall eternize.

Psalm 70

Deus in adjutorium

Lord, hie thee me to save;
   Lord, now to help me haste:

82 ciphers] zeros   86 engrossèd] noted in legal records   96 loose] set free, release   99 Zion] house of the God of Israel   102 in fee] as a fiefdom 104 stay] residence

Psalm 70   1 hie] hasten

Shame let them surely have
 And of confusion taste,
  That hold my soul in chase.   5
   Let them be forcèd back,
   And no disgraces lack,
  That joy in my disgrace.

Back forcèd let them be
 And for a fair reward   10
Their own foul ruin see
  Who laugh and laugh out hard
  When I most inly moan.
   But mirth and joy renew
   In them thy paths ensue°   15
  And love thy help alone.

Make them with gladness sing:
 To God be ever praise.
And fail not me to bring,
  My downcast state to raise.   20
   Thy speedy aid and stay
   In thee my succour grows;
   From thee my freedom flows:
  Lord, make no long delay.

Psalm 71

In te, Domine, speravi

Lord, on thee my trust is grounded:
Leave me not with shame confounded;
 But in justice bring me aid.
Let thine ear to me be bended:
Let my life from death defended   5
 Be by thee in safety stayed.

15 ensue] follow 21 stay] support 22 succour] assistance
Psalm 71 6 stayed] supported

Be my rock, my refuge tower,
Show thy unresisted power,
    Working now thy wonted will:
  Thou, I say, that never feignest°   10
  In thy biddings but remainest
    Still my rock, my refuge still.

O my God, my sole help-giver,
From this wicked me deliver,
    From this wrongful, spiteful man: 15
  In thee trusting, on thee standing,
  With my childish understanding,
    Nay, with life my hopes began.

Since imprisoned in my mother
Thou me freed'st, whom have I other   20
    Held my stay or made my song?
  Yea, when all me so misdeemèd,
  I to most a monster seemèd,
    Yet in thee my hope was strong.

Yet of thee the thankful story   25
Filled my mouth; thy gracious glory
    Was my ditty long the day.
  Do not then, now age assaileth,
  Courage, verdure, virtue faileth,
    Do not leave me cast away.   30

They by whom my life is hated,
With my spies have now debated°
    Of their talk, and, lo, the sum:
  'God', say they, 'hath him forsaken.
  Now pursue, he must be taken;   35
    None will to his rescue come'.

---

9 wonted] accustomed   10 feignest] dissembles   14 wicked] wicked person
21 stay] support   22 misdeemèd] misjudged   27 ditty] song lyrics, theme
long the day] all day long   29 verdure] freshness   32 my spies] those who spy
on me

O my God, be not absented;
O my God, now, now presented
    Let in haste thy succours be:
  Make them full disgracèd, shamèd,   40
  All dismighted, all defamèd,
    Who this ill intend to me.

As for me, resolved to tarry
In my trust, and not to vary:
    I will heap thy praise with praise   45
  Still with mouth thy truths recounting,
  Still thy aids, though much surmounting
    Greatest sum that number lays.

Nay, my God, by thee securèd
Where will I not march assurèd?   50
    But thy truth, what will I hold,
  Who by thee from infant cradle°
  Taught still more, as still more able,
    Have till now thy wonders told?

Now that age hath me attainted,   55
Age's snow my head hath painted,
    Leave me not, my God, forlorn.
  Let me make thy might's relation,°
  To this coming generation,
    To this age as yet unborn.   60

God, thy justice highest raisèd,
Thy great works as highly praisèd,
    Who thy peer, O God, doth reign?
  Thou into these woes dost drive me;
  Thou again shalt hence revive me.   65
    Lift me from this deep again.

---

39 succours] assistance   40 full] fully, completely   41 dismighted] rendered
powerless   defamèd] slandered   51 But] except for   53 able] competent
55 attainted] tainted or stained

Thou shalt make my greatness greater,
Make my good with comfort better;
 Thee my lute, my harp shall sing:°
Thee, my God, that never slidest   70
From thy word but constant bidest,
 Jacob's holy heav'nly king.

So my lips all joy declaring,
So my soul no honour sparing,
 Shall thee sing by thee secure,   75
So my tongue all times, all places,
Tell thy wreaks and their disgraces,
 Who this ill to me procure.

Psalm 72

Deus, judicium

Teach the king's son, who king himself shall be,
 Thy judgements, Lord, thy justice make him learn:
To rule thy realm as justice shall decree,
 And poor men's right in judgement to discern.
   Then fearless peace   5
   With rich increase
    The mountains proud shall fill:°
   And justice shall
   Make plenty fall
    On every humble hill.   10

Make him the weak support, th'oppressed relieve,
 Supply the poor, the quarrel-pickers quail:
So ageless ages shall thee reverence give,
 Till eyes of heav'n, the sun and moon, shall fail.
   And thou again   15
   Shalt blessings rain,
    Which down shall mildly flow,

77 wreaks] acts of vengeance
Psalm 72 12 quail] bring into subjection

As show'rs thrown
On meads new mown
   Whereby they freshly grow.   20

During his rule the just shall aye be green,
   And peaceful plenty join with plenteous peace:
While of sad night the many-formèd queen°
   Decreased shall grow, and grown again decrease.
      From sea to sea   25
      He shall survey
         All kingdoms as his own:
      And from the trace
      Of Pison's race,°
         As far as land is known.   30

The desert-dwellers at his beck shall bend;
   His foes them suppliant at his feet shall fling:
The kings of Tharsis homage gifts shall send;
   So Seba, Saba, every island king.
      Nay, all ev'n all   35
      Shall prostrate fall,
         That crowns and sceptres wear:
      And all that stand
      At their command,
         That crowns and sceptres bear.°   40

For he shall hear the poor when they complain;
   And lend them help, who helpless are oppressed:
His mercy shall the needy sort sustain;
   His force shall free their lives that live distressed.
      From hidden sleight   45
      From open might
         He shall their souls redeem:
      His tender eyes
      Shall highly prize,
         And dear their blood esteem.   50

---

19 meads] meadows   21 aye] always   32 them] themselves   45 sleight]
trickery

So shall he long, so shall he happy live;
    Health shall abound, and wealth shall never want:
They gold to him, Arabia gold, shall give,
    Which scantness dear, and dearness maketh scant.
        They still shall pray   55
        That still he may
            So live, and flourish so:
        Without his praise
        No nights, no days,
            Shall passport have to go.   60

Look how the woods, where interlacèd trees
    Spread friendly arms each other to embrace,
Join at the head, though distant at the knees,
    Waving with wind, and lording on the place:
        So woods of corn   65
        By mountains borne
            Shall on their shoulders wave;
        And men shall pass
        The numbrous grass,
            Such store each town shall have.   70

Look how the sun, so shall his name remain;
    As that in light, so this in glory one:
All glories that, at this all lights shall stain;
    Nor that shall fail, nor this be overthrown.
        The dwellers all   75
        Of earthy ball
            In him shall hold them blest:
        As one that is
        Of perfect bliss
            A pattern to the rest.   80

O God who art, from whom all beings be;
    Eternal Lord, whom Jacob's stock adore,
All wondrous works are done by only thee,

---

68 pass] surpass   69 numbrous] abundant   73 stain] throw into the shade, eclipse

Blessed be thou, most blessed evermore.
And let thy name,   85
Thy glorious fame,
No end of blessing know:
Let all this round
Thy honour sound,
So, Lord, oh, be it so.   90

Psalm 73

Quam bonus Israel

It is most true that God to Israel,°
I mean to men of undefilèd hearts,
Is only good, and naught but good imparts.
Most true, I see, albe almost I fell
From right conceit into a crooked mind   5
And from this truth with straying steps declined:°
For, lo, my boiling breast did chafe and swell
When first I saw the wicked proudly stand,
Prevailing still in all they took in hand.°
And sure no sickness dwelleth where they dwell: 10
Nay, so they guarded are with health and might,
It seems of them Death dares not claim his right.

They seem as privileged from others' pain:
The scourging plagues which on their neighbours fall,
Torment not them, nay, touch them not at all.   15
Therefore with pride, as with a gorgeous chain,
Their swelling necks encompassèd they bear;
All clothed in wrong, as if a robe it were:°
So fat become, that fatness doth constrain
Their eyes to swell; and if they think on aught,   20
Their thought they have, yea, have beyond their thought.°
They wanton grow, and in malicious vein

88 round] earth

Psalm 73 3 only] uniquely   naught] nothing   4 albe] although
7 chafe] become angry   20 aught] anything

Talking of wrong, pronounce as from the skies!
So high a pitch° their proud presumption flies.

Nay, heav'n itself, high heav'n, escapes not free   25
    From their base mouths; and in their common talk
    Their tongues no less than all the earth do walk.
Wherefore ev'n godly men, when so they see
    Their horn of plenty freshly flowing still,°
    Leaning to them, bend from their better will.   30
And thus, they reasons frame:° 'How can it be
    That God doth understand, that he doth know,
    Who sits in heav'n, how earthly matters go?'
See here the godless crew, while godly we
    Unhappy pine,° all happiness possess: 35
    Their riches more, our wealth still growing less.°

Nay, ev'n within myself, myself did say,
    'In vain my heart I purge, my hands in vain°
    In cleanness washed I keep from filthy stain,°
Since thus afflictions scourge me every day: 40
    Since never a day from early east is sent,
    But brings my pain, my check, my chastisement.'
And shall I then these thoughts in words bewray?°
    Oh, let me, Lord, give never such offence
    To children thine that rest in thy defence.   45
So then I turned my thoughts another way,
    Sounding° if I this secret's depth might find;
    But cumbrous° clouds my inward sight did blind.

Until at length nigh weary of the chase,
    Unto thy house I did my steps direct:°   50
    There, lo, I learned what end did these expect,
And what? But that in high, but slippery place,
    Thou didst them set, whence, when they least of all

24 pitch] height (in falconry)   31 frame] contrive   35 pine] languish
43 bewray] reveal, expose   47 Sounding] measuring   48 cumbrous] obstructing

To fall did fear, they fell with headlong fall.
For how are they in less than moment's space   55
    With ruin overthrown, with frightful fear
    Consumed so clean, as if they never were?
Right as a dream, which waking doth deface:
    So, Lord, most vain thou dost their fancies make,
    When thou dost them from careless sleep awake.   60

Then for what purpose was it, to what end,
    For me to fume with malcontented heart,
    Tormenting so in me each inward part?
I was a fool (I can it not defend)
    So quite deprived of understanding might,   65
    That as a beast I bare me in thy sight.
But as I was, yet did I still attend,
    Still follow thee, by whose upholding hand,
    When most I slide, yet still upright I stand.
Then guide me still, then still upon me spend   70
    The treasures of thy sure advice, until
    Thou take me hence into thy glory's hill.

Oh, what is he will teach me climb the skies,°
    With thee, thee good, thee goodness to remain?
    No good on earth doth my desires detain.   75
Often my mind and oft my body tries
    Their weak defects: but thou, my God, thou art
    My endless lot and fortress of my heart.
The faithless fugitives who thee despise,
    Shall perish all, they all shall be undone,   80
    Who leaving thee to whorish idols run.
But as for me, naught better in my eyes
    Than cleave to God, my hopes in him to place,°
    To sing his works while breath shall give me space.°

---

59 fancies] imaginings   60 careless] without care   62 fume] exhibit anger
66 bare me] behaved   76 tries] tests   83 cleave] cling   84 space] time

Psalm 74
Ut quid, Deus

O God, why hast thou thus
      Repulsed, and scattered us?
Shall now thy wrath no limits hold?
      But ever smoke and burn,
      Till it to ashes turn   5
The chosen flock of thy dear fold?

Ah! Think with milder thought
      On them, whom thou hast bought,
And purchasèd from endless days:
      Think of thy birthright lot,   10
      Of Zion, on whose plot,
Thy sacred house supported stays.

Come, Lord, oh, come with speed,
      This sacrilegious seed
Root quickly out, and headlong cast: 15
      All that thy holy place
      Did late adorn and grace,
Their hateful hands have quite defaced.

Their beastly trumpets roar,
      Where heav'nly notes before   20
In praises of thy might did flow:
      Within thy temple they
      Their ensigns oft display,
Their ensigns, which their conquest show.

As men with axe on arm   25
      To some thick forest swarm,
To lop the trees which stately stand:
      They to thy temple flock,

11 Zion] house of the God of Israel   12 stays] remains

       And spoiling, cut and knock
The curious works of carving hand.   30

Thy most, most holy seat
       The greedy flames do eat,
And have such ruthless ruins wrought,
       That all thy house is rased,
       So rased, and so defaced,   35
That of that all, remaineth naught.°

Nay, they resolvèd are,
       We all alike shall fare,
All of one cruel cup shall taste.
       For not one house doth stand   40
       Of God in all the land,
But they by fire have laid it waste.

We see the signs no more,
       We wont to see before,
Nor any now with sprite divine   45
       Amongst us more is found,
       Who can to us expound,
What term these dolours shall define.

How long, O God, how long
       Wilt thou wink at the wrong   50
Of thy reviling, railing foe?
       Shall he that hates thy name,
       And hated paints with shame,
So do, and do for ever so?

Woe us! What is the cause   55
       Thy hand his help withdraws?
That thy right hand far from us keeps?
       Ah, let it once arise,

---

30 curious] elaborate   34 rased] erased   36 naught] nothing
44 wont] were accustomed   45 sprite] spirit   48 term] period of time
dolours] sorrows   53 paints with shame] blasphemes

To plague thine enemies,
Which now embosomed idly sleeps. 60

Thou art my God, I know,
My king, who long ago
Didst undertake the charge of me:
And in my hard distress
Didst work me such release, 65
That all the earth did wond'ring see.

Thou by thy might didst make
That seas in sunder brake,
And dreadful dragons which before
In deep or swam or crawled, 70
Such mortal strokes appalled,
They floated dead to every shore.°

Thou crushed that monster's head,°
Whom other monsters dread,
And so his fishy flesh didst frame 75
To serve as pleasing food
To all the ravening brood,
Who had the desert for their dam.

Thou wondrously didst cause
Repealing nature's laws 80
From thirsty flint a fountain flow°
And of the rivers clear,
The sandy beds appear,
So dry thou mad'st their channels grow.

The day arrayed in light, 85
The shadow-clothèd night,
Were made, and are maintained by thee;
The sun and sun-like rays,
The bounds of nights and days,
Thy workmanship no less they be. 90

71 appalled] weakened　　75 frame] create　　78 dam] mother　　84 mad'st]
made

To thee the earth doth owe,
    That earth in sea doth grow,
And sea doth earth from drowning spare:
    The summer's corny crown,
    The winter's frosty gown,   95
Naught but thy badge, thy livery are.°

Thou then still one, the same,
    Think how thy glorious name
These brain-sick men's despite have borne,
    How abject enemies   100
    The Lord of highest skies,
With cursèd taunting tongues have torn.

Ah! Give no hawk the pow'r
    Thy turtle to devour,
Which sighs to thee with mourning moans: 105
    Nor utterly out-rase
    From tables of thy grace
The flock of thy afflicted ones.

But call thy league to mind,
    For horror all doth blind,   110
No light doth in the land remain:
    Rape, murder, violence,
    Each outrage, each offence,
Each where doth range and rage and reign.

Enough, enough we mourn;   115
    Let us no more return
Repulsed with blame and shame from thee:
    But succour us oppressed,
    And give the troubled rest,
That of thy praise their songs may be.   120

99 despite] contempt   104 turtle] turtledove   106 out-rase] erase
107 tables] writing tablets   114 Each where] everywhere   118 succour] help

Rise, God, plead thine own case,
    Forget not what disgrace
These fools on thee each day bestow:
    Forget not with what cries
    Thy foes against thee rise,   125
Which more and more to heav'n do grow.

Psalm 75

Confitebimur tibi

Thee, God, oh, thee, we sing, we celebrate:
Thy acts with wonder who but doth relate?
    So kindly nigh thy name our need attendeth.
Sure I, when once the charge I undergo
Of this assembly, will not fail to show   5
    My judgements such, as justest rule commendeth.

The people loose, the land I shaken find;
This will I firmly prop, that straitly bind;
    And then denounce my uncontrollèd pleasure:
Brag not you braggarts, you your saucy horn   10
Lift not, lewd mates, no more with heavens scorn,
    Dance on in words your old repining measure.

Where sun first shows; or last enshades his light;
Divides the day; or pricks the midst of night;
    Seek not the fountain whence preferment springeth.   15
God's only fixèd course that all doth sway,
Limits dishonour's night, and honour's day,
    The king his crown, the slave his fetters bringeth.°

A troubled cup is in Jehovah's hand,
Where wine and winy lees compounded stand,   20
    Which frankly filled, as freely he bestoweth;

8 straitly] tightly   9 denounce] announce   10 horn] emblem of power and might   12 repining] complaining   14 pricks] pierces, hurries   20 lees] dregs

Yet for their draught ungodly men doth give,
Gives all (not one except) that lewdly live,
    Only what from the dregs by wringing floweth.

And I secure shall spend my happy times   25
In my, though lowly, never-dying rhymes,°
    Singing with praise the God that Jacob loveth.
My princely care shall crop ill-doers low,
    In glory plant, and make with glory grow
    Who right approves, and doth what right approveth.   30

Psalm 76

Notus in Judea

Only to Judah God his will doth signify;
    Only in Jacob is his name notorious;
His restful tent doth only Salem dignify;°
    On Zion only stands his dwelling glorious;
        Their bow, and shaft, and shield, and sword he
            shiverèd,   5
        Drave war from us, and us from war deliverèd.

Above proud princes, proudest in their thievery,
    Thou art exalted high, and highly glorified:
Their weak attempt, thy valiant delivery,
    Their spoil, thy conquest meet to be historified.   10
        The mighty handless grew as men that slumberèd
        For hands grew mightless, sense and life encumberèd.

Nay, God, O God, true Jacob's sole devotion,
    Thy check the very cars and horses mortified,
Cast in dull sleep, and quite deprived of motion.   15
    Most fearful God, oh, how must he be fortified!
        Whose fearless foot to bide thy onset tarrieth,
        When once thy wrath displayèd ensign carrieth.

---

3 Salem] Jerusalem   4 Zion] house of the God of Israel   5 shaft] arrow
shiverèd] shattered   6 Drave] drove   12 encumberèd] burdened
14 cars] chariots   mortified] subdued, killed   17 bide] abide

From out of heav'n thy justice judgement thunderèd
 When good by thee were saved, and bad were punishèd,   20
While earth at heav'n with fear and silence wonderèd.
 Yea, the most rageful in their rage astonishèd
  Fell to praise thee: whom thou, however furious
  Shalt eft restrain, if fury prove injurious.

Then let your vows be paid, your off'rings offerèd   25
 Unto the Lord, O you of his protection:°
Unto the fearful let your gifts be profferèd,
 Who loppeth princes' thoughts, prunes their affection.°
  And so himself most terrible doth verify,
  In terrifying kings, that earth doth terrify.°   30

Psalm 77

Voce mea ad Dominum

To thee my crying call,
 To thee my calling cry°
 I did, O God, address,
 And thou didst me attend:
  To nightly anguish thrall.   5
 From thee I sought redress;
 To thee incessantly
 Did praying hands extend.

All comfort fled my soul;
 Yea, God to mind I called,   10
 Yet calling God to mind
 My thoughts could not appease:
  Naught else but bitter dole
 Could I in thinking find;
 My sprite with pain appalled,   15
 Could entertain no ease.

24 eft] again

Psalm 77 5 thrall] captive   13 Naught] nothing   dole] sorrow
15 sprite] spirit

Whole troops of busy cares,
    Of cares that from thee came,
    Took up their restless rest
    In sleepy sleepless eyes: 20
        So lay I all oppressed,
    My heart in office lame,
    My tongue as lamely fares,°
    No part his part supplies.

At length with turnèd thought   25
    Anew I fell to think
    Upon the ancient times
    Upon the years of old:
        Yea, to my mind was brought,
    And in my heart did sink,   30
    What in my former rhymes
    Myself of thee had told.°

Lo, then to search the truth
    I sent my thoughts abroad;
    Meanwhile my silent heart   35
    Distracted thus did plain:°
        'Will God no more take ruth?
    No further love impart?
    No longer be my God?
    Unmovèd still remain?   40

'Are all the conduits dry
    Of his erst flowing grace?
    Could rusty teeth of time
    To naught his promise turn?
        Can mercy no more climb   45
    And come before his face?
    Must all compassion die?
    Must naught but anger burn?

22 in office lame] unable to perform its function   36 plain] complain
37 ruth] compassion   42 erst] formerly

'Then, lo, my wrack I see,'
  Say I, 'and do I know   50
  That change lies in his hand,
  Who changeless sits aloft?
    Can I aught understand,
  And yet unmindful be,
  What wonders from him flow?   55
  What works his will hath wrought?'

Nay, still thy acts I mind;
  Still of thy deeds I muse;
  Still see thy glory's light
  Within thy temple shine.   60
    What god can any find
  (For term them so they use)
  Whose majesty, whose might,
  May strive, O God, with thine?

Thou only wonders dost;   65
  The wonders by thee done,
  All earth do wonder make,
  As when thy hand of old°
    From servitude unjust
  Both Jacob's sons did take,   70
  And sons of Jacob's son,
  Whom Jacob's sons had sold.°

The waves thee saw, saw thee,°
  And fearful fled the field;
  The deep with panting breast   75
  Engulfèd quaking lay:
    The clouds thy fingers pressed,
  Did rushing rivers yield;
  Thy shafts did flaming flee
  Through fi'ry airy way,   80

49 wrack] ruin   53 aught] anything   57 mind] remember
79 shafts] arrows

Thy voice's thund'ring crash
 From one to other pole,
 Twixt roof of starry sphere
 And earth's then trembling floor,
  While light of lightnings' flash   85
 Did pitchy clouds enclear,°
 Did round with terror roll,
 And rattling horror roar.

Meanwhile through dusty deep
 On sea's discovered bed,   90
 Where none thy trace could view,
 A path by thee was wrought:
  A path whereon thy crew
 As shepherds use their sheep,
 With Aaron Moses led,   95
 And to glad pastures brought.°

Psalm 78

Attendite, popule

A grave discourse to utter I intend;
The age of time I purpose to renew;°
You, O my charge, to what I teach attend;
Hear what I speak, and what you hear ensue.
The things our fathers did to us commend,   5
The same are they I recommend to you,
  Which though but heard we know most true to be:
  We heard, but heard, of who themselves did see.

Which never let us so ungrateful grow,
As to conceal from such as shall succeed: 10
Let us the praises of Jehovah show,
Each act of worth, each memorable deed
Chiefly since he himself commanded so,

86 enclear] illuminate
Psalm 78 4 ensue] follow 6 recommend] commend again (Rathmell)

Giving a law to Jacob and his seed,
     That fathers should this use to sons maintain,   15
     And sons to sons, and they to theirs again.°

That while the young shall over-live the old,
And of their brood some yet shall be unborn;
These memories in memory enrolled
By fretting time may never thence be worn   20
That still on God their anchor, hope may hold;°
From him by no despairful tempest torn;
     That with wise hearts and willing minds they may
     Think what he did, and what he bids obey;

And not ensue their fathers' froward trace,   25
Whose steps from God rebelliously did stray,
A wayward, stubborn, stayless, faithless race;
Such as on God no hold by hope could lay
Like Ephraim's sons, who durst not show their face,
But from the battle fearful fled away: 30
     Yet bare, as men of warlike excellence,
     Offending bows, and armour for defence.

And why? They did not hold inviolate°
The league of God: nor in his paths would go.
His famous works, and wonders they forgat,   35
Which often hearing well might cause them know
The works and wonders which, in hard estate°
He did of old unto their fathers show:
     Whereof all Egypt testimony yields,
     And of all Egypt, chiefly Zoan fields,°   40

There where the deep did show his sandy floor,°
And heapèd waves an uncouth way enwall:
Whereby they passed from one to other shore,
Walking on seas, and yet not wet at all.

---

15 use] ritual   20 fretting] wasting   25 froward] recalcitrant   trace]
course of action   27 stayless] unsettled   31 bare] bore   32 Offending] for
offence   35 forgat] forgot   42 uncouth] marvellous   enwall] wall in

He led them so, a cloud was them before   45
While light did last: when night did darkness call,
    A flaming pillar glitt'ring in the skies
    Their lodestar was, till sun again did rise.

He rived the rocks, and from their piercèd sides,
To give them drink, whole seas of water drew: 50
The desert sand no longer thirst abides,
The trickling springs to such huge rivers grew.
Yet not content their fury further slides,
In those wild ways they anger God anew.
    As thirst before, now hunger stirs their lust   55
    To tempting thoughts, bewraying want of trust,

And fond conceits begetting fonder words:
'Can God', say they, 'prepare with plenteous hand
Deliciously to furnish out our boards
Here in this waste, this hunger-starvèd land?   60
We see indeed the streams, the rock affords;
We see in pools the gathered waters stand:
    But whither bread and flesh so ready be
    For him to give as yet we do not see.'

This heard, but heard with most displeasèd ear,   65
That Jacob's race he did so dearly love,
Who in his favour had no cause to fear,°
Should now so wav'ring, so distrustful prove;
The rakèd sparks in flame began appear,
And stayèd choler fresh again to move;   70
    That from his trust their confidence should swerve,
    Whose deeds had shown, he could and would preserve.

Yet he unclosed the garners of the skies,
And bade the clouds ambrosian manna rain:°
As morning frost on hoary pasture lies,   75

48 lodestar] guiding star   49 rived] split   51 abides] endures
56 bewraying] exposing   57 fond] foolish   59 boards] tables
69 rakèd] covered up, as in a fire   70 stayèd] held in check   choler] anger
73 garners] storehouses   74 ambrosian] heavenly   75 hoary] white

So strawèd lay each where this heav'nly grain.
The finest cheat that princes dearest prize,
The bread of heav'n could not in fineness stain:
    Which he them gave, and gave them in such store,
    Each had so much, he wished to have no more.   80

But that he might them each way satisfy,
He slipped the rains to east and southern wind;
These on the clouds their utmost forces try,
And bring in rain of admirable kind.
The dainty quails that freely wont to fly,   85
In forcèd show'rs to drop were now assigned:
    And fell as thick as dust on sun-burnt field,
    Or as the sand the thirsty shore doth yield.

So all the plain, whereon their army lay,
As far abroad as any tent was pight,   90
With feathered rain was watered every way,
Which show'ring down did on their lodgings light.
Then fell they to their easy gotten prey,
And fed till fullness vanquished had delight:
    Their lust still flamed, still God the fuel brought   95
    And fed their lust, beyond their lustful thought.

But fully filled, not fully yet content,
While now the meat their weary chaps did chew:
God's wrathful rage upon these gluttons sent,
Of all their troops the principalest slew.   100
Among all them of Israel's descent
His stronger plague the strongest overthrew.
    Yet not all this could wind them to his will,
    Still worse they grew, and more untoward still.

Therefore he made them waste their weary years   105
Roaming in vain in that unpeopled place,

76 strawèd] strewn, scattered   each where] everywhere   77 cheat] wheat bread
78 stain] eclipse   82 slipped] let go   85 wont] were accustomed
90 pight] pitched   98 chaps] jaws   104 untoward] perverse

Possessed with doubtful cares, and dreadful fears;
But if at any time Death showed his face,
Then, lo, to God they sued and sued with tears:
Then they returned, and early sought his grace;   110
    Then they professed, and all did mainly cry
    In God their strength, their hope, their help did lie.

But all was built upon no firmer ground
Than fawning mouths, and tongues to lying trained:
They made but shows, their heart was never sound,   115
Disloyal once, disloyal still remained.
Yet he (so much his mercy did abound)
Purgèd the filth, wherewith their souls were stained:
    Destroyed them not, but oft revoked his ire,
    And mildly quenched his indignation's fire.   120

For kind compassion callèd to his mind,
That they but men, that men but mortal were,
That mortal life, a blast of breathing wind,
As wind doth pass, and passed no more appear,
And yet (good God) how oft this crooked kind   125
Incensed him in the desert everywhere,
    Again repined, and murmurèd again,
    And would in bounds that boundless pow'r contain!

Forsooth, their weak remembrance could not hold
His hand, whose force above all mortal hands   130
To Egypt's wonder did itself unfold,
Loosing their fetters and their servile bands:
When Zoan plains where crystal rivers rolled,
With all the rest of those surrounded lands,
    Saw wat'ry clearness changed to bloody gore,   135
    Pining with thirst in midst of wat'ry store.

Should I relate of flies the deadly swarms?
Of filthy frogs the odious annoy?
Grasshoppers' waste, and caterpillars' harms,

111 mainly] loudly   129 Forsooth] truly   138 annoy] annoyance

Which did their fruits, their harvest hope enjoy?   140
How hail and lightning breaking off the arms
Of vines and figs, the bodies did destroy?
     Lightning and hail, whose flamy, stony blows
     Their beasts no less and cattle overthrows?

These were but smokes of after-going fire: 145
Now, now his fury breaketh into flame;
Now dole and dread, now pine and pain conspire
With angry angels' wreak and wrack to frame.
Naught now is left to stop his stayless ire;
So plain a way is opened to the same.   150
     Abroad goes Death, the uttermost of ills,
     In house, in field, and men and cattle kills.

All that rich land, whereover Nilus trails
Of his wet robe the slimy, seedy train,°
With millions of mourning cries bewails   150
Of every kind their first begotten slain.
Against this plague no wealth, no worth prevails:
Of all that in the tents of Ham remain,°
     Who of their house the props and pillars were,
     Themselves do fall, much less can others bear.   160

Meanwhile, as while a black tempestuous blast
Drowning the earth, in sunder rents the skies,
A shepherd wise to house his flock doth haste,
Taking near ways, and where best passage lies:
God from this ruin, through the barren waste   165
Conducts his troops in such or safer wise;
     And from the seas his sheep he fearless saves,
     Leaving their wolves entombèd in the waves,°

But them leaves not until they were possessed
Of this his hill, of this his holy place,   170
Whereof full conquest did him Lord invest,

---

147 dole] sorrow   148 wreak and wrack] vengeance and ruin   frame] make
149 Naught] nothing   stayless] ceaseless   154 seedy] containing seeds
168 wolves] enemies

When all the dwellers fled his people's face,
By him subdued, and by his hand oppressed:
Whose heritage he sharèd to the race,
  The twelve-fold race of godly Israel,   175
  To lord their lands, and in their dwellings dwell.

But what avails? Not yet they make an end
To tempt high God, and stir his angry gall:
From his prescript another way they wend,
And to their fathers' crooked by-paths fall.   180
So with vain toil distorted bows we bend:
Though levelled right, they shoot not right at all.
  The idol honour of their damnèd groves,
  When God it heard, his jealous anger moves.

For God did hear, detesting in his heart,   185
The Israelites a people so perverse:
And from his seat in Silo did depart
The place where God did erst with men converse,
Right well content that foes on every part
His force captive his glory should reverse;   190
  Right well content (so ill content he grew)
  His people's blood should tyrant's blade imbrue.

So the young men the flame of life bereaves;
The virgins live despaired of marriage choice;°
The sacred priests fall on the bloody glaives;   195
No widow left to use her wailing voice.
But as a knight, whom wine or slumber leaves,°
Hearing alarm, is rousèd at the noise,
  So God awakes: his haters fly for fear,
  And of their shame eternal marks do bear.   200

But God chose not, as he before had chose,
In Joseph's tents, or Ephraim to dwell:
But Judah takes, and to mount Zion goes,

173 oppressed] crushed 179 prescript] command wend] turn
184 jealous] vehement 188 erst] formerly 192 imbrue] stain with blood
195 glaives] swords 203 Zion] house of the God of Israel

To Zion mount, the mount he lovèd well.
There he his house did castle-like enclose;   205
Of whose decay no after times shall tell:
> While her own weight shall weighty earth sustain,
> His sacred seat shall here unmoved remain.

And where his servant David did attend
A shepherd's charge, with care of fold and field;   210
He takes him thence and to a nobler end
Converts his cares, appointing him to shield
His people which of Jacob did descend,
And feed the flock his heritage did yield:
> And he the pains did gladly undergo,   215
> Which heart sincere, and hand discreet did show.°

Psalm 79

Deus, venerunt

The land of long by thee possessèd,
The heathen, Lord, have now oppressèd:
Thy temple holily maintainèd
Till now, is now, profanely stainèd.
> Jerusalem quite spoiled and burnèd,   5
> > Hath suffered sack
> > And utter wrack,
> To stony heaps her buildings turnèd.

The lifeless carcasses of those
That lived thy servants, serve the crows:°   10
The flock, so dearly loved of thee,
To ravening beasts dear food they be.
> Their blood doth stream in every street
> > As water spilled:
> > Their bodies killed   15
> With sepulture can nowhere meet.

7 wrack] ruin   16 sepulture] burial

To them that hold the neighbour places
We are but objects of disgraces:
On every coast who dwell about us,
In every kind deride and flout us.   20
     Ah, Lord! When shall thy wrath be ended?
          Shall still thine ire,
           As quenchless fire,
In deadly ardour be extended?

Oh, kindle there thy fury's flame,   25
Where lives no notice of thy name:
There let thy heavy anger fall,
Where no devotions on thee call.
     For thence, they be who Jacob eat,
          Who thus have rased,   30
          Have thus, defaced,
Thus desert laid his ancient seat.

Lord, rid us from our sinful cumbers,
Count not of them the passèd numbers:
But let thy pity soon prevent us,   35
For hard extremes have nearly spent us.
     Free us, O God, our freedom giver;
          Our misery
          With help supply:
And for thy glory us deliver.   40

Deliver us, and for thy name
With mercy clothe our sinful shame:
Ah! Why should this their byword be,
'Where is your God? Where now is he?'
     Make them, and us on them behold,   45
          That not despised,
          But dearly prized,
Thy wreakful hand our blood doth hold.

30 rased] erased   32 desert laid] destroyed   33 cumbers] burdens
34 passèd] former   35 prevent] anticipate   48 wreakful] vengeful

Where grace and glory thee enthroneth,
Admit the groans the prisoner groaneth: 50
The poor condemned for death reservèd
Let be by thee in life preservèd.
    And for our neighbours, Lord, remember
           Th'opprobrious shame
           They lent thy name 55
With sev'n-fold gain to them thou render.

So we thy servants, we thy sheep,
Whom thy looks guide, thy pastures keep:
Till death define our living days,
Will never cease to sound thy praise. 60
    Nay, when we leave to see the sun,
           The after-goers
           We will make knowers°
From age to age what thou hast done.

Psalm 80

Qui regis Israel

Hear, thou great herdsman that dost Jacob feed;
    Thou Joseph's shepherd, shine from cherubs' throne:
In Ephraim, Benjamin, Manasses' need,
    Awake thy power, and make thy puissance known.
    Free us distressèd, raise us overthrown, 5
        Reduce us strayed, O God, restore us banished:
Display thy face's skies on us, thine own,°
    So we shall safely dwell, all darkness vanished.

Lord God of hosts, what end, what mean appears
    Of thy wrath's fume against thy people's cry, 10
Whom thou with tears for bread, for drink with tears
    So dietest, that we abandoned lie,

---

54 opprobrious] disgraceful   59 define] end
Psalm 80 3 Ephraim, Benjamin, Manasses] tribes of Israel   4 puissance] power
6 Reduce] lead or bring back   10 fume] smoke

To foes of laughter, and to dwellers by,
　　A field of brawl. But God, restore us banished;
Display on us thy face's clearèd sky,　　　　　　　　15
　　So we shall safely dwell all darkness vanished.

A vine thou didst translate from Zoan plains,
　　And weeding them that held the place of old,
Nor planting care didst slack, nor pruning pains,
　　To fix her roots, whom fields could not enfold.°　　20
　　The hills were cloakèd with her pleasing cold;
　　　　With cedar's state her branches' height contended:
　　Scarce here the sea, the river there controlled
　　　　Her arms, her hands, so wide she both extended.

Why hast thou now thyself dishedged this vine,　　　25
　　Carelessly left to passengers in prey?
Unseemly rooted by the wood-bred swine,
　　Wasted by other beasts that wildly stray?
　　O God, return, and from thy starry stay
　　　　Review this vine, reflect thy looking hither;°　　30
　　This vineyard see, whose plot thy hand did lay,
　　　　This plant of choice, ordainèd not to wither.°

Consumed with flames, with killing axes hewn
　　All at thy frown they fall, and quail, and die:°
But heap thou might, on thy elected one,°　　　　　　35
　　That stablished man in whom we may affy.
　　Then we preserved, thy name shall magnify
　　　　Without revolt, Lord God, restore us banished:
　　Display on us thy face's clearèd sky,
　　　　So we shall safely dwell, all darkness vanished.　　40

---

13 of laughter] laughing　　14 brawl] clamour, struggle　　17 translate] transplant
Zoan] Egypt　　19 slack] neglect　　27 rooted] uprooted　　wood-bred swine]
wild boars　　29 stay] residence　　36 stablished] established　　affy] trust

Psalm 81

Exultate Deo

All gladness, gladdest hearts can hold,
 In merriest notes that mirth can yield,
Let joyful songs to God unfold
  To Jacob's God our sword and shield.
    Muster hither music's joys,   5
    Lute, and lyre, and tabret's noise:
  Let no instrument be wanting,
  Chasing grief, and pleasure planting.

When every month beginning takes,
 When fixèd times bring sacred days,   10
When any feast his people makes,
  Let trumpet's tunes report his praise.°
    This to us a law doth stand,
    Pointed thus by God's own hand;
  Of his league a sign ordainèd,   15
  When his plagues had Egypt painèd.

There heard I, erst unheard by me,
 The voice of God, who thus did say:°
'Thy shoulder I from burthen free,
  Free set thy hand from bakèd clay.°   20
    Vexèd, thou my aid didst crave;
    Thunder-hid I answer gave:
  Till the streams where strife did move thee,
  Still I did with trial prove thee.

'I bade thee then attentive be,   25
 And told thee thus: "O Israel,
This is my covenant that with thee
  No false, nor foreign god shall dwell.
    I am God, thy God, that wrought

6 tabret's] of a small tabor or drum 14 Pointed] appointed
17 erst] formerly 19 burthen] burden

That thou wert from Egypt brought: 30
 Open me thy mouth; to feed thee
I will care, naught else shall need thee."

'But, ah, my people scorned my voice,
 And Israel rebellèd still:
So then I left them to the choice   35
 Of froward way and wayward will.
   Why, alas? Why had not they
   Heard my voice, and held my way?
 Quickly I their foes had humbled,
 All their haters headlong tumbled.   40

'Subdued by me who them annoyed,
 Had served them now in base estate:
And of my grant they had enjoyed
 A lease of bliss with endless date.°
   Flour of the finest wheat   45
   Had been now their plenteous meat:
 Honey them from rocks distillèd
 Fillèd had, yea, overfillèd.'°

Psalm 82

Deus stetit

Where poor men plead at princes' bar,
 Who gods (as God's vicegerents) are:°
The God of gods hath his tribunal pight,
 Adjudging right
Both to the judge, and judgèd wight.°   5

 'How long will ye just doom neglect?
 How long', saith he, 'bad men respect?
You should his own unto the helpless give,
 The poor relieve,
Ease him with right, whom wrong doth grieve. 10

32 naught] nothing 36 froward] recalcitrant
Psalm 82 1 bar] bar of justice 2 vicegerents] those appointed by God to govern
3 pight] pitched 5 wight] person 6 doom] judgement

'You should the fatherless defend;
    You should unto the weak extend
Your hand, to loose and quiet his estate°
    Through lewd men's hate
Entangled now in deep debate.   15

'This should you do. But what do ye?
    You nothing know, you nothing see:
No light, no law; fie, fie, the very ground
    Becomes unsound,
So right, wrong, all, your faults confound.°   20

'Indeed to you the style I gave
    Of gods, and sons of God, to have.
But err not, princes: you as men must die;
    You that sit high,
Must fall, and low, as others lie.'°   25

Since men are such, O God, arise:
    Thyself most strong, most just, most wise,
Of all the earth king, judge, disposer be,
    Since to decree
Of all the earth belongs to thee.   30

Psalm 83

Deus, quis similis

Be not, oh, be not silent still;
    Rest not, O God, with endless rest:
        For, lo, thine enemies
        With noise and tumult rise;
Hate doth their hearts with fierceness fill,   5
    And lift their heads who thee detest.

Against thy folk their wits they file
    To sharpest point of secret sleight:

14 lewd] wicked   18 fie, fie] reproachful exclamation   21 style] title
Psalm 83 8 sleight] trickery

A world of traps and trains
They forge in busy brains, 10
That they thy hid ones may beguile,
Whom thy wings shroud from searching sight.

Come, let us of them nothing make;
Let none them more a people see:
Stop we their very name 15
Within the mouth of fame.
Such are the counsels these men take;
Such leagues they link, and these they be:

First, Edom's sons, then Ishmael,°
With Moab, Agar, Gebal's train; 20
With these the Ammonites
The fierce Amalekites,
And who in Palestina dwell,°
And who in tents of Tyre remain.

Ashur, though further off he lie, 25
Assisteth Lot's incestuous brood.°
But, Lord, as Jabin thou
And Sisera didst bow;°
As Midian did fall and die
At Endor walls, and Kison flood; 30

As Oreb, Zeb, and Zeba strong,
As Salmana who led thy foes°
(Who meant, nay, said no less
Than that they would possess
God's heritage) became as dung: 35
So, Lord, oh, so, of these dispose.

Torment them, Lord, as tossèd balls,°
As stubble scattered in the air,
Or as the branchy brood
Of some thick mountain wood, 40

9 trains] snares, treachery   39 branchy brood] trees

To naught, or naught but ashes falls,
　　When flames do singe their leafy hair:

So with thy tempest them pursue,
　　So with thy whirlwind them affright,
　　　　So paint their daunted face,°
　　　　With pencil of disgrace,
That they at length to thee may sue,
　　And give thy glorious name his right.

Add fear and shame, to shame and fear;°
　　Confound them quite, and quite deface;
　　　　And make them know that none
　　　　But thou, and thou alone,
Dost that high name Jehovah bear,
　　High placed above all earthly place.

Psalm 84

Quam dilecta

　　How lovely is thy dwelling,
Great God, to whom all greatness is belonging!
　　To view thy courts far, far from any telling°
My soul doth long, and pine with longing.
　　　　Unto the God that liveth,
　　　　The God that all life giveth,°
　　My heart and body both aspire,
　　Above delight, beyond desire.

　　Alas! The sparrow knoweth
The house where free and fearless she resideth:
　　Directly to the nest the swallow goeth,
　Where with her sons she safe abideth.
　　　　Oh, altars thine, most mighty
　　　　In war, yea, most almighty:
　　Thy altars, Lord: Ah! Why should I
　　From altars thine excluded lie?°

45

50

5

10

15

41 naught] nothing　　45 daunted] subdued　　50 deface] discredit, defame

Oh, happy who remaineth
Thy household-man and still thy praise unfoldeth!
Oh, happy who himself on thee sustaineth,
Who to thy house his journey holdeth!   20
    Me seems I see them going
    Where mulberries are growing:
How wells they dig in thirsty plain,°
And cisterns make, for falling rain.

Me seems I see augmented   25
Still troop with troop, till all at length discover
Zion, where to their sight is represented
The Lord of hosts, the Zion lover.
    O Lord, O God, most mighty
    In war, yea, most almighty: 30
Hear what I beg; hearken, I say,
O Jacob's God, to what I pray.

Thou art the shield us shieldeth:
Then, Lord, behold the face of thine anointed.
    One day spent in thy courts more comfort yieldeth   35
Than thousands otherwise appointed.
    I count it clearer pleasure
    To spend my age's treasure
Waiting a porter at thy gates,
Than dwell a lord with wicked mates.   40

Thou art the sun that shineth;
Thou art the buckler, Lord, that us defendeth:
    Glory and grace Jehovah's hand assigneth,
And good without refusal sendeth
    To him who truly treadeth   45
    The path to pureness leadeth.°
O Lord of might, thrice blessed he,
Whose confidence is built on thee.

27 Zion] house of the God of Israel   represented] presented   42 buckler]
small, round shield

Psalm 85

Benedixisti, Domine

Mighty Lord, from this thy land,
    Never was thy love estranged:
Jacob's servitude thy hand°
    Hath, we know, to freedom changed.
      All thy people's wicked parts   5
        Have been banished from thy sight;
        Thou on them hast curèd quite
      All the wounds of sinful darts.°
          Still thy choler quenching so,
          Heat to flame did never grow.   10

Now then, God, as heretofore,°
    God, the God that dost us save,
Change our state, in us no more
    Let thine anger object have.
      Wilt thou thus for ever grieve?   15
        Wilt thou of thy wrathful rage
        Draw the thread from age to age?°
      Never us again relieve?
          Lord, yet once our hearts to joy
          Show thy grace, thy help employ.   20

What speak I? Oh, let me hear
    What he speaks: for speak he will
Peace to whom he love doth bear,
    Lest they fall to folly still.
      Ever nigh to such as stand   25
        In his fear, his favour is:
        How can then his glory miss
      Shortly to enlight our land?
          Mercy now and Truth shall meet:
          Peace with kiss shall Justice greet.   30

9 choler] anger   28 enlight] enlighten, illuminate

Truth shall spring in every place,
   As the herb, the earth's attire:
Justice's long-absent face
    Heav'n shall show, and earth admire.
     Then Jehovah on us will   35
      Good on good in plenty throw:
      Then shall we in gladness mow,
    Whereas now in grief we till.°
       Then before him in his way
       All go right, not one shall stray.   40

Psalm 86

Inclina, Domine

Eternal Lord, thine ear incline;
   Hear me most helpless, most oppressèd:
This client save, this servant thine,
    Whose hope is whole to thee addressèd.
     On me, Jehovah, pity take: 5
      For daily cry to thee I make.
    Thy servant's soul from depth of sadness
    That climbs to thee, advance to gladness.°

O Lord, I know thee good and kind,
   On all that ask much mercy spending: 10
Then hear, O Lord, with heedful mind
    These careful suits of my commending.
     I only call when much I need;
      Needs of thy help I then must speed:
    A god like whom (if gods be many)°   15
    Who is, or doth, there is not any.

And therefore, Lord, before thy face
   All nations which thy hand hath framèd,
Shall come with low adoring grace,

32 herb] vegetation

Psalm 86 3 client] dependant   4 whole] wholly   14 speed] succeed
19 low] humble

And praise the name upon thee namèd.   20
   For thou art great, and thou alone
     Dost wonders, God, done else by none:
Oh, in thy truth my path discover,
And hold me fast thy fearing lover.

Lord, all my heart shall sing of thee: 25
   By me thy name shall still be praisèd,
Whose goodness richly poured on me
   From lowest pit my soul hath raisèd.
     And now again mine enemies
      Do many, mighty, proud arise: 30
By whom with hate my life is chasèd,
While in their sight thou least art placèd.

But thou, Jehovah, swift to grace,
   On light entreaty pardon showest:
To wrath dost go a heavy pace,   35
   And full with truth and mercy flowest.
     Then turn and take of me remorse;
      With strength my weakness reinforce:
Who in thy service have attended,
And of thy handmaid am descended.°   40

Oh, let some token of thy love
   Be eminently on me placèd;
Some cognisance, to teach and prove,
   That thine I am, that by thee gracèd;
     To dye their cheeks in shameful hue   45
      That now with spite my soul pursue,
Eye-taught how me thou dost deliver,°
My endless aid and comfort giver.

---

23 discover] reveal   35 heavy] slow   36 full] fully
43 cognisance] badge worn by a household retainer

Psalm 87

Fundamenta eius

Founded upon the hills of holiness
    God's city stands: who more love beareth°
To gates of Zion high in lowliness,
    Than all the towns that Judah reareth.
        City of God, in God's decree   5
        What noble things are said of thee!

'I will', saith he, 'henceforth be numberèd
    Egypt and Babel with my knowers;°
That Palestine and Tyre, which cumberèd
    The fathers, with the after-goers   10
        Shall join; so Ethiope from whence
        The born shall be, as born from hence.'

Yea, this, men shall of Zion signify:
    To him, and him it gave first breathing;
Which highest God shall highly dignify,   15
    Eternal stay to it bequeathing.
        Jehovah this account shall make,
        When he of his shall muster take.

That he and he, who ever namèd be
    Shall be as born in Zion namèd;°   20
In Zion shall my music framèd be,
    Of lute and voice most sweetly framèd:
        'I will', saith he, 'to Zion bring
        Of my fresh fountains every spring.'

---

3 Zion] house of the God of Israel   9 cumberèd] burdened
14 first breathing] life   16 stay] endurance   bequeathing] giving

Psalm 88

Domine Deus

My God, my Lord, my help, my health,
    To thee my cry
    Doth restless fly,
        Both when of sun the day
        The treasures doth display,°   5
And night locks up his golden wealth.

Admit to presence what I crave:°
    Oh, bow thine ear
    My cry to hear,
        Whose soul with ills and woes   10
        So flows, so overflows,
That now my life draws nigh the grave.

With them that fall into the pit
    I stand esteemed:
    Quite forceless deemed,   15
        As one who free from strife,
        And stir of mortal life,
Among the dead at rest doth sit.

Right like unto the murdered sort,
    Who in the grave   20
    Their biding have:
        Whom now thou dost no more
        Remember as before,
Quite, quite cut off from thy support.

Thrown down into the grave of graves   25
    In darkness deep
    Thou dost me keep:

---

1 health] salvation   13 pit] grave   15 forceless deemed] judged weak
17 stir] activity   21 biding] dwelling   25 grave of graves] deepest, darkest
grave

Where lightning of thy wrath
Upon me lighted hath,
All overwhelmed with all thy waves.   30

Who did know me, whom I did know,
    Removed by thee
    Are gone from me:
        Are gone? That is the best:
        They all me so detest,   35
That now abroad I blush to go.

My wasted eye doth melt away
    Fleeting amain
    In streams of pain
        While I my prayers send,   40
        While I my hands extend,
To thee, my God, and fail no day.°

Alas, my Lord, will then be time,°
    When men are dead,
    Thy truth to spread?   45
        Shall they, whom death hath slain,
        To praise thee live again,
And from their lowly lodgings climb?

Shall buried mouths thy mercies tell?
    Dust and decay   50
    Thy truth display?
        And shall thy works of mark
        Shine in the dreadful dark?
Thy justice where oblivions dwell?

Good reason then I cry to thee,°   55
    And ere the light
    Salute thy sight,
        My plaint to thee direct.

38 amain] quickly   39 streams of pain] tears   52 of mark] notable
54 oblivions] things forgotten   58 plaint] complaint

Lord, why dost thou reject
My soul, and hide thy face from me? 60

Aye me, alas, I faint, I die,
    So still, so still,
      Thou dost me fill,
        And hast from youngest years,
          With terrifying fears, 65
That I in trance amazed do lie.

All over me thy furies passed;
    Thy fears my mind
      Do fretting bind,
        Flowing about me so, 70
          As flocking waters flow:
No day can overrun their haste.

Who erst to me were near and dear
    Far now, oh, far
      Disjoinèd are, 75
        And when I would them see,
          Who my acquaintance be,
As darkness they to me appear.

Psalm 89

Misericordias Domini

The constant promises, the loving graces,
    That cause our debt, eternal Lord, to thee,
Till ages shall fill up their still-void spaces,
    My thankful song's unaltered theme shall be.
    For of thy bounty thus my thoughts decree: 5
It shall be fully built, as fairly founded;
    And of thy truth attesting heav'ns shall see
The boundless periods, though theirs be bounded.°

69 fretting] chafing, rubbing   71 flocking] flooding   72 overrun] outrun
73 erst] once
Psalm 89 1 constant] faithful

'Lo, I have leagued', thou saist, 'with my elected,
    And thus have to my servant David sworn: 10
Thy offspring kings, thy throne in state erected
    By my support all threats of time shall scorn.'
    And, Lord, as running skies with wheels unworn°
Cease not to lend this wonder their commending:
    So with one-minded praise no less adorn   15
This truth the holy troops thy court attending.

For who among the clouds with thee compareth?
    What angel there thy paragon doth reign?
Whose majesty, whose peerless force declareth
    The trembling awe of thine immortal train.   20
    Lord God, whom hosts redoubt, who can maintain
With thee in pow'rfulness a rival's quarrel?
    Strongest art thou, and must to end remain,
Whom complete faith doth armour-like apparel.°

Thy lordly check the sea's proud courage quailèd,   25
    And highly swelling lowly made reside;
To crush stout Pharaoh thy arm prevailèd:
    What one thy foe did undispersed abide?
    The heav'n, the earth, and all in bosom wide
This huge round engine clips, to thee pertaineth:°   30
    Which firmly basèd, not to shake, or slide,
The unseen hinge of north and south sustaineth.

For north and south were both by thee created,
    And those cross points our bounding hills behold,
Tabor and Hermon, in whose joy related°   35
    Thy glorious grace from west to east is told.
    Thy arm all pow'r, all puissance doth enfold;
Thy lifted hand a might of wonder showeth:

---

15 one-minded] single-minded   16 holy troops] angels   21 redoubt] fear,
stand in awe of   25 quailèd] cowered   27 stout] strong   28 one thy foe]
one of thy foes   30 engine] world   clips] clasps   32 hinge] earth's axis
37 puissance] power

Justice and Judgement do thy throne uphold;
Before thy presence Truth with Mercy goeth.° 40

Happy the people, who with hasty running
    Post to thy court when trumpets triumph blow:
On paths enlighted by thy face's sunning
    Their steps, Jehovah, unoffended go.
    Thy name both makes them glad and holds them so; 45
High thought into their hearts thy justice poureth:
    The worship of their strength from thee doth flow,
And in thy love their springing empire flow'reth.

For by Jehovah's shield stand we protected,°
    And thou gav'st Israel their sacred king, 50
What time in vision thus thy word directed
    Thy lovèd prophet: 'Aid I will you bring°
    Against that violence your state doth wring
From one among my folk by choice appointed,
    David my servant: him to act the thing 55
Have I with holy oil myself anointed.

'My hand shall bide his never-failing pillar,
    And from mine arm shall he derive his might:
Not closely undermined by cursèd willer,
    Nor overthrown by foe in open fight. 60
    For I will quail his vexers in his sight;
All that him hate by me shall be mischancèd,
    My truth my clemency on him shall light,
And in my name his head shall be advancèd:

'Advancèd so that twixt the wat'ry borders 65
    Of seas and floods this noble land define,
All shall obey, subjected to the orders,
    Which his imperious hand for laws shall sign.
    He unto me shall say: "Thou father mine,
Thou art my God, the fort of my salvation": 70

---

44 unoffended] unhindered (Rathmell)   53 wring] oppress   59 willer] one who wills

And I my first-born's room will him assign,°
More highly throned than king of greatest nation.

'While circling time, still ending and beginning,
 Shall run the race where stop nor start appears:
My bounty towards him, not ever linning,   75
 I will conserve nor write my league in years.°
 Nay, more, his sons, whom father's love endears,
Shall find like bliss for legacy bequeathèd;
 A steadfast throne, I say, till heav'nly spheres
Shall faint in course, where yet they never breathèd.°   80

'Now if his children do my laws abandon,
 And other paths than my plain judgements choose:
Break my behests, profanely walk at randon,
 And what I bid with froward heart refuse.
 I mean indeed on their revolt to use   85
Correcting rod, their sin with whips to chasten:
 Not in their fault my love's defect excuse
Nor loose the promise, once my faith did fasten.

'My league shall hold, my word persist unchangèd:
 Once sworn I have, and sworn in holiness,   90
Never shall I from David be estrangèd,
 His seed shall ever bide, his seat no less.
 The day's bright guide, the night's pale governess
Shall claim no longer lease of their enduring:°
 Whom I behold as heav'nly witnesses   95
In termless turns, my termless truth assuring.'

And yet, oh, now by thee abjected, scornèd,°
 Scorched with thy wrath is thy anointed one:
Hated his league, the crown him late adornèd,
 Pulled from his head, by thee, augments his moan.   100
 Razed are his forts, his walls to ruin gone;
Not simplest passenger but on him preyeth;

75 linning] ceasing   80 breathèd] paused   83 behests] commands randon]
random (French)   84 froward] recalcitrant   96 termless] endless
97 abjected] rejected

His neighbours laugh; of all his haters none,
But boasts his wrack and at his sorrow playeth.

Takes he his weapon? Thou the edge rebatest.   105
    Comes to the field to fight? Thou mak'st him fly.
Would march with kingly pomp? Thou him unstatest.
    Ascend his throne? It overthrown doth lie:°
    His age's spring and prime of jollity,
Winter of woe before the day defineth;°   110
    For praise, reproach, for honour, infamy,
He overloaden bears, and bearing pineth.

How long, O Lord, what still in dark displeasure
    Wilt thou thee hide? And shall thine angry thought
Still flame? Oh, think how short our age's measure;   115
    Think if we all created were for naught,
    For who is he whom birth to life hath brought,
But life to death, and death to grave subjecteth?
    From this necessity (let all be sought)
No privilege exempts, no age protecteth.°   120

Kind Lord, where is the kindness once thou swarest,
    Swarest in truth thy David's stock should find?
Show, Lord, yet show thou for thy servant carest,
    Holding those shames in unforgetting mind,
    Which we embosomed bear of many a kind;°   125
But all at thee and at thy Christ directed:°
    To endless whom be endless praise assigned,
Be this, again I say, be this effected.

Psalm 90

Domine, refugium

Thou our refuge, thou our dwelling,
    O Lord, hast been from time to time:

---

104 wrack] ruin   105 rebatest] dulls   107 unstatest] deprive of position
109 jollity] cheerfulness   110 defineth] represents the extent of or brings to an end
116 naught] nothing

Long ere mountains proudly swelling
  Above the lowly dales did climb;
    Long ere the earth, embowled by thee   5
      Bare the form it now doth bear:
    Yea, thou art God for ever, free
      From all touch of age and year.

Oh, but man by thee created,
  As he at first of earth arose,   10
When thy word his end hath dated,
  In equal state to earth he goes.°
    Thou saist, and saying mak'st it so:°
      'Be no more, oh, Adam's heir;
    From whence you came, dispatch to go,   15
      Dust again, as dust you were.'°

Grant a thousand years be sparèd
  To mortal men of life and light:
What is that to thee comparèd?
  One day, one quarter of a night.   20
    When death upon them storm-like falls,
      Like unto a dream they grow:
    Which goes and comes as fancy calls,
      Naught in substance all in show.°

As the herb that early groweth,   25
  Which leavèd green and flow'red fair
Evening change with ruin moweth,
  And lays to roast in withering air:
    So in thy wrath we fade away,
      With thy fury overthrown,   30
    When thou in sight our faults dost lay,
      Looking on our sins unknown.

Therefore in thy angry fuming,
  Our life of days his measure spends:°

---

3 ere] before   5 embowled] given spherical form   6 Bare] bore   34 his] its

All our years in death consuming,   35
   Right like a sound that sounded ends.
      Our days of life make seventy years,
         Eighty, if one stronger be:
      Whose crop is labours, dolours, fears,
         Then away in post we flee.   40

Yet who notes thy angry power
   As he should fear so fearing thee?
Make us count each vital hour.
   Make thou us wise, we wise shall be.
      Turn, Lord: shall these things thus go still?   45
         Let thy servants peace obtain:
      Us with thy joyful bounty fill,
         Endless joys in us shall reign.

Glad us now as erst we grievèd;
   Send years of good for years of ill: 50
When thy hand hath us relievèd,
   Show us and ours thy glory still.
      Both them and us not one exempt,
         With thy beauty beautify:
      Supply with aid what we attempt,   55
         Our attempts with aid supply.

Psalm 91

Qui habitat

   To him the highest keeps
      In closet of his care,
   Who in th'Almighty's shadow sleeps,
      For one affirm I dare.°
         Jehovah is my fort,   5
      My place of safe repair:

---

39 dolours] sorrows   40 in post] in haste   43 vital] living   49 erst]
once

My God in whom of my support
All hopes reposèd are.

From snare the fowler lays
   He shall thee sure untie: 10
The noisome blast that plaguing strays
   Untouched shall pass thee by.
      Soft hived with wing and plume°
      Thou in his shroud shalt lie
         And on his truth no less presume,   15
         Than most in shield affy;

Not moved with frightful night
   Nor arrow shot by day:
Though plague, I say, in darkness fight,
   And waste at noontide slay.   20
      Nay, albe thousands here,
      Ten thousands there decay:
         That ruin to approach thee near,
         Shall find no force nor way.

But thou shalt live to see,   25
   And seeing to relate,
What recompenses sharèd be
   To every godless mate.
      When once thou mak'st the Lord
      Protector of thy state;   30
         And with the highest canst accord
         To dwell within his gate:

Then ill, nay, cause of ill,
   Shall far excluded go;
Naught thee to hurt, much less to kill,   35
   Shall near thy lodging grow.
      For angels shall attend

---

9 fowler] hunter of fowl   11 noisome] offensive   13 hived] sheltered
16 affy] trust   20 waste] disease, destruction   21 albe] although
35 Naught] nothing

By him commanded so:
  And thee in all such ways defend,
As his directions show.   40

To bear thee with regard
  Their hands shall both be spread:
Thy foot shall never dash too hard,
  Against the stone misled.°
    So thou on lions go   45
So on the aspic's head:
    On lionet shalt hurtless so
And on the dragon tread.

'Lo, me', saith God, 'he loves,
  I therefore will him free: 50
My name with knowledge he approves,
  That shall his honour be.
    He asks when pains are rife,
And straight received doth see
    Help, glory, and his fill of life,   55
With endless health from me.'

Psalm 92

Bonum est confiteri

Oh, lovely thing,
  To sing and praises frame,°
To thee, O Lord, and thy high name
  With early spring
  Thy bounty to display,   5
Thy truth when night hath vanquished day,
  Yea, so to sing,
  That ten-stringed instrument
With lute, and harp, and voice consent.°

46 aspic's] snake's 47 lionet] lion cub 51 approves] confirms 53 rife]
widespread

Psalm 92 2 frame] compose 4 spring] day-spring, dawn 9 consent]
harmonize

> For, Lord, my mind 10
> Thy works with wonder fill;
> Thy doings are my comfort still.
> What wit can find,°
> How bravely thou hast wrought?
> Or deeply sound thy shallow'st thought?° 15
> The fool is blind,°
> And blindly doth not know,
> How like the grass the wicked grow.

> The wicked grow
> Like frail though flow'ry grass:° 20
> And fall'n, to wrack past help do pass.
> But thou not so,
> But high thou still dost stay:
> And, lo, thy haters fall away.
> Thy haters, lo, 25
> Decay and perish all;
> All wicked hands to ruin fall.

> Fresh oilèd I
> Will lively lift my horn,
> And match the matchless unicorn; 30
> Mine eye shall spy
> My spies in spiteful case;°
> Mine ear shall hear my foes' disgrace.
> Like cedar high
> And like date-bearing tree, 35
> For green and growth, the just shall be.°

> Where God doth dwell
> Shall be his spreading place:°
> God's courts shall his fair boughs embrace.
> Ev'n then shall swell 40
> His blossoms fat and fair,

---

21 wrack] ruin   23 stay] remain   29 horn] emblem of power and might
32 My spies] those that spy on me

When agèd rind the stock shall bear.
    And I shall tell
  How God, my rock, is just,
So just, with him is naught unjust.   45

Psalm 93

Dominus regnavit

Clothed with state and girt with might,°
    Monarch-like Jehovah reigns:
He who earth's foundation pight,
    Pight at first, and yet sustains.
    He whose stable throne disdains   5
Motion's shock, and age's flight:
    He who endless one remains,
One, the same, in changeless plight.

Rivers, yea, though rivers roar,
    Roaring though sea-billows rise;   10
Vex the deep, and break the shore,
    Stronger art thou, Lord of skies.°
    Firm and true thy promise lies
Now and still, as heretofore:
    Holy worship never dies   15
In thy house where we adore.

Psalm 94

Deus ultionum

God of revenge, revenging God, appear:
  To recompense the proud, earth's judge arise.
How long, O Lord, how long, unpunished bear
    Shall these vile men their joys, their jollities?
    How long thus talk, and talking tyrannize?   5

---

42 rind] bark   45 naught] nothing
Psalm 93 3 pight] pitched   6 Motion's] change's   8 plight] condition

Cursedly do and doing proudly boast?
    This people crush by thee affected most?
This land afflict, where thy possession lies?°

For these the widow and the stranger slay:
    These work the orphan's deadly overthrow.   10
'God shall not see', then in their thoughts they say,
    'The God of Jacob, he shall never know.'
    Oh, fools, this folly when will you forgo,
        And wisdom learn? Who first the ear did plant,
        Shall he himself not hear? Sight shall he want,   15
From whose first workmanship the eye did grow?°

Who checks the world shall he not you reprove?
    Shall knowledge lack, who all doth knowledge lend?
Nay, ev'n the thoughts of men who reigns above,
    He knows, and knows they more than vainly end.°   20
    Then blest who in thy school his age doth spend;°
        Whom thou, O Lord, dost in thy law inform.
        Thy harbour shall him shroud from ruin's storm,
While pits are digged where such men shall descend.

For sure the Lord his folk will not forsake,   25
    But ever prove to his possession true;
Judgement again the course of Justice take,
    And all right hearts shall God their guide ensue.
    See, if you doubt: against the cankered crew,
        Those mischief-masters, who for me did stand?   30
        The Lord, none else, but for whose aiding hand,
Silence by now had held my soul in mew:

But Lord, thy goodness did me then uphold,
    Ev'n when I said, 'Now, now I faint, I fall':
And quailèd in mind-combats manifold°   35
    Thy consolations did my joys recall.
    Then what society hold'st thou at all,

17 checks] reprimands   21 age] life   29 cankered] corrupt
32 in mew] in confinement

What friendship with the throne of misery?
　　Which law pretends, intends but injury,°
And justice doth unjust vexation call?   40

To council where conspirèd caitiffs flock
　　The just to slay, and faultless blood to spill?
Oh, no: My God Jehovah is my rock,
　　My rock of refuge, my defensive hill,
　　He on their heads shall well repay their ill;   45
　　　　Jehovah, lo, the God in whom we joy,
　　　　Destroy them shall, shall them at once destroy:
And what the mean? Their own malicious will.

Psalm 95

Venite, exultemus

Come, come, let us with joyful voice
　　Record and raise
　　Jehovah's praise:
Come, let us in our safety's rock rejoice.°
　　　　Into his presence let us go   5
　　　　　And there with psalms our gladness show,
　　For he is God, a God most great,
　　Above all gods a king in kingly seat.

What lowest lies in earthy mass,
　　What highest stands,   10
　　Stands in his hands:
The sea is his, and he the sea-wright was.
　　　　He made the sea, he made the shore:
　　　　　Come, let us fall, let us adore;
　　Come, let us kneel with awful grace,   15
　　Before the Lord, the Lord our maker's face.

---

41 caitiffs] base persons   48 mean] means
Psalm 95 15 awful] full of awe

He is our God, he doth us keep:
    We by him led,
    And by him fed,
His people are, we are his pasture's sheep.   20
       Today if he some speech will use,
       Do not, oh, do not you refuse
    With hardened hearts his voice to hear,
    As Masha now, or Meriba it were.°

'Where me your fathers', God doth say,°   25
    'Did ang'ring move,
    And tempting prove:
Yet oft had seen my works before that day.
       Twice twenty times my post the sun,
       His yearly race to end had run,   30
    While this fond nation bent to ill,
    Did tempt, and try, and vex and grieve me still.

'Which when I saw, thus said I, "Lo,
    These men are mad,
    And too, too bad   35
Err in their hearts; my ways they will not know."
       Thus therefore unto them I swear
       (I angry can no more forbear):
    "The rest for you I did ordain,
    I will so work you never shall obtain." '   40

Psalm 96

Cantate Domino

Sing and let the song be new,
    Unto him that never endeth:
Sing, all earth and all in you.
    Sing to God and bless his name,

29 post] messenger

Of the help, the health he sendeth, 5
    Day by day new ditties frame.

Make each country know his worth;
    Of his acts the wondered story
Paint unto each people forth.
        For Jehovah great alone 10
      All the gods, for awe and glory
        Far above doth hold his throne.°

For but idols what are they,
    Whom besides mad earth adoreth?
He the skies in frame did lay; 15
        Grace and Honour are his guides;
    Majesty his temple storeth;
        Might in guard about him bides.

Kindreds, come, Jehovah give,
    Give Jehovah all together, 20
Force and fame whereso you live.
        Give his name the glory fit:
    Take your off'rings, get you thither,
        Where he doth enshrinèd sit.

Go adore him in the place 25
    Where his pomp is most displayèd:°
Earth, oh, go with quaking pace.
        Go proclaim Jehovah king:
    Stayless world shall now be stayèd;
        Righteous doom his rule shall bring. 30

Starry roof, and earthy floor,
    Sea and all thy wideness yieldeth:
Now rejoice and leap and roar.
        Leafy infants of the wood,°
    Fields and all that on you fieldeth,° 35
        Dance, oh, dance, at such a good.

6 ditties] songs   frame] compose   29 Stayless] ever-changing

For Jehovah cometh, lo!
    Lo, to reign Jehovah cometh:
Under whom you all shall go.
        He the world shall rightly guide: 40
    Truly as a king becometh,
        For the people's weal provide.

Psalm 97

Dominus regnavit

Jehovah comes to reign!
Rejoice, O earthy main:
    You isles with waves enclosèd,
    Be all to joy disposèd.
        Clouds him round on all sides,   5
        And pitchy darkness hides.
          Justice and Judgement stand
          As props on either hand,
        Whereon his throne abides.

The fire before him goes,   10
To ashes turns his foes:
    His flashing lightnings maketh,°
    That earth beholding quaketh.
        The mountains at his sight,
        His sight that is by right   15
          The Lord of all this all,
          Do fast on melting fall,
        As wax by fire's might.

The heav'ns his justice tell,
No less they all that dwell   20
    And have on earth their being
    Are glad his glory seeing.
        Shame then, shame may you see,

---

42 weal] good
Psalm 97 2 main] mainland   5 round] surround

That idol-servers be
    And trust in idols' place.   25
But let before his face
    All angels bow their knee.°

When Zion this did hear,
How did her joys appear!
    How were to mirth invited   30
    All towns in Judah sited!°
        For thou, Lord, rulest right;
        Thou throned in glory bright
            Sitt'st high: they all by thee
            Be ruled who rulers be,°   35
        Thy might above all might.

Who love God, love him still:
And haters be of ill.
    For he their lives preserveth,
    Whom he as his reserveth.   40
    Now light and joy is sown
    To be by good men mown.
        You just with joyful voice
        Then in the Lord rejoice:
        His holiness make known.   45

Psalm 98

Cantate Domino

Oh, sing Jehovah, he hath wonders wrought,
    A song of praise that newness may commend:°
His hand, his holy arm alone have brought
    Conquest on all that durst with him contend.
    He that salvation his elect attend,   5
        Long hid, at length hath set in open view:°

28 Zion] house of the God of Israel   31 sited] located
Psalm 98 4 durst] dare

And now the unbelieving nations taught°
    His heavn'ly justice yielding each their due.

His bounty and his truth the motives were,°
    Promised of yore to Jacob and his race   10
Which every margin of this earthy sphere
    Now sees performèd in his saving grace.
    Then earth, and all possessing earthy place,
        Oh, sing, oh, shout, oh, triumph, oh, rejoice:
Make lute a part with vocal music bear,°   15
    And entertain this king with trumpets' noise.

Roar, sea, and all that trace the briny sands;
    Thou total globe and all that thee enjoy;
You streamy rivers, clap your swimming hands;
    You mountains, echo each at other's joy.   20
    See on the Lord this service you employ,°
        Who comes of earth the crown and rule to take:°
And shall with upright justice judge the lands,
    And equal laws among the dwellers make.

Psalm 99

Dominus regnavit

What if nations rage and fret?
What if earth do ruin threat?
    Lo! Our state Jehovah guideth,
    He that on the cherubs rideth.°

Great Jehovah Zion holds,   5
High above what earth enfolds:
    Thence his sacred name with terror,
    Forceth truth from tongues of error.

10 of yore] long ago
Psalm 99 1 fret] worry   5 Zion] house of the God of Israel

Throned he sits a king of might,
Mighty so, as bent to right: 10
    For how can but be maintainèd
    Right by him who right ordainèd?

Oh, then come, Jehovah sing;
Sing our God, our Lord, our king:
    At the footstool set before him   15
    (He is holy), come, adore him.

Moses erst and Aaron so
(There did high in priesthood go),°
    Samuel so unto him crying,
    Got their suits without denying.°   20

But from cloudy pillar then
God did deign to talk with men:
    He enacting, they observing,
    From his will there was no swerving.

Then our God Jehovah, thou,   25
Unto them thy ear didst bow:
    Gracious still and kindly hearted,
    Though for sin they somewhile smarted.

Oh, then come, Jehovah sing:
Sing our God, our Lord, our king.   30
    In his Zion mount before him
    (He is holy), come, adore him.

Psalm 100
Jubilate Deo

O all you lands, the treasures of your joy
    In merry shout upon the Lord bestow:°

17 erst] once   28 somewhile] at one time   31 Zion mount] location of
God's house

Your service cheerfully on him employ,
   With triumph song into his presence go.
   Know first that he is God; and after know   5
This God did us, not we ourselves create:
   We are his flock, for us his feedings grow;
We are his folk, and he upholds our state.
With thankfulness, oh, enter then his gate:
       Make through each porch of his your praises ring.   10
All good, all grace, of his high name relate,
       He of all grace and goodness is the spring.
Time in no terms his mercy comprehends;
From age to age his truth itself extends.

Psalm 101

Misericordiam et judicium

When, now appointed king, I king shall be,
       What mercy then, what justice use I will,
I here, O Lord, in song protest to thee.

Till that day come thou me the crown shalt give,
       Deep study I on virtue will bestow: 5
And pure in heart at home retirèd live.°

My lowly eye shall level at no ill:
       Who fall from thee with me not one shall stand;
Their ways I shall pursue with hatred still.

Mischievous heads far off from me shall go;   10
       Malicious hearts I never will admit;°
And whisp'ring biters all will overthrow.

---

7 feedings] food, pastures   13 terms] limits   comprehends] contains
Psalm 101 7 lowly] humble   level at] aim   12 whisp'ring biters] slandering
deceivers

Ill shall I brook the proud ambitious band,
    Whose eyes look high, whose puffèd hearts do swell,
But for truth-tellers seek and search the land.   15

Such men with me my counsellors shall sit;
    Such evermore my officers shall be:
Men speaking right and doing what is fit.

No fraudulent within my house shall dwell:
    The cunning, coining tongue shall in my sight   20
Be not endured, much less accepted well.°

As soon as I in all the land shall see
    A wicked wretch, I shall him hate outright;
And of vile men Jehovah's city free.

Psalm 102

Domine, exaudi

    O Lord, my praying hear:
        Lord, let my cry come to thine ear.
    Hide not thy face away,
        But haste, and answer me,
    In this my most, most miserable day,   5
        Wherein I pray, and cry to thee.

    My days as smoke are past:
        My bones as flaming fuel waste,
    Mown down in me (alas)
        With scythe of sharpest pain.   10
    My heart is withered like the wounded grass;°
        My stomach doth all food disdain.

    So lean my woes me leave,
        That to my flesh my bones do cleave:

13 brook] tolerate   19 fraudulent] fraudulent person   20 coining] counter-
feiting, lying   24 Jehovah's city] Jerusalem

And so I bray and howl,°   15
  As use to howl and bray
The lonely pelican and desert owl,°
  Like whom I languish long the day.

    I languish so the day,
      The night in watch I waste away;   20
    Right as the sparrow sits,
      Bereft of spouse, or son,°
    Which irked alone with dolour's deadly fits
      To company will not be won.

      As day to day succeeds,   25
        So shame on shame to me proceeds
      From them that do me hate,
        Who of my wrack so boast,
      That wishing ill, they wish but my estate,
        Yet think they wish of ills the most.° 30

        Therefore my bread is clay,
          Therefore my tears my wine allay:
        For how else should it be,
          Sith thou still angry art,°
        And seem'st for naught to have advancèd me,   35
          But me advancèd to subvert?

          The sun of my life-days
            Inclines to west with falling rays,
          And I as hay am dried,
            While yet in steadfast seat   40
          Eternal thou eternally dost bide,
            Thy memory no years can fret.

            Oh, then at length arise:
              On Zion cast thy mercy's eyes.

15 bray] cry of horses, oxen, deer   18 long the day] all day long
23 dolour's] sorrow's   28 wrack] misfortune   32 allay] dilute   34 Sith] since
35 naught] nothing   37 life-days] life   42 fret] diminish   44 Zion] house of
the God of Israel

Now is the time that thou   45
   To mercy shouldst incline
Concerning her: O Lord, the time is now
   Thyself for mercy didst assign.

   Thy servants wait the day
    When she, who like a carcass lay°   50
Stretched forth in ruin's bier,
   Shall so arise and live,
That nations all Jehovah's name shall fear,
   All kings to thee shall glory give.

   Because thou hast anew   55
    Made Zion stand, restored to view
Thy glorious presence there,
   Because thou hast, I say,
Beheld our woes and not refused to hear
   What wretched we did plaining pray,   60

   This of record shall bide°
    To this and every age beside:
And they commend thee shall
   Whom thou anew shalt make,
That from the prospect of thy heav'nly hall   65
   Thy eye of earth survey did take,

   Heark'ning to prisoners' groans,
    And setting free condemnèd ones:
That they, when nations come,°
   And realms to serve the Lord,
In Zion and in Salem might become   70
   Fit means his honour to record.

   But what is this if I
    In the mid way should fall and die?
My God, to thee I pray,   75

---

49 wait] await   51 bier] tomb   60 plaining] complaining   62 beside]
besides   74 mid way] middle age

Who canst my prayer give:
Turn not to night the noontide of my day,
    Since endless thou dost ageless live.

    The earth, the heaven stands°
      Once founded, formèd by thy hands: 80
They perish, thou shalt bide;
    They old, as clothes, shall wear,
Till changing still, full change shall them betide,°
    Unclothed of all the clothes they bear.

    But thou art one, still one: 85
      Time interest in thee hath none.
Then hope, who godly be,
    Or come of godly race:
Endless your bliss, as never ending he,
    His presence your unchangèd place.   90

Psalm 103

Benedic, anima

    My soul, my heart,°
    And every inward part,
Praise high Jehovah, praise his holy name;
    My heart, my soul,°
      Jehovah's name extol: 5
      What gracious he
      Doth, and hath done for thee,
Be quick to mind, to utter be not lame.

    For his free grace°
    Doth all thy sins deface   10
He cures thy sickness, healeth all thy harm.
    From greedy grave
    That gapes thy life to have,

---

83 betide] befall   85 one] unique, pre-eminent   86 interest] legal right
Psalm 103 8 lame] halting, ineffectual   10 deface] blot out

He sets thee free:
>> And kindly makes on thee   15
All his compassions, all his mercies swarm.

> He doth thee still
>> With flowing plenty fill:
He eagle-like doth oft thy age renew.°
>>> The Lord his right   20
>>> Unto the wrongèd wight
>>> Doth ever yield:
>>> And never cease to shield
With justice them, whom guile and fraud pursue.

> His way and trade   25
>> He known to Moses made,
His wonders to the sons of Israel
>>> The Lord, I mean
>>> Jehovah, who doth lean
>>> With mildest will   30
>>> To ruth and mercy still,
As slow to wrath, as swift to doing well.

> When he doth chide
>> He doth not chiding bide:
His anger is not in his treasures laid.   35
>>> He doth not serve
>>> Our sins, as sins deserve:
>>> Nor recompense
>>> Unto us each offence,
With due revenge in equal balance weighed.   40

> For look how far
>> The sphere of farthest star
Drowns that proportion earthly centre bears:°
>>> So much, and more
>>> His never empty store°   45

---

21 wight] person   25 trade] path   31 ruth] compassion   34 bide] continue

Of grace and love
Beyond his sins doth prove,°
Who ever him with due devotion fears.

Nay, look how far
From east removèd are   50
The western lodgings of the weary sun:
So far, more far,
From us removèd are,
By that great love
Our faults from him do prove,   55
Whatever faults and follies we have done.

And look how much
The nearly touching touch
The father feels towards his son most dear,
Affects his heart,   60
At every froward part
Played by his child:
So merciful, so mild,
Is he to them that bear him awful fear.

Our potter he°   65
Knows how his vessels we
In earthy matter lodged this fickle form:
Fickle as glass,
As flow'rs, that fading pass,
And vanish so,   70
No not their place we know,
Blasted to death with breath of blust'ring storm.

Such is our state;
But far in other rate,°
God's endless justice and his mercy stand,   75
Both on the good,

---

61 froward] recalcitrant   64 awful] full of awe   67 fickle] fragile

And their religious brood;
Who uncontrolled
Sure league with him do hold,
And do his laws, not only understand.° 80

Jehovah great
Sits throned in starry seat:
His kingdom doth all kingdoms comprehend.
You angels strong,
That unto him belong, 85
Whose deeds accord
With his commanding word,
Praises and thanks upon Jehovah spend.

Spirits of might,
You that his battles fight,
You ministers that willing work his will; 90
All things that he
Hath wrought, whereso they be,
His praise extol:
Thou with the rest, my soul, 95
Praises and thanks spend on Jehovah still.

Psalm 104

Benedic, anima mea

Make, O my soul, the subject of thy song
Th'eternal Lord: O Lord, O God of might,
To thee, to thee, all royal pomps belong;
Clothèd art thou in state and glory bright.°
For what is else this eye-delighting light 5
But unto thee a garment wide and long?
The vaulted heaven but a curtain right,
A canopy, thou over thee hast hung?

77 brood] children   78 uncontrolled] unlimited, numberless
83 comprehend] include
Psalm 104 3 pomps] magnificent celebrations   4 state] splendour

The rafters that his parlour's roof sustain,
    In chevron he on crystal waters binds:°   10
He on the winds, he on the clouds doth reign,
    Riding on clouds, and walking on the winds,
    Whose wingèd blasts, his word as ready finds
To post from him, as angels of his train,°
    As to effect the purposes he minds   15
He makes no less the flamy fire fain.

By him the earth a steadfast base doth bear,°
    And steadfast so, as time nor force can shake,
Which once round waters garment-like did wear,
    And hills in seas did lowly lodging take.   20
    But seas from hills a swift descent did make,
When swelling high by thee they chidden were:
    Thy thunder's roar did cause their conduits quake,
Hast'ning their haste with spur of hasty fear.

So waters fled, so mountains high did rise,   25
    So humble valleys deeply did descend,°
All to the place thou didst for them devise,
    Where bounding seas with unremovèd end,°
    Thou badst they should themselves no more extend,
To hide the earth which now unhidden lies: 30
    Yet from the mountains' rocky sides didst send
Springs' whisp'ring murmurs, rivers' roaring cries.

Of these the beasts which on the plains do feed
    All drink their fill; with these their thirst allay
The asses wild and all that wildly breed;   35
    By these in their self-chosen mansions stay°
    The free-born fowls, which through the empty way
Of yielding air wafted with wingèd speed,
    To art-like notes of nature-tunèd lay
Make earless bushes give attentive heed.°   40

14 post] hasten   16 fain] eager   19 once] i.e. at creation   22 chidden]
rebuked   23 conduits] rivers   29 badst] commanded   34 allay] satisfy
36 mansions] i.e. nests

Thou, thou of heav'n the windows dost unclose,°
  Dewing the mountains with thy bounty's rain:
Earth great with young her longing doth not lose;°
  The hopeful ploughman, hopeth not in vain.
  The vulgar grass, whereof the beast is fain,°   45
The rarer, herbman for himself hath chose:
  All things in brief, that life in life maintain,
From earth's old bowels fresh and youngly grows:°

Thence wine, the counter-poison unto care;°
  Thence oil, whose juice unplaits the folded brow;°   50
Thence bread, our best, I say not daintiest fare,
  Prop yet of hearts, which else would weakly bow;
  Thence, Lord, thy leavèd people bud and blow,°
Whose princes thou, thy cedars, dost not spare°
  A fuller draught of thy cup to allow,   55
That highly raised above the rest they are.

Yet highly raised they do not proudly scorn
  To give small birds an humble entertain,°
Whose brickle nests are on their branches borne,°
  While in the firs the storks a lodging gain.   60
  So highest hills rock-loving goats sustain
And have their heads with climbing traces worn,°
  That safe in rocks the coneys may remain,°
To yield them caves, their rocky ribs are torn.

Thou mak'st the moon, the empress of the night,   65
  Hold constant course with most inconstant face:
Thou mak'st the sun, the chariot-man of light,°
  Well know the start and stop of daily race.
  When he doth set and night his beams deface,°
To roam abroad wood-burgesses delight,   70
  Lions, I mean, who roaring all that space,
Seem then of thee to crave their food by right.

---

41 unclose] open   45 vulgar] ordinary   fain] fond   48 bowels] interior
of body   49 counter-poison] antidote   50 unplaits] unwrinkles   53 leavèd
people] trees   blow] bloom   58 entertain] entertainment   59 brickle]
brittle   63 coneys] rabbits

When he returns they all from field retire,
  And lay them down in cave, their home, to rest:
They rest, man stirs to win a workman's hire,   75
  And works till sun have wrought his way to west.
  Eternal Lord, who greatest art and best,
How I amazed thy mighty works admire!
  Wisdom in them hath every part possessed,
Whereto in me, no wisdom can aspire.°   80

Behold the earth: how there thy bounties flow!
  Look on the sea extended hugely wide:°
What wat'ry troops swim, creep, and crawl and go,°
  Of great and small, on that, this, every side!
  There the sail-wingèd ships on waves do glide; 85
Sea-monsters there their plays and pastimes show:°
  And all at once in seasonable tide
Their hungry eyes on thee their feeder throw.

Thou giv'st, they take; thy hand itself displays,
  They fillèd feel the plenties of thy hand: 90
All darkened lie deprivèd of thy rays,
  Thou tak'st their breath, not one can longer stand.°
  They die, they turn to former dust and sand,
Till thy life-giving sprite do must'ring raise
  New companies, to reinforce each band,   95
Which still supplièd, never whole decays.°

So may it, oh, so may it ever go,
  Jehovah's works his glorious gladness be,
Who touching mountains, mountains smoking grow,
  Who eyeing earth, earth quakes with quivering knee.° 100
  As for myself, my silly self, in me
While life shall last, his worth in song to show
  I framèd have a resolute decree,
And thankful be, till being I forgo.°

Oh, that my song might good acceptance find: 105
    How should my heart in great Jehovah joy!
Oh, that some plague this irreligious kind,
    Ingrate to God, would from the earth destroy!
    Meanwhile, my soul, incessantly employ
To high Jehovah's praise my mouth and mind: 110
    Nay, all (since all his benefits enjoy)
Praise him whom bands of time nor age can bind.°

Psalm 105

Confitemini Domino

Jehovah's praise, Jehovah's holy fame
    Oh, show, oh, sound, his acts to all relate:
To him your songs, your psalms unto him frame;
    Make your discourse, his wonders celebrate.
Boast, ye God-searchers, in his sacred name,   5
    And your contracted hearts with joy dilate:
      To him, his ark, his face, let be intended
      Your due inquest, with service never ended.

Record, I say, in special memory
    The miracles he wrought, the laws he gave,   10
His servants you O Abraham's progeny,
    You Jacob's sons, whom he doth chosen save.
We first and most on him, our God, rely:
    Albe no bounds his jurisdiction have;°
      And he eternally that treaty mindeth,   15
      Which him to us untermèd ages bindeth:

A treaty first with Abraham begun,
    After again by oath to Isaac bound,
Lastly to Isaac's God-beholding son
    Confirmed, and made inviolably sound.   20
I give in fee (for so the grant did run)°

3 frame] compose   8 inquest] quest   14 Albe] although   16 untermèd]
unlimited

Thee and thine heirs the Canaanean ground:
    And that when few they were, few, unregarded,
    Yea, strangers too, where he their lot awarded.

They strangers were and roamed from land to land,   25
    From realm to realm, though seatless, yet secure;
And so remote from wrong of meaner hand
    That kings for them did sharp rebuke endure:
'Touch not, I charge you, my anointed band,
    Nor to my prophets least offence procure.'°   30
    Then he for Famine spake: scarce had he spoken,
    When Famine came, the staff of bread was broken.°

But he for them to Egypt had foresent
    The slave-sold Joseph kindly to prepare:
Whose feet if fretting irons did indent,   35
    His soul was clogged with steely bolts of care,
Till fame abroad of his divining went,
    And heav'nly saws such wisdom did declare;
    That him a message from the king addressèd
    Of bondage rid, of freedom repossessèd.°   40

No sooner freed, the monarch in his hands
    Without control both house and state doth lay;
He rulers rules, commanders he commands;
    Wills and all do: prescribes and all obey.
While thus in terms of highest grace he stands,   45
    Lo, Israel to Egypt takes his way,
    And Jacob's line from Holy Sem descended,
    To sojourn comes where Ham his tents extended.°

Who now but they in strength and number flow?
    Raised by their God their haters far above?   50
For, changed by him, their entertainers grow
    With guile to hate, who erst with truth did love.

26 seatless] homeless   35 fretting] gnawing, chaffing   36 clogged] fettered
38 saws] commands, sayings   51 entertainers] hosts   52 erst] formerly

But he with sacred Moses wills to go°
    Aaron his choice, those mischiefs to remove:
        By whose great works their sender's glory blazèd   55
        Made Ham's whole land with frightful signs amazèd.

Darkness from day the wonted sun doth chase
    (For both he bids and neither dares rebel);
Late wat'ry Nilus looks with bloody face:°
    How fishes die, what should I stand to tell?°   60
Or how of noisome frogs the earth-bred race
    Croak where their princes sleep, not only dwell?°
        How lice and vermin heav'nly voice attending
        Do swarming fall, what quarter not offending?

No rainy cloud but breaks in stony hail;   65
    For cheerful lights dismayful lightnings shine,
Not shine alone, their fi'ry strokes assail
    Each taller plant; worst fares the fig and vine
Nor, called, to come do caterpillars fail
    With locusts more than counting can define: 70
        By these the grass, the grace of fields is wasted,
        The fruits consumed by owners yet untasted.

Their eldest-born, that country's hopeful spring,
    Prime of their youth, his plague doth lastly wound;
Then rich with spoil, he out his folk doth bring;   75
    In all their tribes not one a weakling found.
Egypt once wished, now fears, their tarrying,
    And gladly sees them on their journey bound:
        Whom God in heat a shading cloud provideth
        In dark with lamp of flamy pillar guideth.   80

Brought from his store at suit of Israel
    Quails in whole bevies each remove pursue;
Himself from skies, their hunger to repel,
    Candies the grass with sweet congealèd dew.

57 wonted] habitual   61 noisome] offensive   82 bevies] flocks
84 Candies] encrusts

He wounds the rock, the rock doth, wounded, well: 85
  Welling affords new streams to channels new.
   All for God's mindful will cannot be driven,
   From sacred word once to his Abraham given.

So then in joyful plight, his lovèd bands,
  His chosen troops with triumph on he trains: 90
Till full possession of the neighbour lands,
  With painless harvest of their thankless pains,
He safely leaves in their victorious hands,
  Where naught for them to do henceforth remains,
   But only to observe and see fulfillèd,   95
   What he (to whom be praise) hath said and willèd.

Psalm 106

Confitemini Domino

Where are the hymns, where are the honours due
  To our good God, whose goodness knows no end?
Who of his force can utter what is true?
  Who all his praise, in praises comprehend?
   Oh, blessed they whose well-advisèd sight   5
Of all their life the level straight do bend,
  With endless aiming at the mark of right.°

Lord, for the love thou dost thy people bear,
  Grant thought of me may harbour in thy mind:
Make me with them thy safety's liv'ry wear,   10
  That I may once take notice in what kind
   Thy kindness is on thine elected shown;°
That I may gladness in their gladness find,
  Boasting with them, who boast to be thine own.

Indeed we have as our forefathers done   15
  Done ill, done wrong, unjustly, wickedly:

---

90 trains] leads 94 naught] nothing
Psalm 106 10 liv'ry] livery, court uniform

For (that I may begin where they begun)
    Thy works in Egypt, naught they passèd by.
      Quite out of thought thy many bounties fell,
    And at the sea they did thy patience try: 20
      At the Red Sea, they did, I say, rebel.

Yet God (oh, goodness) savèd for his name°
    These mutineers that this his might might show,
For he the waters did rebuking blame,
    The waters left at his rebuke to flow   25
      On sandy deep as on the desert sands,
    Unwet in waves he made his people go:
      Setting them safe from all their haters' hands.

For look how fast their foes did them pursue,
    So fast, more fast the sea pursued their foes: 30
All drent, all dead, not one left of the crew.
    Then, lo, belief, then thankfulness arose
      In faithless, graceless hearts: but in a trice
    Oblivion all remembrance overgrows
      Of his great works, or care of his advice.   35

For gluttonous they flesh in desert crave,
    That they forsooth might try th'Almighty's might:
As gluttons fits, they flesh in desert have,
    For fully fed, yet fared in pining plight.°
      What should I utter how from Moses they   40
    And holy Aaron sacred in God's sight,
      Through envy sought to take the rule away?

The very earth such mischief grieved to bear
    And opening made her gaping throat the grave,
Where Dathan and Abiram buried were,°   45
    Buried alive with tents and all they have,
      Whose complices the flash of angry fire
    Surprisèd so, none could from burning save,
      In ashes raked they found their treason's hire.

18 naught] nothing   31 drent] drowned   33 trice] instant
37 forsooth] truly   47 complices] accomplices

A molten god they did in Horeb frame,   50
    And what? Forsooth, the suckling of a cow;
Their heav'nly glory changed to beastly shame,
    They more than beasts, before a beast did bow.
        A calf, nay, image of a calf they served,
        Whose highest worship, hay they should allow.°   55
        God was forgot, who had them so preserved;

Preserved them so by miracles of might,
    Done in the plains where fertile Nilus flows;
And wondered works, which fearfully did fright,
    The ochre banks their passage did enclose.°   60
        Therefore their wrack he meant; which while he meant
        Moses his chosen in the gap arose,
        And turned his wrath from wrackful punishment.

What more? The land that well deserved desire
    With fond disdain mistrustful they reject: 65
Their tents do flame with hot rebellious fire,
    Jehovah's words received with no respect.
        For which he in the desert overthrew
        Themselves, their sons, with fathers' fault infect,
        Scattered, exiled, no certain country knew.   70

For they to Peór, filthy idol, went,°
    And what had been to dead things sacrificed,
Forbidden food, abominably spent.
        So God with anger mightily surprised
        His hurtful hand against their health did raise: 75
        But Phinehas, justice done, their lives reprised,°
        And for that justice purchased endless praise.

Could this suffice? Nay, farther at the brook,
    The brook of brawl, they did the Lord incense:
Which then his name of their contention took,°   80
    Where Moses self did smart for their offence

---

50 frame] make   61 wrack] ruin   65 fond] foolish
69 infect] infected with   76 reprised] reprieved   79 brawl] strife

For inly angered that he rashly spake,
   Forgetting due respect and reverence,
      Which for his rashness God did angry make.

After, their sons came to that lovely land,   85
   No better minded, albe better blest,
Would not root out, as stood with his command
      The pagan plants, who then the place possessed.
        But grew together up, and did as they,
      In idol service forward as the best: 90
        In idol service root of their decay.

For they both sons and daughters offerèd
   Unto their gods. Gods? No, they devils were:
Whose guiltless blood, which wastefully they shed,
      Imbrued the idols Canaan did bear.   95
        The land defilèd was with murders done,
      Whiles they in works no filthiness forbear,
        And in conceits a-whoring mainly run.

So God incensèd grew against his own,
   And plainly did his heritage detest: 100
Left them to be by strangers overthrown,
      Lorded by foes, by enemies oppressed.
        Often he freed them by his force divine:
      But when their wits would give his wrath no rest,
        Left them at length in worthy plagues to pine.°   105

He left them long yet left them not at last
   But saw their woes, and heard their wailful cries
Which made him call to thought his cov'nant past.
      So changed, not only in himself did rise
        Repentant pity of their passèd pains: 110
      But their captivers' now relenting eyes
        His ruth of them to tender yielding trains.°

---

82 inly] inwardly   86 albe] although   87 stood] was consistent
88 plants] inhabitants   95 Imbrued] stained with blood   100 heritage] God's
chosen people   112 ruth] pity   trains] leads

Go on, O God, as them, so us to save,
    Rally thy troops that widely scattered be,
That their due thanks, thy holiness may have;   115
    Their glorious praise, thy heav'nly pow'r may see.
    O God of Israel, our God, our Lord,
    Eternal thanks be to eternal thee:
        Let all the earth with praise approve my word.

Psalm 107

Confitemini Domino

Oh, celebrate Jehovah's praise,
    For gracious he and good is found;
And no precinct, no space of days
    Can his great grace and goodness bound.
    Say you with me, with me resound   5
        Jehovah's praise with thankfulness,
    Whose bands of peril he unbound,
        When tyrant's hate did you oppress.

How many, and how many times,°
    From early east, from evening west,   10
From thirsty coasts, from frosty climes,
    Hath he dispersèd brought to rest!
    How many saved, who deep distressed
        And straying far from path and town,
    With want and drought so sore were pressed   15
        That drought well near their lives did drown!°

They cried to him in woeful plight;
    His succour sent did end their woe.
From error trained he led them right,°
    And made to peopled places go.   20
    Such then in song his mercies show,
        His wonders done to men display,

---

1 praise] praiseworthiness   3 precinct] boundary   12 dispersèd] those who have been dispersed   15 pressed] oppressed   16 well near] nearly

Who in the hungry hunger so,
    So doth in thirsty thirst allay.

How many fast imprisoned lie   25
    In shade of death and horror blind,
Whose feet as iron fetters tie,
      So heavy anguish clogs their mind,
      Whom though the Lord did rebels find,
        Despising all he did advise;   30
      Yet when their heart with grief declined
        Now helpless quite and hopeless lies!

They cry to him in woeful plight;°
    His succour sent doth end their woe.
From death to life, from dark to light   35
      With broken bolts he makes them go.°
      Such then in song his mercy show,
        His wonders done to men display;
      The gates of brass who breaketh so,
        So makes the iron yield them way.   40

How many wantonly misled,
    While fools, they follow Folly's train,
For sin confinèd to their bed,
      This guerdon of their folly gain!
      Their loathing soul doth food refrain,   45
        And hardly, hardly failing breath
      Can now his ending gasp restrain
        From ent'ring at the gate of death.

They cry to him in woeful plight;
    His succour sent doth end their woe.   50
His word puts all their pain to flight
      And free from sickness makes them go.
      Such then in song his mercy show,

24 allay] satisfy   41 wantonly] recklessly   44 guerdon] reward
45 refrain] give up

His wonders done to men display;
   Tell gladly of his works they know   55
And sacrifice of praises pay.

How many mounting wingèd tree°
   For traffic leave retiring land
And on huge waters busied be,
     Which bankless flow on endless sand!   60
   These, these indeed, well understand,
     Informed by their fear-open eye,
   The wonders of Jehovah's hand
     While on the waves they rocking lie.

He bids and straight on moisty main   65
   The blust'ring tempest falling flies:
The stars do drop bedashed with rain,
     So huge the waves in combat rise.°
   Now ship with men do touch the skies:
     Now down, more down than centre falls;   70
   Their might doth melt, their courage dies,
     Such hideous fright each sense appals.

For now the whirlwind makes them wheel:
   Now stopped in midst of broken round,
As drunkards use, they stagg'ring reel,   75
     Whose head-lame feet can feel no ground.°
   What helps to have a pilot sound,
     Where wisdom wont to guide the stern,
   Now in despairful danger drowned,
     With wisdom's eye can naught discern?°   80

They cry to him in woeful plight;
   His succour sent doth end their woe.
Of seas and winds he parts the fight;

---

57 wingèd tree] sailing ship   58 traffic] transportation   60 bankless] without restraint   67 bedashed] splashed   70 centre] earth's centre   72 appals] dismays   78 wont] was accustomed to   80 naught] nothing

To wishèd port with joy they row.
Such then in song his mercies show, 85
   His wonders done to men display:
Make people's press his honour know,
   At princes' thrones his praise bewray.

How many wheres doth he convert
   Well-watered grounds to thirsty sand, 90
And salts the soil for wicked heart°
   The dwellers bear that till the land!
How oft again his gracious hand
   To wat'ry pools doth deserts change
And on the fields that fruitless stand 95
   Makes trickling springs unhopèd range!

Suppose of men that live in want
   A colony he there do make:
They dwell, and build, and sow, and plant,
   And of their pains great profit take. 100
His blessing doth not them forsake,
   But multiplies their children's store:
Nay, ev'n their cattle, for their sake,
   Augments in number more and more.

They stand while he their state sustains: 105
   Then comes again that harmful day
Which brings the interchange of pains
   And their increase turns to decay.
Nor strange: for he exilèd stray°
   Makes greatest kings, scorned where they go: 110
The same from want the poor doth weigh,
   And makes like herds their houses grow.

See this, and joy this thus to see,
   All you whose judgements judge aright;
You whose conceits distorted be, 115

87 press] crowd   88 bewray] reveal   89 wheres] places
111 weigh] lift, raise   114 aright] justly   115 conceits] thoughts

Stand mute, amazèd at the sight.
How wise were he, whose wisdom might
  Observe each course the Lord doth hold,
To light in men his bounty's light,
  Whose providence doth all enfold!   120

Psalm 108

Paratum cor meum

To sing and play my heart is bent,
  Is bent God's name to solemnize.
Thy service, O my tongue, present:
  Arise, my lute; my harp, arise.°
  Myself will up with dawning skies,   5
    And so in song report thy praise.
    No ear but shall conceive my lays
  As far as earth extended lies.

For, Lord, the heav'ns however high,
  Are lower far than thy sweet grace: 10
Thy truth on steadfast wings doth fly,
  Aspiring up to cloudy space.
  Oh, then thyself in highest place
    Above the heav'ns, Jehovah, show:
    And thence on all this earth below
  Display the sunbeams of thy face

To set thy dearly lovèd free,
  To help and hear me when I pray.
'Hark, hark, so shall, so shall it be,'
  Himself doth from his temple say.   20
  Then make we here a merry stay,
    And let me part out Sichem's fields:
    The land that Succoth's valley yields,
  By perch and pole divided lay.

7 lays] songs   21 stay] residence   24 perch . . . pole] units of measure

Mine Gilead is, Manasses mine;° 25
   Ephraim's arms shall guard the king;
My law shall Judah right define,
   While I my shoe at Edom fling.
   Thee, Moab, I will humbled bring
     To wash my feet in servile place: 30
     Thou, Palestine, my late disgrace,
   Triumphèd, shalt my triumph sing.°

But who shall cause us Edom take,
   And enter Edom's strongest town;
Who, but thou, God, used to forsake 35
   Our troops, and at our suits to frown?
   Then help us ere distressed we drown:
     Who trusts in man doth vainly trust.
     In only God prevail we must,
   He, he shall tread our haters down. 40

Psalm 109

Deus laudem

Since thus the wicked, thus the fraudulent,
   Since liars thus enforce my blame,
     O God, God of my praise,
Be not in silence pent:
     For their malicious words against me raise 5
   Engines of hate, and causeless batt'ry frame.°

Causeless? Aye me! Quite contrary to cause,
   My love they do with hate repay:
     With treason's lawless spite
They answer friendship's laws 10
     And good with ill, and help with harm requite:
   What resteth now, but that to thee I pray?

4 pent] confined   6 Engines] plots   batt'ry] battery, bombardment
frame] contrive

I pray then what? That lorded at command°
    Of some vile wretch I may him see:
        That fitly still his foe   15
To thwart his good may stand;
        That judged from judgement, he condemned may go,
        Yea, to his plague, his prayer turnèd be.

That speedy death cut off his woeful life,
    Another take his place and port: 20
        His children fatherless,
And husbandless his wife,
        May wand'ring beg, and beg in such distress
        Their beggared homes may be their best resort.

That usurers may all he hath ensnare,°   25
    And strangers reap what he hath sown:
        That none him friend at all,
None with compassion's care
        Embrace his brood, but they to wrack may fall,
        And fall'n may lie in following age unknown.   30

That not his own alone but every crime
    Of father's, and forefather's hand,
        May in God's sight abide:
Yea, to eternal time
        Sin of his mother and his mother's side   35
        May in his mind, who is eternal, stand.

That he and they so far may be forgot,
    That neither print of being leave
        What human nature will:
For he remembered not,°   40
        But sought a wretch inhumanly to spill
        And would of life an humbled heart bereave.

He lovèd mischief; mischief with him go:
    He did no good; then do him none.

29 wrack] ruin   41 spill] slay

Be wretchedness his cloak, 45
Into him soaking so
    As water drunken inwardly doth soak
    As oil through flesh doth search the hidden bone.

Be woe, I say, his garment large and wide,
    Fast girt with girdle of the same. 50
      So be it, be it aye,
Such misery betide
    Unto all such as thirsting my decay,
    Against my soul such deadly falsehood frame.

But thou, O Lord, my Lord, so deal with me 55
    As doth thy endless honour fit:
      And for thy glory's sake
Let me deliverance see,
    For want and woe my life their object make
    And in my breast my heart doth wounded sit. 60

I fade and fail as shade with falling sun:
    And as the grasshopper is tossed,
      Place after place I leese,
While fast hath nigh undone
    The withered knots of my disjointed knees, 65
    And drièd flesh all juice and moisture lost.

Worse yet, alas! I am their scorn, their nod,
    When in their presence I me show.
      But thou, thou me uphold,
My Lord, my gracious God: 70
    Oh, save me in thy mercies manifold,
    Thy hand, thy work, make all men on me know.

They curse me still, but bless thou where they curse:
    They rise, but shame shall bring them down.
      And this my joy shall be, 75

50 Fast girt with girdle] encircled tightly with a belt   51 aye] always
52 betide] happen   63 leese] lose   64 fast] fasting

As bad disgrace or worse
  Shall them attire than ever clothèd me,
 Trailing in train a sinful shameful gown.°

Then, then will I Jehovah's works relate
  Where multitudes their meeting have: 80
   Because still nigh at hand
To men in hard estate
  He in their most extremities doth stand,
 And guiltless lives from false condemners save.

Psalm 110

Dixit Dominus

Thus to my Lord, the Lord did say:°
  'Take up thy seat at my right hand,
  Till all thy foes that proudly stand,
I prostrate at thy footstool lay.
   From me thy staff of might   5
    Sent out of Zion goes:
   As victor then prevail in fight,
    And rule repining foes.

'But as for them that willing yield,
  In solemn robes they glad shall go,   10
  Attending thee when thou shalt show
Triumphantly thy troops in field:
   In field as thickly set
    With warlike youthful train
   As pearlèd plain with drops is wet,   15
    Of sweet Aurora's rain.'°

The Lord did swear, and never he
  What once he sware will disavow:
  'As was Melchizedek so thou°
An everlasting priest shalt be.   20

6 Zion] house of the God of Israel

At hand still ready prest
    To guard thee from annoy,
Shall sit the Lord that loves thee best,
    And kings in wrath destroy.

'Thy realm shall many realms contain;   25
    Thy slaughtered foes thick heapèd lie:
    With crushèd head ev'n he shall die,
Who head of many realms doth reign.
    If passing on these ways
        Thou taste of troubled streams: 30
    Shall that eclipse thy shining rays?
    Nay, light thy glory's beams.'

Psalm 111

Confitebor tibi

At home, abroad, most willingly I will
Bestow on God my praise's utmost skill:
Chanting his works, works of unmatchèd might,
Deemed so by them, who in their search delight.°
Endless the honour to his pow'r pertains,°   5
From end as far his justice eke remains.°
Gracious and good and working wonders so
His wonders never can forgotten go.
In hungry waste he fed his faithful crew,
Keeping his league and still in promise true.   10
Lastly his strength he caused them understand,°
Making them lords of all the heathen's land.
Now what could more each promise, doom, decree,
Of him confirm sure, just, unmoved to be!°
Preserved his folk, his league eternal framed,   15
Quake then with fear when holy he is named.

21 ready prest] prepared   22 annoy] harm
Psalm 111 6 eke] also   7 so] so that   9 waste] desert
10 league] covenant   13 doom] judgement   15 framed] made

Reverence of him is perfect wisdom's well:
Stand in his law, so understand you well.
The praise of him (though wicked hearts repine)
Unbounded bides, no time can it define.   20

Psalm 112

Beatus vir

Oh, in how blessed state he standeth,
    Who so Jehovah feareth,
That in the things the Lord commandeth
    His most delight appeareth!

The branches from that body springing°   5
    On the earth shall freshly flourish:
Their pedigree from good men bringing
    The Lord with bliss will nourish.

The happy house wherein he dwelleth
    Well storèd shall persever: 10
The treasures justly got he telleth,
    Shall bide his own for ever.

For he when woe them over-cloudeth°
    The darkened hearts enlighteth:
His mildness them and mercy shroudeth,   15
    His justice for them fighteth.

He is both good and goodness loveth,°
    Most liberal and lending:
All businesses wherein he moveth
    With sound advice attending.   20

He firmly propped for ever falling,
    His name exempt from dying:

---

17 well] source   18 so] thus   19 repine] complain   20 bides] abides
Psalm 112 11 telleth] tallies   12 bide] abide   19 businesses] activities

Can hear ill news without appalling,
    His heart on God relying.

His heart (I say) which strongly stayèd, 25
    Is free from fear preservèd:
Till on his foes he view displayèd
    The plagues by them deservèd.

He gives where needs, nay, rather straweth,
    His justice never ending: 30
So honour's hand him higher draweth
    With glad applause ascending.°

Of good I mean: for wicked wretches
    Shall seeing fume, and fuming
Consume to naught, their fruitless fetches 35
    To naught with them consuming.

Psalm 113
Laudate, pueri

O you that serve the Lord,
To praise his name accord:
Jehovah now and ever
Commending, ending never,
Whom all this earth resounds, 5
From east to western bounds.

He monarch reigns on high;
His glory treads the sky.
Like him who can be counted,
That dwells so highly mounted? 10
Yet stooping low beholds
What heav'n and earth enfolds.

23 appalling] dismay   25 stayèd] supported   29 straweth] distributes widely
34 fume] show anger   35 naught] nothing   fetches] tricks
Psalm 113 10 highly mounted] placed high in the mountains

From dust the needy soul,
The wretch from miry hole°
He lifts: yea, kings he makes them,   15
Yea, kings his people takes them.
He gives the barren wife
A fruitful mother's life.

Psalm 114

In exitu Israel

At what time Jacob's race did leave of Egypt take,
    And Egypt's barb'rous folk forsake:
Then, then our God, our king, elected Jacob's race
    His temple there and throne to place.°
The sea beheld and fled; Jordan with swift return   5
    To twinnèd spring his streams did turn.°
The mountains bounded so, as fed in fruitful ground
    The fleecèd rams do frisking bound.
The hillocks caprioled so, as wanton by their dams
    We capriole see the lusty lambs.   10
O sea, why didst thou fly? Jordan, with swift return
    To twinnèd spring what made thee turn?
Mountains, why bounded ye, as fed in fruitful ground
    The fleecèd rams do frisking bound?
Hillocks why caprioled ye, as wanton by their dams   15
    We capriole see the lusty lambs?
Nay, you, and earth with you, quake ever at the sight
    Of God Jehovah, Jacob's might.
Who in the hardest rocks, makes standing waters grow
    And purling springs from flints to flow.   20

---

9 caprioled] leaped, skipped   wanton] playing   10 lusty] vigorous
20 purling] rippling, gurgling

Psalm 115

Non nobis, Domine

Not us, I say, not us,
    But thine own name respect, eternal Lord:
And make it glorious,
    To show thy mercy and confirm thy word.
Why, Lord, why should these nations say,   5
Where doth your God now make his stay?

You ask where our God is?
    In heav'n enthroned, no mark of mortal eye.
Nor hath, nor will he miss
    What likes his will, to will effectually.   10
'What are your idols?' we demand:
Gold, silver, works of workmen's hand.°

They mouths, but speechless, have;
    Eyes sightless; ears, no news of noys can tell.
Who them their noses gave,   15
    Gave not their noses any sense of smell.
Nor hands can feel, nor feet can go,
Nor sign of sound their throats can show.

And wherein differ you,
    Who having made them, make of them your trust?   20
But Israel pursue
    Thy trust in God, the target of the just.
O Aaron's house, the like do ye:°
He is their aid, their target he.

All that Jehovah fear,   25
    Trust in Jehovah, he our aid and shield:
He us in mind doth bear,
    He will to us abundant blessings yield.

6 stay] abode   14 noys] annoyances   24 target] shield

Will evermore with grace and good
Bless Jacob's house, bless Aaron's brood.   30

Bless all that bear him awe,
        Both great and small the conduits of his store,
He never dry shall draw,
        But you and yours enrich still more and more.
Blest, oh, thrice blest, whom he hath chose,°   35
Who first with heav'ns did earth enclose.

Where height of highest skies
        Removèd most from floor of lowly ground
With vaulted roof doth rise:°
        Himself took up his dwelling there to found.   40
To mortal men he gracious gave
The lowly ground to hold and have.

And why? His praise to show:
        Which how can dead men, Lord, in any wise,
Who down descending go   45
        Into the place where silence lodgèd lies?
But save us: we thy praise record
Will now and still: Oh, praise the Lord!

Psalm 116

Dilexi quoniam

The Lord receives my cry,
        And me good ear doth give:
Then love him still will I,
        And praise him while I live.
                Fast bound in bonds of death,   5
                        With deadly anguish thrallèd:
                When grief nigh stopped my breath,
                        Upon his name I callèd.

48 still] continually
Psalm 116 2 me good ear doth give] listens to me   6 thrallèd] held in bondage
7 nigh] almost

I called, and thus I said:
    'O Lord, my bands unbind.'   10
I found him prone to aid,
    I found him just and kind,
        The simple's surest guard
          By me of right esteemèd:
        Whom he distressèd hard,   15
          From hard distress redeemèd.

My soul turmoiled with woes,
    Now boldly turn to rest,
Such changes on thee shows
    Who greatest is and best.   20
        My life from death is past,
          Mine eyes have dried their weeping;
        My slipping foot stands fast:
          Myself live in his keeping.

Believing as I spake   25
    (Such woe my wits did blind),
I said when I did quake,
    'I all men liars find':
        Which finding false, to thee°
          What thanks, Lord, shall I render,   30
        Who show'ring bliss on me
          Dost me so truly tender?

'My cup with thanks shall flow
    For freedom from my thrall:
Which I in flames will throw,   35
    And on thy name will call.°
        To thee my vows will pay,
          Thy people all beholding:
        Who dear their deaths dost weigh,
          That are to thee beholden.   40

---

11 prone] inclined   13 simple's] unsuspecting person's   32 tender] cherish

'This I thy servant taste,
 Thy slave thy handmaid's son:
Whose bands thou broken hast,
 And fett'ring chains undone;
  Who unto thee for this   45
   A sacrifice of praising
  To offer will not miss,
   Thy name with honour raising.

'Thou, whom no times enfold,
 Shalt have what I did vow: 50
And they shall all behold,
 Who to thy sceptre bow,
  The place, that holy place,
   Before thy house extended:
  The very middle space   55
   In Zion comprehended.'

Psalm 117

Laudate Dominum

P raise him that aye
R emains the same:
A ll tongues display
I ehovah's fame.
S ing all that share   5
T his earthly ball:
H is mercies are
E xposed to all,
L ike as the word
O nce he doth give,   10
R olled in record,
D oth time outlive.

41 taste] experience 55 middle space] in the midst of
56 Zion] house of the God of Israel comprehended] encompassed
Psalm 117 1 aye] always 4 I ehovah's] Jehovah's 11 R olled] enrolled

Psalm 118

Confitemini Domino

The Lord is good, you see and know;
  Acknowledge then and praise him so:
For so his bounty it extendeth,
No age can say, 'Lo, here it endeth.'

Thou chosen Israel alway,   5
  With me be prest the same to say:
For so his bounty it extendeth,
No age can say, 'Lo, here it endeth.'

You that of sacred Aaron came,
  Be prest with me to say the same: 10
For so his bounty it extendeth,
No age can say, 'Lo, here it endeth.'

And you his fearers all the rest,
  The same to say with me be prest:
For so his bounty it extendeth,   15
No age can say, 'Lo, here it endeth.'

I sometime straitened lay in thrall:
  So lying, I on God did call,
God answer gave me, when I callèd,
And me enlarging, me unthrallèd.   20

Jehovah doth my party take;
  Should fear of man then cause me quake?
Nay, with my friends sith God is placèd,
How can my foes but be disgracèd?

More safe it is on God to stay,   25
  Than confidence on man to lay:

6 prest] eager   17 straitened] constrained   20 unthrallèd] set free
21 party] side   23 sith] since   25 stay] rely

More safe who God his refuge taketh,
Than he who kings his succour maketh.

Of enemies all sorts that be,
   On every part environed me: 30
But I their sinews cut and quailèd,
Jehovah's name so much prevailèd.

They me environed yet again,
   Again they did me straitly strain:
But I their sinews cut and quailèd,   35
Jehovah's name so much prevailèd.

They me environed yet anew,
   And swarming fast like bees they flew.
As fire in thorns they quickly quailèd,
So to their wrack his name prevailèd.   40

Indeed thou sore at me didst thrust:
   Yet by his succour stand I must.
In him my strength, of him my ditty,
He did my soul in thraldom pity.

You righteous troop with me rejoice,   45
   Consort with mine your joyful voice:
Say, 'Praised his hand, yea, double praisèd,
Be his strong hand so highly raisèd.'

For be assured I shall not die;
   But live God's works to testify: 50
Who though he sore did scourging pain me
He hath but scourged, he hath not slain me.

---

30 environed] encircled   31 sinews] tendons, strength   quailèd] destroyed
34 straitly strain] narrowly restrain   40 wrack] ruin   41 sore] forcefully
43 ditty] song   44 thraldom] captivity   46 Consort] harmonize

Who opens to me Justice gate?
 I ent'ring may God's praise relate.°
This gate unto Jehovah showeth   55
By this to him the righteous goeth.

 Here, here, O Lord, I will thee praise,°
 Who didst my life to safety raise:
The stone the builders erst refusèd,
In corner now is laid and usèd.   60

 This workmanship in deed divine
 Doth in our eyes with wonder shine.
God made this day, he did us send it,
In joy and mirth then let us spend it.

 Oh, help us, Lord, oh, help we say,   65
 Oh, prosper, prosper us we pray.
Blest in thy name who coming rideth,
Blest in thy house who dwelling bideth:

 Thy house, Lord, mighty God, whence we
 Both have our light and sight to see: 70
Tie fast the lamb on altar lying,
The cords to hornèd corners tying.

 O God, my mighty God thou art,
 And I to thee will praise impart:
O God, thou art my God, and ever   75
I will extol thee, ceasing never.

 The Lord is good you see and know:
 Acknowledge then and praise him so.
For so his bounty it extendeth,
No age can say, 'Lo, here it endeth.'   80

---

59 erst] formerly   68 bideth] abides   72 hornèd corners] horns of the altar

Psalm 119

Beati immaculati

A

An undefilèd course who leadeth,°
And in Jehovah's doctrine treadeth,
    How blessed he!
    How blest they be
Who still his testimonies keeping,   5
Do seek himself with hearty seeking!°

For whom in walk God's way directeth,°
Sure them no sinful blot infecteth°
    Of deed or word:
    For thou, O Lord,   10
Hast to be done thy laws commanded,
Not only to be understanded.

Oh, were my steps so stayed from swerving,
That I me to thy hests observing
    Might wholly give   15
    Then would I live
With constant cheer, all chances brooking,
To all thy precepts ever looking.

Then would I worship thee sincerely,
When what thy justice bids severely.   20
    Thou shouldst me teach:
    I would no breach
Make of thy law to me betaken:
Oh, leave me not in whole forsaken.

B

By what correcting line,
    May a young man make straight his crooked way?

---

13 stayed] protected   14 hests] commands   17 brooking] profiting by
23 betaken] entrusted   24 in whole] wholly
Psalm 119B 1 correcting line] plumb line

By level of thy lore divine.°
   Sith then with so good cause
     My heart thee seeks, O Lord, I seeking pray,   5
    Let me not wander from thy laws.

Thy speeches have I hid
   Close lockèd up in casket of my heart:
Fearing to do what they forbid.
    But this cannot suffice: 10
     Thou, wisest Lord, who ever-blessed art,
    Yet make me in thy statutes wise.

Then shall my lips declare°
   The sacred laws that from thy mouth proceed:
And teach all nations what they are.°   15
    For what thou dost decree
     To my conceit far more delight doth breed,
    Than worlds of wealth, if worlds might be.

Thy precepts therefore I
   Will my continual meditation make: 20
And to thy paths will have good eye.
    The orders by thee set
     Shall cause me in them greatest pleasure take,
    Nor once will I thy words forget.

C

    Confer, O Lord,
     This benefit on me,
      That I may live, and keep thy word.
Open mine eyes,
     They may the riches see,   5
Which in thy law enfolded lies.

    A pilgrim right
     On earth I wand'ring live:

---

  3 level] an instrument for determining what is 'level', right or true
lore] doctrine   4 Sith] since   17 conceit] thought

Oh, bar me not thy statutes' light.
I waste and spill,   10
   While still I longing grieve,
Grieve longing for thy judgements still.

   Thou proud and high
     Dost low and lowly make:°
       Cursed from thy rule who bend awry.   15
What shame they lay
   On me then from me take:
For I have kept thy will alway.

   Let princes talk,
     And talk their worst of me: 20
       In thy decrees my thoughts shall walk.°
All my delight
   Thy witnessed will shall be:
My counsel to advise me right.

D

Dead as if I were,
   My soul to dust doth cleave:
   Lord, keep thy word, and do not leave
Me here:
     But quicken me anew.   5
    When I did confess
     My sinful ways to thee,
      As then thy ear thou didst to me
    Address:
     So teach me now, thy statutes true.   10

Make that I may know,
   And throughly understand
   What way to walk thou dost command:
Then show

---

10 spill] perish

Psalm 119D 2 cleave] cling, adhere   5 quicken] revive   12 throughly]
thoroughly

Will I thy wonders all.   15
   Very woe and grief
      My soul do melt and fry;
        Revive me, Lord, and send me thy
      Relief;
   And let on me thy comfort fall.   20

From the liar's trace,
   From falsehood's wreathèd way,
      Oh, save me, Lord, and grant I may
Embrace
   The law thou dost commend.   25
      For the path aye right,
        Where truth unfeignèd goes,
         My tongue to tread hath gladly chose:°
      My sight
   Thy judgements doth, as guides, attend.   30

Since therefore, O Lord,
   Still did I, still I do
   So nearly, dearly cleave unto
Thy word:
   All shame from me avert.   35
      Then, lo, lo, then I
        Will tread, yea, running tread
        The trace, which thy commandments lead:
      When thy
   Free grace hath fully freed my heart.   40

E

Explain, O Lord, the way to me,
   That thy divine edicts enfold:
      And I to end will run it right.
Oh, make my blinded eyes to see,

---

17 fry] to burn with emotion   21 trace] path   22 wreathèd] twisted, crooked
26 aye] always   27 unfeignèd] sincerely

And I thy law will hold: yea, hold   5
    Thy law with all my heart's delight.

Oh, be my guide, oh, guide me so,
    I thy commandments' path may pace:
        Wherein to walk my heart is fain.
Oh, bend it then to things that show   10
    True witness of thy might and grace,
        And not to hungry thirst of gain.

Avert mine eye, it may not view
    Of vanity the falsèd face:°
        And strength my treadings in thy trade.   15
Let doings prove thy sayings true
    To him that holds thy servant's place,
        And thee his awe, his fear hath made.

Thou then, my fear, remove the fear
    Of coming blame from careful me: 20
        For gracious are thy judgements still;
Behold, to me thy precepts dear,
    Most dear, and most delightful be:
        Oh, let thy justice aid my will.

F

    Frankly pour, O Lord, on me
    Saving grace, to set me free,
    That supported I may see
    Promise truly kept by thee;

    That to them who me defame,   5
    Roundly I may answer frame,
    Who because thy word and name
    Are my trust, thus seek my shame.

---

9 fain] desirous   15 strength] strengthen   trade] path
20 coming] anticipated

Psalm 119 F 1 Frankly] freely   6 Roundly] plainly, sharply   frame] compose

Thy true word, oh, do not make
Utterly my mouth forsake: 10
Since I thus still waiting wake,
When thou wilt just vengeance take.

Then, lo, I thy doctrine pure,
Sure I hold, will hold more sure:
Naught from it shall me allure,   15
All the time my time shall dure.

Then as brought to widest way
From restraint of straitest stay,
All their thinking night and day:
On thy law my thoughts shall lay.   20

Yea, then unto any king
Witness will I anything
That from thee can witness bring:
In my face no blush shall spring.

Then will I set forth to sight   25
With what pleasure, what delight,
I embrace thy precepts right,
Whereunto all love I plight.

Then will I, with either hand,
Clasp the rules of thy command: 30
There my study still shall stand,
Striving them to understand.

G

Grave deeply in rememb'ring mind
    My trust, thy promise true:°
This only joy in grief I find,
    Thy words my life renew.

15 Naught] nothing   16 dure] endure   18 straitest] narrowest
stay] limit   23 That] I who   28 plight] pledge   29 either] each
Psalm 119 G 1 Grave] engrave

> Though proudly scorned, yet from thy lore 5
I no way have declined:
> I hold for comfort what of yore
Thy dooms, O Lord, defined.

I quake to view how people vile,
> Do from thy doctrine swerve: 10
Thy just edicts ev'n in exile°
> Did me for music serve.
> I keep thy learning, and in night
Record Jehovah's style:
> Observing still thy precepts right, 15
Lo, this I have the while.

H

> High Jehovah, once I say,
> > For my choice and lot I take,
> > I will sure his words obey.
> Hot and hearty suit I make,°
> > Praying thus ev'n to thy face: 5
> > 'Pity me for thy word's sake.
> Every path, and every pace
> > Taught by thee, observing well,
> > To thy rule I frame my race,
> Lest upon delays I dwell, 10
> > But to keep, contend with speed,
> > What to me thy precepts tell.°
> By lewd robbers brought to need
> > From my losses, of thy laws
> > Never did neglect proceed.° 15
> Midnight's watch thy praises cause,
> > While that me from bed and rest
> > Thought of thy just judgements draws.
> Fellowship and friendship's hest,

---

5 lore] teaching   7 of yore] anciently   8 dooms] judgements
Psalm 119 H 3 sure] surely   9 frame] compose   11 contend] contending
13 lewd] wicked   19 hest] command

With thy fearers all I hold,   20
   Such as hold thy biddings best.
Lord, the earth can scarce enfold,
   What thou dost benignly give:
Let me then by thee be told
In thy learning how to live.'   25

I

In all kindness, thou, O Lord,
Hast to me performed thy word:
   This now resteth that I learn
     From thy skill a skilful taste,
   Good from evil to discern,   5
     On thy laws whose trust is placed.

Yet unhumbled I did stray:
Now I will thy words obey.
   Thou that art so highly good
     Nothing can thy goodness reach,   10
   Thou where floweth bounties' flood,
     Willing me thy statutes teach.

What if proud men on me lie?°
I will on thy laws rely.
   Wallow they in their delights,   15
     Fat in body, fat in mind;°
   I the pleasures of my sprites
     Will unto thy doctrine bind.

Now I find the good of woe,
How thy hests it makes me know,   20
   Of whose mouth the lectures true,
     Are alone all wealth to me:
   Millions then, and mines, adieu;°
     Gold and silver, dross you be.

---

20 thy fearers] the godly

Psalm 119 I 3 resteth] remains   4 taste] judgement   17 sprites] spirits
20 hests] commands   24 dross] worthless residue

K

Knit and conformèd by thy hand
    Hath been every part of me:°
Then make me well to understand,
Conceiving all thou dost command.°
      That when me thy fearers see,   5
        They for me may justly joy:
      Seeing what I looked from thee
        On thy word I now enjoy.

O Lord, thy judgements just I know;
    When thy scourges scourgèd me,   10
Thou, in that doing, naught didst show
That might thy promise overthrow.°
      Let me then thy comfort see
        Kindly sent as thou hast said;
      Bring thy mercy's life from thee: 15
        On thy laws my joys are laid.

Let blame and shame the proud betide
    Falsely who subverted me,
Whose meditations shall not slide,°
But fast in thy commandments bide.   20
      So shall I thy fearers see
        On my part who know thy will:
      While I purely worship thee,
        Blot nor blush my face shall fill.

L

Looking and longing for deliverance,
    Upon thy promise, mightless is my mind,
Sightless mine eyes, which often I advance
      Unto thy word,
        Thus praying: 'When, O Lord,   5
      When will it be I shall thy comfort find?'

---

5 thy fearers] the godly   7 looked] expected   8 On thy word] because of thy word   11 naught] nothing   17 betide] happen to   20 fast] firm bide] abide   22 part] side

I like a smokèd bottle am become:
    And yet the wine of thy commandments hold.°
Aye me! When shall I see the total sum
        Of all my woes?
        When wilt thou on my foes
    Make wrongèd me thy just revenge behold?

Their pride hath diggèd pits me to ensnare,
    Which with thy teachings how doth it agree?
True or more truly, truth thy precepts are.
        By falsehood they
        Would make of me their prey:
    Let truth, O Lord, from falsehood rescue me.

Nigh quite consumed by them on earth I lie:
    Yet from thy statutes never did I swerve.
Lord, of thy goodness quicken me, and I
        Will still pursue
        Thy testimonies true,
    And all the biddings of thy lips observe.

M

    Most plainly, Lord, the frame of sky
Doth show thy word decayeth never:
    And constant stay of earth descry
Thy word, that stayed it, stayeth ever.
        For by thy laws they hold their standings,°
    Yea, all things do thy service try:
        But that I joyed in thy commandings,
    I had myself been sure to die.

    Thy word that hath revivèd me
I will retain, forgetting never:
    Let me thine own be saved by thee,
Whose statutes are my studies ever.
        I mark thy will the while their standings

3 descry] declare   4 stayed . . . stayeth] supported . . . remains
5 standings] positions   6 try] prove

Line numbers: 10, 15, 20 (stanza one); 5, 10 (section M)

The wicked take my bane to be:
   For I no close of thy commandings,   15
Of best things else an end I see.

N

Naught can enough declare
   How I thy learning love:
Whereon all day my meditation lies,
   By whose edicts I prove
Far than my foes more wise,   5
   For they a wisdom never-failing are.

My teachers all of old
   May now come learn of me,
Whose studies tend but to thy witnessed will:
   Nay, who most agèd be,   10
Thought therefore most of skill,
   In skill I pass, for I thy precepts hold.

I did refrain my feet
   From every wicked way,
That they might firmly in thy statutes stand.   15
   Nor ever did I stray
From what thy laws command:
   For I of thee have learnèd what is meet.

How pleasing to my taste,
   How sweet thy speeches be!   20
No touch of honey so affects my tongue,
   From whose edicts in me
Hath such true wisdom sprung,°
   That all false ways quite out of love I cast.

15 close] end
Psalm 119 N 1 Naught] nothing   18 meet] appropriate

O

Oh, what a lantern, what a lamp of light
　　Is thy pure word to me
To clear my paths and guide my goings right!
　　　　I sware and swear again,
　　　　I of the statutes will observer be,   5
　　　　　Thou justly dost ordain.

The heavy weights of grief oppress me sore:
　　Lord, raise me by thy word,
As thou to me didst promise heretofore.
　　　　　And this unforcèd praise   10
　　　　　I for an off'ring bring, accept, O Lord,°
　　　　　And show to me thy ways.

What if my life lie naked in my hand,°
　　To every chance exposed!
Should I forget what thou dost me command?   15
　　　　　No, no, I will not stray
　　　　From thy edicts though round about enclosed
　　　　　With snares the wicked lay.

Thy testimonies as mine heritage,
　　I have retainèd still: 20
And unto them my heart's delight engage,
　　　　My heart which still doth bend,
　　　　And only bend to do what thou dost will,
　　　　　And do it to the end.

P

　　People that inconstant be,
　　Constant hatred have from me:°
　　But thy doctrine changeless ever
　　Holds my love that changeth never.
For thou the closet where I hide°   5

7 sore] sorely, intensely
Psalm 119 P 5 closet] private chamber

The shield whereby I safe abide:
My confidence expects thy promise just.
  Hence, away you cursèd crew,
  Get you gone, that rid from you
 I at better ease and leisure,   10
  May perform my God's good pleasure.
O Lord, as thou thy word didst give,
Sustain me so that I may live:
Nor make me blush, as frustrate of my trust.

  Be my pillar, be my stay,°   15
  Safe then I shall swerve no way;
 All my wit and understanding
 Shall then work on thy commanding
For under foot thou tread'st them all
Who swerving from thy precepts fall   20
And vainly in their guile and treason trust.
  Yea, the wicked sort by thee
  All as dross abjected be:
 Therefore what thy proof approveth,
 That my love entirely loveth   25
And such regard of thee I make,
For fear of thee my flesh doth quake:
And of thy laws, thy laws severely just.

Q

Quit and clear from doing wrong,
  Oh, let me not betrayèd be
Unto them, who ever strong
  Do wrongly seek to ruin me.
   Nay, my Lord,   5
   Bail thy servant on thy word:
    And let not these that soar too high,
    By my low stoop yet higher fly.

---

14 frustrate] frustrated 15 stay] support 23 dross] worthless residue
abjected] cast out 24 proof] test
Psalm 119 Q 6 Bail] liberate

Eye doth fail while I not fail
    With eye thy safety to pursue: 10
Looking when will once prevail
    And take effect thy promise true.
      All I crave,
      I at thy mercy's hand would have:
        And from thy wisdom, which I pray 15
        May cause me know thy law and way.

Since thy servant still I stay,
    My understanding, Lord, enlight:
So enlight it that I may
    Thy ordinances know aright. 20
      Now, oh, now,
      The time requires, O Lord, that thou
        Thy law's defence shouldst undertake,
        For now thy law they sorely shake:

Hope whereof makes, that more dear 25
    I thy edicts and statutes hold,
Than if gold to me they were,
    Yea, than they were the purest gold;
      Makes that right
      Are all thy precepts in my sight; 30
        Makes that I hate each lying way,
        That from their truth may cause me stray.

R

Right wonderful thy testimonies be:
    My heart to keep them I therefore bend.
      Their very threshold gives men light,
      And gives men sight,
That light to see: 5
    Yea, ev'n to babes doth understanding lend.°

17 stay] remain   18 enlight] enlighten
Psalm 119 R 2 bend] incline

Opening my mouth: I drank a greedy draught,
    And did on them my whole pleasure place.
        Look then, O Lord, and pity me
        As erst I see   10
Ordained and taught
    By thee for them whose hearts thy name embrace.°

Of all my goings make thy word the guide,
    Nor let injustice upon me reign:
        From them that false accusers be,   15
        Lord, set me free:
So never slide
    Shall I from what thy statutes do ordain.

Shine on thy servant with thy face's beams,
    And throughly me thy commandments teach.   20
        From fountains of whose wat'ry eyes
        Do welling rise
Of tears huge streams,
    Viewing each where thy doctrine's daily breach.

S

    Sure, Lord, thyself art just,
        Thy laws as rightful be:
    What rightly bid thou dost,
        Is firmly bound by thee.
        I flame with zeal to see   5
            My foes thy word forget:
        Pure words, whereon by me
        A servant's love is set.

    Though bare, and though debased
        I yet thy rules retain: 10
    Whose dooms do endless last,
        And doctrine true remain.°

10 erst] formerly   20 throughly] thoroughly   24 each where] everywhere
Psalm 119 S 11 dooms] judgements

In pressure, and in pain
    My joys thy precepts give:
    No date thy judgements deign,°   15
    Oh, make me wise to live.

T

To thee my hearty plaint I send:
    Lord, turn thine ear
    My plaint to hear;
For to thy law my life I bend.
        Since I have invokèd thee,   5
        Let me, Lord, thy succour see:
And what thy ordinances will
I will persist observing still.

My cry more early than the day
    Doth daily rise,°   10
    Because mine eyes
Upon thy promise waiting stay:
        Eyes, I say, which still prevent
        Watches best to watching bent,
Esteeming it but pleasing pains   15
To muse on that thy word contains.

Oh, in thy mercy hear my voice,
    And as thy laws
    Afford the cause
So make me, Lord, revived rejoice.   20
        Lord, thou seest the graceless crew
        Press me near, who me pursue.
As for the doctrine of thy law
They far from it themselves withdraw.

That, Lord, thou seest, and this I see: 25
    Thou everywhere

---

1 plaint] complaint   6 succour] help   12 stay] remain   13 prevent]
anticipate   14 Watches] those on watch   21 graceless crew] godless, those
without grace

To me art near,
For true, nay, truth thy precepts be.
>   Now, though not now first, I know,
>   For I knew it long ago:°   30
That firmly founded once by thee
Thy ordinance no end can see.

V

>   View how I am distressèd,
>   And let me be releasèd:
For look what me thy word hath bidden
Out of my mind hath never slidden.

>   Then be my cause's deemer: 5
>   Be then my soul's redeemer.°
And as good hope thy word doth give me,
Let with good help thy work relieve me.

>   Where wickedness is lovèd,
>   There health is far removèd.°   10
For since thy sole edicts contain it,
Who search not them, how can they gain it?

>   Thy mercies are so many,
>   Their number is not any:°
Then as thou usest, Lord, to use me,   15
Revive me now, and not refuse me.°

>   Exceeding is their number,
>   That me pursue and cumber:
Yet what thy witness hath definèd,
From that my steps have not declinèd.   20

>   I saw, and grievèd seeing
>   Their ways, who wayward being,

---

4 slidden] slid   5 deemer] judge   18 cumber] harass, trouble

With guileful stubbornness withstanded
What by thy speeches was commanded.

Since therefore plain is provèd,   25
   That I thy laws have lovèd:
Look, Lord, and here thy bounty showing
Restore my life now feeble growing.

This in thy doctrine reigneth,
   It naught but truth containeth: 30
This in thy justice brightly shineth,
Thy just edicts no date defineth.°

W

Wronged I was by men of might°
   Hotly chased and hard assailèd;
Little they my heart to fright,
   But, oh, much thy words prevailèd:
Words to me of more delight,   5
Than rich booty won by fight.

Fraud do I with hate detest,
   But with love embrace thy learnings
Sev'n times daily ere I rest,
   Sing thy dooms and right discernings.   10
Whom who love with peace are blest
Plenteous peace without unrest.

Doing what thy precepts will
   I thy help have long expected:
My soul by thy doctrine still,   15
   Lovèd most, is most directed.
Thy edicts my deeds fulfil
Who survey'st my good and ill.

30 naught] nothing
Psalm 119 W 10 dooms] judgements

Y

Yield me this favour, Lord:
My plaint may press into thy sight,
And make me understand aright
   According to thy word.

Admit to sight, I say,   5
The prayer that to thee I send,
And unto me thy help extend,
   Who on thy promise stay.

Then from my lips shall flow
A holy hymn of praise to thee: 10
When I thy scholar taught shall be°
   By thee thy laws to know.

Then shall my tongue declare,
And teach again what thou hast taught:
All whose decrees to trial brought   15
   Most just, nay, justice are.

Oh, then reach out thy hand,
And yield me aid I justly crave,
Since all things I forsaken have
   And chosen thy command.   20

I look, I long, O Lord,
To see at length thy saving grace:
And only do my gladness place,
   In thy glad-making word.

I know my soul shall live,   25
And living, thee due honour yield:
I know thy law shall be my shield
   And me all succour give.

---

2 plaint] complaint   8 stay] rely   28 succour] help

As sheep from shepherd gone
So wander I: oh, seek thy sheep,   30
Who so in mind thy precepts keep,
    That I forget not one.

Psalm 120

Ad Dominum

As to th'Eternal often in anguishes
Erst have I called, never unanswered,
    Again I call, again I calling
    Doubt not again to receive an answer.°

Lord, rid my soul from treasonous eloquence   5
Of filthy forgers craftily fraudulent:
    And from the tongue where lodged resideth
    Poisoned abuse, ruin of believers.

Thou that reposest vainly thy confidence
In wily wronging, say by thy forgery   10
    What good to thee? What gain redoundeth?
    What benefit from a tongue deceitful?

Though like an arrow strongly delivered
It deeply pierce, though like to a juniper
    It coals do cast which quickly fired,   15
    Flame very hot, very hardly quenching?

Ah, God! Too long here wander I banished,
Too long abiding barbarous injury:
    With Kedar and with Mesech harboured.°
    How? In a tent, in a houseless harbour.°   20

Too long, alas, too long have I dwelled here
With friendly peace's furious enemies:°
    Who when to peace I seek to call them,
    Faster I find to the war they arm them.

2 Erst] formerly   11 redoundeth] results   24 them] themselves

Psalm 121

Levavi oculos

What? And do I behold the lovely mountains,
Whence comes all my relief, my aid, my comfort?
Oh, there, oh, there abides the world's Creator,
Whence comes all my relief, my aid, my comfort.°

March, march, lustily on, redoubt no falling:°   5
God shall guide thy goings; the Lord thy keeper
Sleeps not, sleeps not a whit, no sleep, no slumber
Once shall enter in Israel's true keeper.

But whom named I Israel's true keeper?
Whom but only Jehovah: whose true keeping   10
Thy saving shadow is, not ever absent
When present peril his relief requireth.

March then boldly by day: no sun shall hurt thee°
With beams too violently right reflected.
Fear no journey by night: the moony vapours   15
Shall not cast any mist to breed thy grievance.

Nay, from every mishap, from every mischief
Safe thou shalt by Jehovah's hand be guarded:
Safe in all thy goings, in all thy comings,
Now thou shalt by his hand, yea, still be guarded.   20

Psalm 122

Laetatus sum

Oh, fame most joyful! Oh, joy most lively delightful!
Lo, I do hear God's temple, as erst, so again be frequented,
And we within thy porches again glad-wonted abiding,

---

5 redoubt] fear
Psalm 122 2 erst] formerly   3 glad-wonted] habitually cheerful

Lovely Salem shall find: thou city rebuilt as a city,
Late dispersed, but now united in absolute order.   5
Now there shall be the place for God's holy people appointed
First to behold his pledge, then sing almighty Jehovah.
Now there shall be the seat, where not to be justiced only,°
All shall freely resort whom strife, hate, injury vexeth:
But where David's house and offspring heav'nly beloved   10
Shall both judges sit and reign kings throned in honour.
Pray then peace to Salem: to her friends all happy proceeding,
Wish to her walls all rest, to her forts all blessed abundance.
This with cause I do pray, since from these blisses a blessing
My brother and kinsman, my friend and country deriveth.   15
This I do wish and more, if more good rest to be wished
Since our God here builds him an house, almighty Jehovah.

Psalm 123

Ad te levavi oculos meos

Unto thee, oppressed, thou great commander of heaven
    Heav'nly good attending, lift I my earthy seeing.
Right as a waiter's eye on a graceful master is holden;
    As the look of waitress fixed on a lady lieth:
So with erected face, until by thy mercy relieved,°   5
    O Lord, expecting, beg we thy friendly favour.
Scorn of proud scorners, reproach of mighty reproachers
    Our sprites clean ruined fills with an inly dolour.
Then friend us, favour us, Lord, then with mercy relieve us,
    Whose scornful misery greatly thy mercy needeth.   10

Psalm 124

Nisi quia Dominus

Say, Israel, do not conceal a verity,
    Had not the Lord assisted us,

---

4   Salem] Jerusalem   8   justiced] given justice
Psalm 123 2 earthy] earthly   3 waiter's] servant's   4 waitress] handmaid
5 erected] raised   8 sprites] spirits   dolour] sorrow   10 scornful] contemptible

Had not the Lord assisted us what time arose
    Against us our fierce enemies,
Us all at once long since they had devoured up:°   5
    They were so fell, so furious.
If not, the angry gulfs, the streams most horrible°
    Had drowned us: so drowned us,
That in the deep been tombed, at least on the deep
    Had tumbled our dead carcasses.°   10
But, Lord, what honour shall thy people yield to thee,
    From greedy teeth delivered,
Escaped as the fowl, that oft breaking the grin,
    Beguiles the fowler's wiliness?
For sure this is thy work, thy name protecteth us,   15
    Who heav'n and earth hast fashioned.

Psalm 125

Qui confidunt

As Zion standeth very firmly steadfast,
Never once shaking: so on high Jehovah
Who his hope buildeth, very firmly steadfast
                Ever abideth.

As Salem braveth with her hilly bulwarks   5
Roundly enforted: so the great Jehovah
Closeth his servants, as a hilly bulwark
                Ever abiding;

Though tyrant's hard yoke with a heavy pressure
Wring the just shoulders: but a while it holdeth,   10
Lest the best minded by too hard abusing
                Bend to abuses.

---

3 what time] when   5 had devoured] would have devoured   6 fell] fierce
13 grin] snare

Psalm 125 1 Zion] house of the God of Israel   5 Salem] Jerusalem
6 Roundly] in a circular manner, completely   7 Closeth] encloses

As the well-workers, so the right believers,
Lord, favour, further; but a vain deceiver,
Whose wried footing not aright directed 15
                    Wand'reth in error,

Lord him abjected set among the number°
Whose doings lawless, study bent to mischief
Mischief expecteth: but upon thy chosen
                    Peace be for ever. 20

Psalm 126

In convertendo

When long absent from lovely Zion
By the Lord's conduct home we returned,°
We our senses scarcely believing
Thought mere visions moved our fancy.°

Then in our merry mouths laughter abounded, 5
Tongues with gladness loudly resounded
While thus wond'ring nations whispered:
'God with them most royally dealeth.'

Most true: with us thou royally dealest,°
Woe is expired, sorrow is vanished: 10
Now, Lord, to finish throughly thy working
Bring to Jerusalem all that are exiles.

Bring to Jerusalem all that are exiles,
So by thy comfort newly refreshed:
As when southern sunburnt regions 15
Be by cold fountains freshly relieved.

---

13 well-workers] those doing good   15 wried] diverted
Psalm 126 1 Zion] house of the God of Israel   2 conduct] passport
11 throughly] thoroughly

Oft to the ploughman so good hap happ'neth,
What with tears to the ground he bequeathed,
Season of harvest timely returning,
He, before woeful, joyfully reapeth.   20

Why to us may not as haply happen,
To sow our business woefully weeping:
Yet when business grows to due ripeness,
To see our business joyfully reaped?

Psalm 127
Nisi Dominus

The house Jehovah builds not,
We vainly strive to build it:
The town Jehovah guards not,
We vainly watch to guard it.

No use of early rising;   5
As useless is thy watching:
Not aught at all it helps thee
To eat thy bread with anguish.

As unto weary senses
A sleepy rest unaskèd: 10
So bounty cometh uncaused
From him to his beloved.

No, not thy children hast thou
By choice, by chance, by nature;
They are, they are Jehovah's,   15
Rewards from him rewarding.

The multitude of infants
A good man holds, resembleth

17 hap] chance   21 haply] by chance   22 business] labour
Psalm 127 7 aught] anything

The multitude of arrows,
A mighty archer holdeth.   20

His happiness triumpheth
Who bears a quiver of them:
No countenance of haters
Shall unto him be dreadful.

Psalm 128

Beati omnes

All happiness shall thee betide,
    That dost Jehovah fear:
And walking in the paths abide,
      By him first trodden were°
        The labours of thy hands   5
    Desirèd fruit shall bear.
        And where thy dwelling stands,
    All bliss, all plenty there.

Thy wife a vine, a fruitful vine
      Shall in thy parlour spring:°   10
Thy table compass children thine
      As olive plants in ring.
        On thee, I say, on thee:
      That fear'st the heav'nly king,
        Such happiness shall he   15
      He shall from Zion bring.

Yea, while to thee thy breath shall hold,
    Though running longest race,°
Thou Salem ever shalt behold
      In wealth and wishèd case: 20
        And children's children view

---

  1 betide] happen to   11 compass] surround   12 in ring] in a circle
16 Zion] house of the God of Israel   19 Salem] Jerusalem

While Jacob's dwelling place
 No plagues of war pursue,
But gifts of peace shall grace.

Psalm 129

Saepe expugnaverunt

'Oft and ever from my youth,'
 So now Israel may say;
Israel may say for truth,
 'Oft and ever my decay
  From my youth their force hath sought:°   5
  Yet effect it never wrought.

'Unto them my back did yield
 Place and plain (oh, height of woe)
Where as in a ploughèd field,
 Long and deep did furrows go.   10
  But, O just Jehovah, who
  Hast their plough-ropes cut in two!

'Tell me you that Zion hate,
 What you think shall be your end?°
Terror shall your minds amate: 15
 Blush and shame your faces shend.
  Mark the wheat on house's top:°
  Such your harvest, such your crop:

'Wither shall you where you stand.
 Gathered? No: but wanting sap,   20
Filling neither reaper's hand,
 Nor the binder's inbowed lap.
  Nay, who you shall reap or bind,
  Common kindness shall not find.'°

13 Zion] house of the God of Israel 15 amate] dismay 16 shend] disgrace
22 inbowed] bent inwards

Such as travel by the way, 25
    Where as they their pains employ,
Shall not once saluting say,
      'God speed, friends, God give you joy:
        He in whom all blessing reigns,
        Bless yourselves, and bless your pains.' 30

Psalm 130
De profundis

From depth of grief°
    Where drowned I lie,
Lord, for relief
    To thee I cry:
My earnest, vehement, crying, praying, 5
Grant quick, attentive hearing, weighing.

O Lord, if thou
    Offences mark,
Who shall not bow
    To bear the cark? 10
But with thy justice mercy dwelleth,
And makes thy worship more excelleth,°

Yea, makes my soul
    On thee, O Lord,
Dependeth whole, 15
    And on thy word,
Though sore with blot of sin defacèd,
Yet surest hope hath firmly placèd.

Who longest watch,
    Who soonest rise, 20
Can nothing match

6 weighing] considering   8 mark] notice   10 cark] burden
15 whole] wholly   17 sore] severely

    The early eyes,
The greedy eyes my soul erecteth,
While God's true promise it expecteth.

    Then, Israel,   25
        On God attend:
Attend him well,
        Who still thy friend,
In kindness hath thee dear esteemèd,
And often, often erst redeemèd.°   30

    Now, as before,
        Unchangèd he
Will thee restore,
        Thy state will free,
All wickedness from Jacob driving   35
Forgetting follies, faults forgiving.

Psalm 131

Domine, non est

A lofty heart, a lifted eye,
      Lord, thou dost know I never bare:
Less have I borne in things too high
      A meddling mind or climbing care.
      Look how the weanèd babe doth fare: 5
Oh, did I not? Yes, so did I:
      None more for quiet might compare
Ev'n with the babe that weaned doth lie.
      Hear then and learn, O Jacob's race,
      Such endless trust on God to place.   10

---

23 erecteth] lifts up   29 dear esteemèd] highly valued   30 erst] formerly
Psalm 131 4 climbing care] ambitious worrying

Psalm 132

Memento, Domine

Lord, call to mind, nay, keep in mind
    Thy David and thy David's pains:
Who once by oath and vow did bind°
      Himself to him who aye remains,
        That mighty one,   5
        The God in Jacob known.

My house shall never harbour me,
    Nor bed allow my body rest,
Nor eyes of sleep the lodging be,
      Nor eyelids slend'rest slumber's nest: 10
        Until I find
        A plot to please my mind:

I find, I say, my mind to please
    A plot wherein I may erect
A house for him to dwell at ease,   15
      Who is adored with due respect:
        That mighty one
        The God in Jacob known.

The plot thy David then did name,
    We heard at Ephrata it lay: 20
We heard, but bent to find the same,
      Were fain to seek another way:
        Ev'n to the fields,
        That woody Jear yields.°

And yet not there, but here, oh, here   25
    We find now settled what we sought:°
Before the stool thy feet doth bear
    Now ent'ring in, we, as we ought,

Adore thee will,
And duly worship still.   30

Then enter, Lord, thy fixèd rest,
   With Ark the token of thy strength,°
And let thy priests be purely dressed
   In robes of justice laid at length:
     Let them be glad   35
     Thy graceful bliss have had.°

For David once thy servant's sake,
   Do not our kings, his seed reject:
For thou to him this oath didst make,
   This endless oath: 'I will erect,   40
     And hold thy race
     Enthroned in royal place.

'Nay, if thy race my league observe,
   And keep the cov'nants I set down,
Their race again I will preserve   45
   Eternally to wear thy crown:
     No less thy throne
     Shall ever be their own.

'For Zion which I lovèd best,
   I chosen have no seat of change: 50
Here, here shall be my endless rest,
   Here will I dwell, nor hence will range:
     Unto the place
     I bear such love and grace;

'Such grace and love that evermore   55
   A bliss from gracious loving me,
Shall bless her victual, bless her store,
   That ev'n the poor who in her be
     With store of bread
     Shall fully all be fed.   60

43 league] contract   49 Zion] house of the God of Israel   57 victual] food

'In her my priests shall naught annoy:
     Nay, clad they shall with safety be.
Oh, how in her with cause shall joy
     Who there as tenants hold of me
       Whose tenure is   65
       By grace my fields of bliss!°

'Oh, how in her shall sprout and spring,
     The sceptre David's hand did bear!°
How I my Christ, my sacred king,
     As light in lantern placèd there   70
       With beams divine
       Will make abroad to shine!

'But as for them who spite and hate
     Conceive to him, they all shall down,
Downcast by me to shameful state,   75
     While on himself his happy crown
       Shall up to skies
       With fame and glory rise.'°

Psalm 133

Ecce quam bonum

How good, and how beseeming well
     It is that we,
     Who brethren be,
As brethren, should in concord dwell.

Like that dear oil, that Aaron bears,   5
     Which fleeting down
     To foot from crown
Embalms his beard, and robe he wears.

61 naught] nothing   annoy] harm
Psalm 133 1 beseeming well] appropriate

Or like the tears the morn doth shed°
    Which lie on ground   10
    Impearlèd round°
On Zion or on Hermon's head.°

For joined therewith the Lord doth give°
    Such grace, such bliss:
    That where it is,°   15
Men may for ever blessèd live.

Psalm 134

Ecce nunc

You that Jehovah's servants are,
Whose careful watch, whose watchful care,
    Within his house are spent;
    Say thus with one assent:
        'Jehovah's name be praised.'   5
    Then let your hands be raised
        To holiest place,
        Where holiest grace
          Doth aye
           Remain: 10
        And say
          Again,
'Jehovah's name be praised.'
Say last unto the company,
        Who tarrying make   15
        Their leave to take,
'All blessings you accompany,
From him in plenty showerèd,
Whom Zion holds embowerèd,
    Who heav'n and earth of naught hath raised.'°   20

---

12 Zion] hill on which God's house is located

Psalm 134 9 aye] ever   19 Zion] house of the God of Israel   20 naught]
nothing

Psalm 135

Laudate nomen

Oh, praise the name whereby the Lord is known,
 Praise him, I say, you that his servants be;
You whose attendance in his house is shown,
  And in the courts before his house we see,
   Praise God, right termèd God, for good is he: 5
    Oh, sweetly sing
    Unto his name, the sweetest, sweetest thing.

For of his goodness Jacob hath he chose,
 Chose Israel his own domain to be.°
My tongue shall speak, for well my conscience knows, 10
  Great is our God, above all gods is he,
   Each branch of whose inviolate decree°
    Both heav'ns do keep,
    And earth, and sea, and sea's unsounded deep.

From whose extremes drawn up by his command 15
 In flaky mists, the reeking vapours rise,
Then high in clouds incorporate they stand;°
  Last out of clouds rain flows, and lightning flies.
   No less a treasure in his storehouse lies
    Of breathing blasts, 20
    Which oft drawn forth in wind his pleasure wastes.°

He from best man to most despisèd beast
 Egypt's firstborn in one night overthrew:
And yet not so his dreadful shows he ceased,
  But did them still in Egypt's midst renew. 25
   Not only meaner men had cause to rue,
    But ev'n the best
    Of Pharaoh's court, the king among the rest.°

---

14 unsounded] unfathomed, unknown 16 flaky] snowy
reeking] rising, emanating 26 meaner] poorer rue] regret

He many nations, mighty kings destroyed:
  Sehon for one, who ruled the Amorites,   30
And huge-limbed Og, who Basan's crown enjoyed,°
  Yea, all the kingdoms of the Canaanites
  Whose heritage he gave the Israelites,
   His chosen train,
    Their heritage for ever to remain.   35

Therefore, O Lord, thy name is famous still,
  The memory thy ancient wonders got,
Time well to world his message may fulfil°
  And back return to thee, yet never blot
  Out of our thoughts: for how should be forgot 40
   The Lord that so
    Forgives his servant, plagues his servant's foe?

What difference, what unproportioned odds
  To thee these idols gold and silver bear
Which men have made, yet men have made their gods?° 45
  Who though mouth, eye, and ear, and nose they wear
  Yet neither speak, nor look, nor smell, nor hear.
   Oh, idols right
    Who idols make, or idols make your might!

But you that are of Israel's descent,   50
  Oh, praise the Lord: you that of Aaron came;
Oh, praise the Lord, you Levi's house assent
  To praise the Lord; you all his fearers, frame
  Your highest praise, to praise Jehovah's name.
   His praises still,   55
    Salem, resound, resound, O Zion hill.

---

34 train] followers 43 unproportioned odds] inequalities
53 fearers] the godly frame] compose 56 Salem] Jerusalem
56 Zion hill] location of God's house

Psalm 136

Confitemini

Oh, praise the Lord where goodness dwells,
    For his kindness lasteth ever:
Oh, praise the God all gods excels,
    For his bounty endeth never.

Praise him that is of lords the Lord,   5
    For his kindness lasteth ever:
Who only wonders doth afford,
    For his bounty endeth never;

Whose skilful art did vault the skies,
    For his kindness lasteth ever: 10
Made earth above the waters rise,
    For his bounty endeth never;

Who did the luminaries make,
    For his kindness lasteth ever:
The sun of day the charge to take,   15
    For his bounty endeth never;

The moon and stars in night to reign,
    For his kindness lasteth ever:
Who Egypt's eldest born hath slain,
    For his bounty endeth never;   20

And brought out Israel from thence,
    For his kindness lasteth ever:
With mighty hand and strong defence,
    For his bounty endeth never;

Who cut in two the rushy sea,°   25
    For his kindness lasteth ever:

7 afford] perform

And made the middest Jacob's way,
  For his bounty endeth never;

Who Pharaoh and his army drowned,
  For his kindness lasteth ever: 30
And led his folk through desert ground,
  For his bounty endeth never;

Great kings in battle overthrew,
  For his kindness lasteth ever:
Yea, mighty kings most mighty slew,   35
  For his bounty endeth never;

Both Sehon, king of Amorites,
  For his kindness lasteth ever:
And Og, the king of Basanites,°
  For his bounty endeth never;   40

For heritage their kingdoms gave,
  For his kindness lasteth ever:
His Israel to hold and have,
  For his bounty endeth never;

Who minded us dejected low,   45
  For his kindness lasteth ever:
And did us save from force of foe,
  For his bounty endeth never;

Who fills with food each feeding thing,°
  For his kindness lasteth ever: 50
Praise God who is of heav'ns the king,
  For his bounty endeth never.

27 middest] middle

Psalm 137

Super flumina

Nigh seated where the river flows
   That wat'reth Babel's thankful plain,
Which then our tears in pearlèd rows
   Did help to water with their rain,
The thought of Zion bred such woes,   5
   That though our harps we did retain,
      Yet useless and untouchèd there
      On willows only hanged they were.

Now while our harps were hangèd so,
   The men whose captives then we lay,°   10
Did on our griefs insulting go,
   And more to grieve us, thus did say:
'You that of music make such show,
   Come sing us now a Zion lay.'
      Oh, no, we have nor voice, nor hand   15
      For such a song, in such a land.

Though far I lie, sweet Zion hill,
   In foreign soil exiled from thee,
Yet let my hand forget his skill,°
   If ever thou forgotten be: 20
And let my tongue fast gluèd still
   Unto my roof lie mute in me,
      If thy neglect within me spring,
      Or aught I do, but Salem sing.°

But thou, O Lord, shalt not forget   25
   To quit the pains of Edom's race,°
Who causelessly yet hotly set
   Thy holy city to deface,

2 Babel's] Babylon's   5 Zion] house of the God of Israel   14 lay] song
15 nor . . . nor] neither . . . nor   21 fast] firmly   22 my roof] roof of my mouth
23 thy neglect] neglect of thee   24 aught] anything   26 quit] repay
27 set] began

Did thus the bloody victors whet
 What time they entered first the place: 30
  'Down, down with it at any hand°
  Make all plat pays, let nothing stand.'

And, Babylon, that didst us waste,
 Thyself shalt one day wasted be:
And happy he who what thou hast   35
 Unto us done, shall do to thee,
Like bitterness shall make thee taste,
 Like woeful objects cause thee see:
  Yea, happy who thy little ones
  Shall take and dash against the stones. 40

Psalm 138

Confitebor tibi

Ev'n before kings by thee as gods commended,
And angels all, by whom thou art attended,
 In hearty tunes I will thy honour tell.°

The palace where thy holiness doth dwell,°
Shall be the place, where falling down before thee, 5
With reverence meet I prostrate will adore thee.

There will I sing how thou thy mercy sendest,
And to thy promise due performance lendest,
 Whereby thy name above all names doth fly.

 There will I sing, how when my careful cry 10
Mounted to thee, my care was straight releasèd,
My courage by thee mightily increasèd.

---

29 whet] encourage 30 What time] when 32 plat pays] flat place (French)
33 waste] lay waste, destroy 37 Like] similar
Psalm 138 6 meet] appropriate

Sure, Lord, all kings that understand the story
Of thy contract with me, naught but thy glory°
   And means shall sing whereby that glory grew,   15

Whose highly seated eye yet well doth view
With humbled look the soul that lowly lieth,
And far aloof aspiring things espieth.°

On every side though tribulation grieve me,
Yet shalt thou aid, yet shalt thou still relieve me,   20
   From angry foe thy succour shall me save.

Thou, Lord, shalt finish what in hand I have:
Thou, Lord, I say, whose mercy lasteth ever,
Thy work begun shall leave unended never.

Psalm 139

Domine, probasti

O Lord, in me there lieth naught,
   But to thy search revealèd lies:°
      For when I sit
      Thou markest it;°
   No less thou notest when I rise: 5
Yea, closest closet of my thought
   Hath open windows to thine eyes.

Thou walkest with me when I walk,
   When to my bed for rest I go,
      I find thee there,   10
      And everywhere:
   Not youngest thought in me doth grow,
No, not one word I cast to talk,
   But yet unuttered thou dost know.°

14 naught] nothing   16 highly seated] seated on high   18 espieth] spies, sees
21 succour] help

Psalm 139 6 closet] private chamber

If forth I march, thou go'st before;   15
   If back I turn, thou com'st behind:
      So forth nor back
      Thy guard I lack,
   Nay, on me too, thy hand I find.°
Well I thy wisdom may adore,   20
   But never reach with earthy mind.°

To shun thy notice, leave thine eye,
   Oh, whither might I take my way?
      To starry sphere?°
      Thy throne is there.   25
To dead men's undelightsome stay?
There is thy walk, and there to lie
   Unknown, in vain I should assay.°

O sun, whom light nor flight can match,°
   Suppose thy lightful, flightful wings   30
      Thou lend to me,
      And I could flee
   As far as thee the evening brings:
Ev'n led to west he would me catch,
   Nor should I lurk with western things.°   35

Do thou thy best, O secret night,
   In sable veil to cover me:
      Thy sable veil
      Shall vainly fail.
With day unmasked my night shall be,°   40
For night is day, and darkness light,
   O father of all lights, to thee.°

Each inmost piece in me is thine:
   While yet I in my mother dwelt,
      All that me clad   45
      From thee I had.

---

17 So forth nor back] neither forth nor back   18 guard] protection
21 earthy] earthly   26 undelightsome] unpleasant   stay] residence
28 assay] attempt   30 flightful] well adapted for flight   35 lurk] hide

Thou in my frame hast strangely dealt;
Needs in my praise thy works must shine
   So inly them my thoughts have felt.

Thou how my back was beam-wise laid   50
  And raft'ring of my ribs dost know:
     Know'st every point
     Of bone and joint,
  How to this whole these parts did grow,
In brave embroid'ry fair arrayed,   55
  Though wrought in shop both dark and low.°

Nay, fashionless, ere form I took,
  Thy all and more beholding eye
     My shapeless shape
     Could not escape: 60
  All these, with times appointed by,
Ere one had being, in the book
  Of thy foresight, enrolled did lie.°

My God, how I these studies prize,°
  That do thy hidden workings show   65
     Whose sum is such,
     No sum so much:°
  Nay, summed as sand they sumless grow!
I lie to sleep, from sleep I rise,
  Yet still in thought with thee I go.   70

My God, if thou but one wouldst kill,
  Then straight would leave my further chase
     This cursèd brood
     Inured to blood:°
  Whose graceless taunts at thy disgrace   75
Have aimèd oft, and hating still
  Would with proud lies, thy truth outface.

---

47 my frame] the forming of my body   49 inly] inwardly   55 brave] rich
56 shop] i.e. womb   57 ere] before   77 outface] contradict

Hate not I them, who thee do hate?
　　Thine, Lord, I will the censure be.
　　　　Detest I not   80
　　　　　The cankered knot,
　　Whom I against thee banded see?
O Lord, thou know'st in highest rate
　　I hate them all as foes to me.

Search me, my God, and prove my heart,   85
　　Examine me, and try my thought:
　　　　And mark in me
　　　　If aught there be
　　That hath with cause their anger wrought.
If not (as not) my life's each part,   90
　　Lord, safely guide from danger brought.

Psalm 140

Eripe me, Domine

Protect me, Lord, preserve me, set me free
From men that be so vile, so violent:
In whose intent both force and fraud doth lurk
My bane to work; whose tongues are sharper things
Than adder's stings; whose rusty lips enclose   5
A poison's hoard, such in the aspic grows.

Save, I say, Lord, protect me, set me free
From those that be so vile, so violent:
Whose thoughts are spent in thinking how they may
My steps betray, how net of foul mishap°   10
May me entrap, how hid in traitor grass
Their cunning cord may catch me as I pass.

But this, O Lord, I hold: my God art thou;
Thou ear wilt bow, what time thy aid I pray

81 cankered] corrupt   87 mark] observe   88 aught] anything
Psalm 140 3 lurk] hide   4 bane] destruction   6 aspic] asp

In thee my stay, Jehovah; thou dost arm° 15
Against all harm, and guard my head in field.
Oh, then to yield these wicked their desire,
Do not accord: for still they will aspire.°

But yield, O Lord, that ev'n the head of those
That me enclose, of this their hot pursuit 20
May taste the fruit: with deadly venom stung
Of their own tongue, lo, lo, I see they shall,°
Yea, coals shall fall, yea, flames shall fling them low°
Aye unrestored to drown in deepest woe.°

For liars, Lord, shall never firmly stand, 25
And from the land who violently live
Mischief shall drive: but well I know the poor
Thou wilt restore, restore th'afflicted wight,
That in thy sight the just may houses frame,
And glad record the honour of thy name. 30

Psalm 141

Domine, clamavi

To thee, Jehovah, thee, I lift my crying voice,
Oh, banish all delay, and let my plaintful noise,
  By thy quick-hearing ear be carefully respected.
    As sweet perfume to skies let what I pray ascend:
    Let these uplifted hands, which praying I extend, 5
  As evening sacrifice be unto thee directed.

Ward well my words, O Lord (for that is it I pray),
A watchful sentinel at my mouth's passage lay:
  At wicket of my lips stand aye a faithful porter;
    Incline me not to ill, nor let me loosely go 10

15 stay] support   18 accord] consent   aspire] be proud
28 wight] person   29 frame] construct

Psalm 141 2 plaintful] lamenting   7 Ward] guard   9 wicket] gate
aye] ever

A mate in work with such, whence no good work doth grow,
And in their flatt'ring baits, let me be no consorter.°

But let the good man wound, most well I shall it take,°
Yea, price of his rebukes as dearest balm shall make,
    Yea, more shall for him pray, the more his words shall
        grieve me,   15
        And as for these, when once the leaders of their crew
        By thee be brought to stoop, my words most sweetly true
Shall in the rest so work, that soon they shall believe me.

Meanwhile my bones the grave, the grave expects my bones,
So broken, hewn, dispersed, as least respected stones,   20
    By careless mason drawn from cave of worthless quarry,°
        But thou, O Lord, my Lord, since thus thy servant's eye
        Replete with hopeful trust doth on thy help rely,
Fail not that trustful hope, that for thy help doth tarry.

Oh, so direct my feet they may escape the hands   25
Of their entangling snare, which for me pitchèd stands:
    And from the wicked nets for me with craft they cover.
        Nay, for these fowlers once, thyself a fowler be,
        And make them foully fall where nets are laid by thee,
But where for me they lay, let me leap freely over.   30

Psalm 142

Voce mea ad Dominum

My voice to thee itself extremely straining,
    Cries praying, Lord; again it crying prayeth.
Before thy face the cause of my complaining,
    Before thy face my case's map it layeth.
        Wherein my soul is painted   5

12 consorter] partner   17 stoop] bow down

In doubtful way a stranger:
But, Lord, thou art acquainted,
　　And know'st each path, where stick the toils of danger.
　　　For me, mine eye to every coast directed,
　　　　　Lights not on one that will so much as know me:° 　10
　　　My life by all neglected,
　　　　　Ev'n hope of help is now quite perished from me.

Then with good cause to thee my spirit flieth,
　Flieth, and saith: 'O Lord, my safe abiding
Abides in thee: in thee all-only lieth 　　　　　　　　　15
　Lot of my life, and plot of my residing.'
　　Alas, then yield me hearing,
　　　For wearing woes have spent me:
　　And save me from their tearing,
　　　Who hunt me hard, and daily worse torment me. 　20
　　　　Oh, change my state, unthrall my soul enthrallèd:
　　　　　Of my escape then will I tell the story;
　　　　And with a crown enwallèd
　　　　　Of godly men, will glory in thy glory.

Psalm 143

Domine, exaudi

Hear my entreaty, Lord; the suit, I send,
With heed attend.
　　And as my hope and trust is°
　　　Reposèd whole in thee,
　　So in thy truth and justice 　　　　　　　　　　5
　　　Yield audience to me.°
　　　　And make not least beginning
　　　　　To judge thy servant's sinning:
　　　　　For, Lord, what living wight
　　　　　Lives sinless in thy sight? 　　　　　　　10

---

8 toils] snares, traps　　15 all-only] alone　　18 wearing] fatiguing, wearying
21 unthrall . . . enthrallèd] set free . . . captive　　23 enwallèd] walled in
Psalm 143 1 suit] petition　　9 wight] person

Oh, rather look with ruth upon my woes,
Whom ruthless foes
    With long pursuit have chasèd,
       And chased at length have caught,
    And caught, in tomb have placèd   15
       With dead men out of thought.
          Aye me! What now is left me?
          Alas! All knowledge reft me,
             All courage faintly fled,
             I have nor heart nor head.   20

The best I can is this, nay, this is all:
That I can call
    Before my thoughts, surveying
       Time's evidences old,
    All deeds with comfort weighing   25
       That thy handwriting hold.°
          So hand and heart conspiring
          I lift, no less desiring
             Thy grace I may obtain,
             Than drought desireth rain.   30

Leave then delay, and let his cry prevail,°
Whom force doth fail.
    Nor let thy face be hidden
       From one who may compare
    With them whose death hath bidden   35
       Adieu to life and care.
          My hope, let mercy's morrow
          Soon chase my night of sorrow.
             My help, appoint my way,°
             I may not wand'ring stray.°   40

My cave, my closet where I wont to hide
In troublous tide:
    Now from these troubles save me,

---

11 ruth] compassion   16 thought] remembrance   18 reft] taken from
20 nor . . . nor] neither . . . nor   21 can] can do   41 closet] private chamber
wont] am accustomed   42 tide] time

And since my God thou art,
Prescribe how thou wouldst have me 45
Perform my duty's part.
And lest awry I wander
In walking this Meander,°
Be thy right sprite my guide
To guard I go not wide.° 50

Thy honour, justice, mercy crave of thee,
O Lord, that me
Revived thou shouldst deliver
From pressure of my woes,
And in destruction's river 55
Engulf and swallow those°
Whose hate thus makes in anguish
My soul afflicted languish:
For meet it is so kind
Thy servant should thee find. 60

Psalm 144
Benedictus Dominus

Praised be the Lord of might,
My rock in all alarms,
By whom my hands do fight,
My fingers manage arms,
My grace, my guard, my fort, 5
On whom my safety stays:
To whom my hopes resort
By whom my realm obeys.°

Lord, what is man that thou
Shouldst tender so his fare? 10
What hath his child to bow

49 sprite] spirit   59 meet] appropriate
Psalm 144 10 tender . . . his fare] pay his passage

Thy thoughts unto his care?
Whose nearest kin is naught,
    No image of whose days
More lively can be thought,   15
    Than shade that never stays.

Lord, bend thy archèd skies
    With ease to let thee down;
And make the storms arise
    From mountains' fuming crown.   20
Let follow flames from sky,
    To back their stoutest stand:
Let fast thy arrows fly,
    Dispersing thickest band.

Thy heav'nly help extend   25
    And lift me from this flood:
Let me thy hand defend
    From hand of foreign brood
Whose mouth no mouth at all,
    But forge of false intent,   30
Whereto their hand doth fall
    As aptest instrument.°

Then in new song to thee
    Will I exalt my voice:
Then shall, O God, with me   35
    My ten-stringed lute rejoice.
Rejoice in him, I say,
    Who royal right preserves
And saves from sword's decay
    His David that him serves.   40

O Lord, thy help extend,
    And lift me from this flood:
Let me thy hand defend

---

13 naught] nothing   16 stays] remains   20 fuming] smoking
32 aptest] most suitable

From hand of foreign brood
Whose mouth no mouth at áll,   45
    But forge of false intent,
Whereto their hand doth fall
    As aptest instrument.°

So then our sons shall grow
    As plants of timely spring: 50
Whom soon to fairest show
    Their happy growth doth bring.
As pillars both do bear
    And garnish kingly hall:
Our daughters straight and fair,   55
    Each house embellish shall.°

Our store shall aye be full,
    Yea, shall such fullness find,
Though all from thence we pull,
    Yet more shall rest behind.   60
The millions of increase
    Shall break the wonted fold:
Yea, such the sheepy press,
    The streets shall scantly hold.°

Our herds shall brave the best;   65
    Abroad no foes alarm;
At home to break our rest,
    No cry, the voice of harm.
If blessed term I may
    On whom such blessings fall: 70
Then blessed, blessed they
    Their God Jehovah call.

57 aye] ever   60 rest] remain   62 wonted] accustomed

Psalm 145

Exaltabo te

My God, my king, to lift thy praise
   And thank thy most thank-worthy name
I will not end, but all my days
   Will spend in seeking how to frame
   Records of thy deservèd fame   5
      Whose praise past-praise, whose greatness such,°
      The greatest search can never touch.

Not in one age thy works shall die,
   But elder eft to younger tell
Thy praiseful pow'r: among them I   10
   Thy excellences all excel°
   Will muse and mark; my thoughts shall dwell
      Upon the wonders wrought by thee,
      Which wrought beyond all wonder be.

Both they and I will tell and sing   15
   How forceful thou, and fearful art:
Yea, both will willing witness bring
   And unto coming times impart
   Thy greatness, goodness, just desert:
      That all who are, or are to be,   20
      This hymn with joy shall sing to thee.

Jehovah doth with mildness flow,
   And full of mercy standeth he:
Great doubt if he to wrath more slow,
   Or unto pardon prompter be.   25
   For naught is from his bounty free:
      His mercies do on all things fall
      That he hath made, and he made all.

4 frame] compose   9 eft] again   26 naught] nothing

Thus, Lord, all creatures thou hast wrought,
    Though dumb, shall their Creator sound: 30
But who can utt'rance add to thought,
    They most whom special bonds have bound
    (For best they can, who best have found)
        Shall blaze thy strength, and glad relate
        Thy more than glorious kingdom's state;°   35

That all may know the state, the strength,
    Thy more than glorious kingdom shows,
Which longest time to timeless length
    Leaves undefined; nor age's close
    As age to age succeeding grows   40
        Can with unsteadfast change procure°
        But still it must, and steadfast dure.

Thou dost the faint from falling stay,
    Nay, more, the fall'n again dost raise:
On thee their looks all creatures lay,   45
    Whose hunger in due time allays
    Thy hand, which when thy will displays,
        Then all that on the air do feed,
        Receive besides what food they need.

Each way, each working of thy hand   50
    Declare thou art both just and kind,
And nigh to all dost alway stand
    Who thee invoke, invoke with mind,
    Not only mouth: oh, they shall find,
        He will his fearers' wish fulfil,   55
        Attend their cry, and cure their ill.

He will his lovers all preserve;
    He will the wicked all destroy:
To praise him then as these deserve,

---

30 sound] celebrate   34 blaze] proclaim   42 dure] endure
43 stay] support   46 allays] satisfies   55 his fearers] the godly

Oh, thou my mouth thy might employ: 60
Nay, all that breathe, record with joy
  His sacred name's eternal praise,
  While race you run of breathing days.°

Psalm 146

. Lauda, anima mea

Up, up, my soul, advance Jehovah's praise.°
  His only praise: for fixèd is in me
To praise Jehovah all my living days
  And sing my God, until I cease to be.
    Oh, let not this decree°   5
      A fond conceit deface,
        That trust thou may'st in earthy prince's place:
          That any son of man
          Can thee preserve, for not himself he can.°

His strength is none: if any, in his breath,   10
  Which vapoured forth to mother earth he goes:
Nay, more, in him, his thoughts all find their death.
  But blessed he, who for his succour knows
    The God that Jacob chose:
      Whose rightly levelled hope   15
      His God Jehovah makes his only scope,
        So strong, he built the skies,°
        The fields, the waves, and all that in them lies.

He endless true doth yield the wrongèd right,
  The hungry feeds, and sets the fettered free: 20
The lame to limbs, the blind restores to sight,
  Loveth the just, protects who strangers be.
    The widow's pillar he,

---

63 breathing] living
Psalm 146 6 conceit] thought   7 earthy] earthly   13 succour] help

He orphans doth support:
But heavy lies upon the godless sort. 25
   He everlasting reigns:
   Zion, thy God from age to age remains.

Psalm 147

Laudate Dominum

Sing to the Lord: for what can better be,
   Than of our God that we the honour sing?°
With seemly pleasure what can more agree,
   Than praiseful voice, and touch of tunèd string?
   For, lo, the Lord again to form doth bring 5
     Jerusalem's long ruinated walls:
And Jacob's house, which all the earth did see
     Dispersèd erst, to union now recalls.
       And now by him their broken hearts made sound,
       And now by him their bleeding wounds are bound. 10

For what could not, who can the number tell
   Of stars, the torches of his heav'nly hall?
And tell so readily, he knoweth well
   How every star by proper name to call.
   What great to him, whose greatness doth not fall 15
     Within precincts? Whose pow'r no limits stay?°
Whose knowledges all number so excel,
     Not numb'ring number can their number lay?
       Easy to him to lift the lowly just:
       Easy to down proud wicked to the dust. 20

Oh, then Jehovah's causeful honour sing,
   His, whom our God we by his goodness find;
Oh, make harmonious mix of voice and string

---

27 Zion] house of the God of Israel

Psalm 147 8 erst] formerly   11 tell] count   16 precincts] boundaries
16 stay] hinder   18 lay] express   21 causeful] well-founded

To him, by whom the skies with clouds are lined:
   By whom the rain from clouds to drop assigned   25
      Supples the clods of summer-scorchèd fields,
Fresheth the mountains with such needful spring,
     Fuel of life to mountain cattle yields,
        From whom young ravens careless old forsake,
        Croaking to him of alms their diet take.°   30

The stately shape, the force of bravest steed
   Is far too weak to work in him delight:
No more in him can any pleasure breed
   In flying footman foot of nimblest flight.
     Nay, which is more, his fearers in his sight   35
      Can well of nothing, but his bounty brave,
Which never failing, never lets them need,
     Who fixed their hopes upon his mercies have.
        O, then Jerusalem, Jehovah praise,
        With honour due thy God, O, Zion, raise.   40

His strength it is thy gates doth surely bar;
   His grace in thee thy children multiplies:
By him thy borders lie secure from war,
   And finest flour thy hunger satisfies.
     Nor means he needs: for fast his pleasure flies,   45
      Borne by his word, when aught him list to bid.
Snow's woolly locks by him wide scattered are,
     And hoary plains with frost, as ashes, hid.
        Gross icy gobbets from his hand he flings,
        And blows a cold too strong for strongest things.   50

He bids again, and ice in water flows
   As water erst in ice congealèd lay:
Abroad the southern wind, his melter, goes,
   The streams relenting take their wonted way.

26 Supples] softens   35 his fearers] the godly   40 Zion] house of the God of Israel
46 aught] anything   list] desire   49 Gross] large   gobbets] lumps
54 wonted] accustomed

Oh, much is this, but more I come to say,   55
   The words of life he hath to Jacob told:
Taught Israel, who by his teaching knows
   What laws in life, what rules he wills to hold.
     No nation else hath found him half so kind,
     For to his light what other is not blind.°   60

Psalm 148

Laudate Dominum

Inhabitants of heav'nly land,
   As loving subjects praise your king:
You that among them highest stand,
   In highest notes Jehovah sing.
     Sing, angels all on careful wing,°   5
      You that his heralds fly,
   And you whom he doth soldiers bring
      In field his force to try.

Oh, praise him, sun, the sea of light,
   Oh, praise him, moon, the light of sea.°   10
You pretty stars in robe of night
   As spangles twinkling, do as they.
     Thou sphere within whose bosom play
      The rest that earth emball,°
   You waters banked with starry bay,   15
     Oh, praise, oh, praise him all.

All these, I say, advance that name,
   That doth eternal being show:°
Who bidding, into form and frame,
   Not being yet, they all did grow,   20
     All formèd, framèd, founded so,
      Till age's utmost date,°

8 try] test

They place retain, they order know,
   They keep their first estate.

When heav'n hath praised, praise earth anew:°					25
   You dragons first, her deepest guests;
Then soundless deeps, and what in you
   Residing low or moves or rests;
   You flames affrighting mortal breasts;
     You stones that clouds do cast;					30
   You feathery snows from winter's nests;
     You vapours, sun's appast;

You boist'rous winds, whose breath fulfils
   What in his word his will sets down;
Ambitious mountains, courteous hills;					35
   You trees that hills and mountains crown,
   Both you that proud of native gown
     Stand fresh or tall to see,
   And you that have your more renown,
     By what you bear, than be;°					40

You beasts in woods untamed that range,
   You that with men familiar go;
You that your place by creeping change,
   Or airy streams with feathers row;
   You stately kings, you subjects low,					45
     You lords and judges all,
   You others whose distinctions show,
     How sex or age may fall:

All these, I say, advance that name
   More high than skies, more low than ground.					50
And since advancèd by the same,
   You Jacob's sons, stand chiefly bound;
   You Jacob's sons, be chief to sound
     Your God Jehovah's praise.

27 soundless] unfathomable   28 or . . . or] either . . . or
30 stones] hailstones   32 appast] food   37 native gown] foliage

So fits them well on whom is found,   55
  Such bliss on you he lays.

Psalm 149

Cantate Domino

In an erst unusèd song
  To Jehovah lift your voices:
Make his favourites among
  Sound his praise with cheerful noises.°
    Jacob, thou with joy relate   5
    Him that hath reframed thy state:
  Sons whom Zion entertaineth,
  Boast in him who on you reigneth.

Play on harp, on tabret play;
  Dance Jehovah public dances:°   10
He their state that on him stay,
  Most afflicted, most advances.
    Oh, how glad his saints I see!
    Ev'n in bed how glad they be!
  Heav'nly hymns with throat unfolding,   15
  Swords in hand twice-edgèd holding,

Plague and chastise that they may°
  Nations such as erst them painèd:
Yea, their kings in fetters lay,
  Lay their nobles fast enchainèd,   20
    That the doom no stay may let
    By his sentence on them set.
  Lo, what honour all expecteth
  Whom the Lord with love affecteth!

1 erst] formerly   7 Zion] house of the God of Israel   8 on you] over you
9 tabret] small tabor or drum   11 stay] rely   21 doom] judgement
stay] delay   let] prevent

Psalm 150

Laudate Dominum

Oh, laud the Lord, the God of hosts commend,
 Exalt his pow'r, advance his holiness:
 With all your might lift his almightiness;
Your greatest praise upon his greatness spend.

Make trumpet's noise in shrillest notes ascend;   5
 Make lute and lyre his lovèd fame express:
 Him let the pipe, him let the tabret bless,
Him organs' breath, that winds or waters lend.

Let ringing timbrels so his honour sound,
 Let sounding cymbals so his glory ring,   10
That in their tunes such melody be found,
 As fits the pomp of most triumphant king.

 Conclude: by all that air or life enfold,°
 Let high Jehovah highly be extolled.

---

7 tabret] small tabor or drum 9 timbrels] tambourines

EXPLANATORY NOTES

Geneva = The Geneva Bible (1560, revised 1587, 1599), containing numerous interpretative marginal glosses. Old Version = *The Whole Book of Psalms* (1562 and constantly reprinted), popularly known as Sternhold and Hopkins, the metrical version of the Psalms sung in English worship and devotion. Parker = *The Whole Psalter* (1567), the metrical version of the Psalms by Archbishop Matthew Parker. BCP = The Book of Common Prayer (1549, revised 1552, 1559), regularly including the Psalter as translated (1535) by Miles Coverdale and included in the 1539 Great Bible. The Psalter comprises a collection of 150 songs or Psalms. The numbering of the Hebrew Bible, followed in the Sidneys' versions, is from Psalm 10 to Psalm 148 one ahead of the Greek and Vulgate versions, in which Psalms 9 and 10 and 114 and 115 are joined but Psalms 116 and 147 are divided into two separate Psalms.

DEDICATORY POEMS

John Donne's 'Upon the Translation of the Psalms by Sir Philip Sidney, and the Countess of Pembroke His Sister' expresses profound appreciation of the Sidneian *Psalms* by one of the age's greatest poets and most prominent churchmen, and—as Gary Stringer has suggested ('Donne's Dedication of the Sidney Psalter,' *John Donne Journal*, 27 (2008), 197–211—may have been written about 1625 as a preface to a projected edition. Donne's poem was first printed in the 1635 edition of his collected *Poems* and was very likely set into type from a manuscript written in Donne's autograph, one of only a handful of Donne poems of which this can be said. On grounds that the accidentals in that edition may be largely authorial, the modernized rendition presented here retains most of the original's punctuation, the capitals on (especially) words referring to the deity, and the emphatic italics in lines 22 and 45. Only two substantive emendations have been made to the text: line 41: 'reformed. Would' emended from 'reform'd; Would'; line 46: 'this Moses' emended from 'thy *Moses*'. This edition of the Sidney Psalter includes the Donne poem as a dedicatory poem, even though it never appeared as such in manuscript or print, because it serves this function, and may have been intended to by its author.

'Even now that care' and 'To the Angel Spirit of the Most Excellent Sir Philip Sidney' are Dedicatory Poems in Tixall.

THE PSALMS OF DAVID

Psalm 1

The translations of Sir Philip Sidney begin here.

This Psalm acts as a preface to the whole Psalter, summarizing its moral teachings and celebrating the happiness of the godly in contrast to the ruin of the ungodly. Strong emphasis is placed upon personal moral choice, in which the virtuous will ultimately enjoy a rooted existence and a productive life while the wicked will lack roots and suffer ruinous death.

   3 *Ne for bad mates*: nor for undesirable company.

   5 *God's law*: either the Torah (Hebrew for the first five books of the Bible, or more generally, divine teachings) or divine authority and instruction.

7–8 *He shall be . . . neighbours be*: cf. Psalm 52. 29–32.

  13 *like chaff with wind*: like chaff dispersed by the wind from the threshing floor.

Psalm 2

A royal Psalm addressed to rebellious kings. They are exhorted to embrace the absolute authority of God. See also Psalm 110. This Psalm has also been endowed with a messianic significance and within a New Testament context (cf. Matthew 3: 17) can be taken as referring to Christ.

1–2 *mean/To mutter murmurs*: an alliterative imitation of the murmuring being described.

   6 *anointed king*: the divinely authorized power of the King of Israel was confirmed through anointing.

   8 *yokes*: 'cords' in both BCP and Geneva. Cf. Matthew. 11: 30.

  11 *with breath of wrathful fire*: echoed in lines 28–9.

Psalm 3

A morning prayer of the Psalmist when falsely accused, often taken to refer to David's flight from his son Absalom. The Psalm laments the power of malicious enemies but concludes with an expression of resolute trust in God's love.

  10 *build*: build your hopes.

Psalm 4

An evening prayer (see lines 19–20 and 31–5), assumed (in Geneva) to have been composed under the same circumstances as Psalm 3, in which the Psalmist pleads for Divine support and reproves his enemies. The Psalm concludes with an expression of absolute trust in God's love.

  16 *tremble then with awful will*: be deeply moved with religious awe or desire.

  22 *on justice stayed*: desire for justice is limited by what can be achieved by just means.

  35 *nest*: Philip Sidney's addition, borrowing a familiar metaphor from other Psalms.

Psalm 5

The Psalmist's prayer professes his loyalty to God and appeals for vengeance against the Lord's wicked and foolish enemies.

   7 *prime*: the first of the lesser offices of the Roman breviary, usually 6 a.m. or sunrise.

8 *waiting*: adopted from Geneva's 'I will wait'.

19 *knees of my heart will fold*: replacing 'worship' in the BCP and Geneva with this emblematic image, derived from the Wedderburns' popular *Spiritual Sangis* (see *The Poems of Philip Sidney*, ed. William A. Ringler, Jr. (Oxford: Clarendon Press, 1962), 510).

25–30 *For in their mouth . . . the thinkers' ruin be*: linking the sources of sin, *souls* (line 26), and *thoughts* (line 30), with the routes through which sinfulness may be verbally expressed: *mouth* (line 25), *throat* (line 27), and *tongue* (line 28).

33 *trust on thee do bend*: fasten or place their trust in God.

Psalm 6

The first of the seven Penitential Psalms (6, 32, 38, 51, 102, 130, 143), a terminology used since the seventh century CE to denote Psalms of special relevance to repentance. Here the Psalmist appeals to God in his extreme sickness but ultimately hopes through faith to triumph over his enemies. Sickness was often interpreted as a sign of God's displeasure but here the Psalmist attributes it to the malice of his *swarm of foes* (line 23).

5 *mercy*: from the Hebrew *hesed*, usually translated as 'mercy' or 'love', denoting God's Divine fidelity and eternal love towards humans.

14–16 *For death . . . A heav'nly story?*: there are no psalms or songs of praise in the world of the dead.

Psalm 7

The Psalmist protests his innocence under persecution and calls on God for vengeance against the malice of his enemies.

4 *he*: a reference to a specific enemy. David had been accused of traitorous conspiracy against his sovereign by King Saul or by Cush, one of his courtiers.

10 *unkind for friendly part*: repaid friendship with evil.

16 *in wrath thyself up set*: prepare to act in anger.

Psalm 8

The glory and munificence of God are magnified through his works and by his love for humankind. The Psalmist is very much aware of the smallness of humankind in comparison with the infinite grandeur of the Creator.

1–2 *O Lord . . . doth shine*: the repetition of these first two lines at the end of the Psalm follows BCP.

5–6 *From sucklings . . . from babies' tongue*: out of the mouths of babes and infants, recalling the children who acclaimed Christ's entry into Jerusalem. The phrase also emphasizes for Christians the natural state of innocence into which humankind is born.

12 *life no life*: God is the source of life.

13–24 *what is this man . . . reignèd*: although frail and sinful, man was yet made in the image and likeness of God. As the appointed ruler over natural creation he should joyfully celebrate his position between the spiritual and material worlds.

29–32 *The bird . . . his rule embraceth*: cf. BCP: 'The fowls of the air, and the fishes of the sea: and whatsoever walketh through the paths of the seas'.

Psalm 9

This Psalm, proclaiming the execution of God's judgement on the wicked, and Psalm 10 were originally one poem (as in the Greek and Vulgate). They formed a single acrostic poem with each verse beginning with a successive letter of the Hebrew alphabet (although several letters were omitted). They were perhaps composed after the death of David's son Absalom, or to commemorate the death of Goliath, the champion of Gath (1 Samuel 17). Both Psalms seems to focus upon a hope for God's intercession on behalf of the helpless and oppressed.

42 *Of Zion's daughter*: in mythology cities were sometimes personified as a female or queen, representing the spouse of the god of the city.

51 For then the Lord is revealed to reign in Divine judgement.

53 *When wicked souls be turned to hellish pain*: Philip turns the literal Hell of the Psalm into a metaphorical and psychological one.

Psalm 10

The Psalmist laments the withdrawal of God's support and the deeds of the wicked who persecuted him during God's absence. He earnestly supplicates for Divine intervention.

15–16 *he fancies this:/The name of God a fable is*: the wicked act in denial of Divine providence, as though there is no God at all.

Psalm 11

A simple but moving song of trust. The virtuous and innocent man is hunted like a bird but places his confidence in God's protection over those who seek sanctuary in the Temple.

10 *ground-plot's fall*: the destruction of foundations, implicitly suggesting the collapse of the foundations of lawful society and public order. Cf. Psalm 82. 18.

17–24 *The Lord doth search . . . to God inclinèd*: a powerful rendition of the traditional opposition of God's vanquishing wrath and embracing love.

Psalm 12

Despairing of human support perhaps during the reign of King Saul, David chooses to depend absolutely upon God's promises. The Psalm is not simply a cry for vengeance but more an expression of hope that God's justice will hold sway over the earth.

12 *brave*: Mary's substitution of *brave* for Philip's *bold* obliterates his apparently intended polyptoton: *bold emboldened*.

20–21 *Pure . . . hath spent his earthy parts*: God's word is like silver found already pure in the earth rather than having to be refined by smelting.

25 *each side*: Philip's rendering of the Bible's 'on every side'.

Psalm 13

In extreme distress perhaps through illness, the Psalmist laments the apparent delay in Divine intervention but ends by joyfully reaffirming his absolute trust in God's mercy.

1 *How long . . . forgotten be?*: BCP opens: 'How long wilt thou forget me (O Lord) for ever?'

Psalm 14

The Psalmist laments the folly of the godless man but confirms God's power to punish and reward just human behaviour. This version follows Geneva and omits verses 5–7 of BCP. See also Psalm 53 for virtually an exact duplicate of this Psalm.

1 *foolish*: wicked or ignorant of virtue.

8 *clayey*: referring to Adam's creation out of dust.

14 *These cannibals*: a figure of speech derived from the prophets. The term 'cannibals' was only introduced into English during the mid-sixteenth century, following contact with Caribbean natives.

Psalm 15

The Psalmist describes the virtues required of a righteous man who wishes to dwell in the presence of God. The Psalm may be read as an Israelite seeking admission to the court of the Temple and enquiring as to appropriate behaviour within God's precincts.

11 *biting usury*: the prohibition of usury, viewed here as *biting* or harmful, since assistance to the poor should be viewed as a charitable gift, is found in Exodus 22: 24–5, Leviticus 25: 36–7, and Deuteronomy 23: 19–20.

Psalm 16

The Psalmist reveals his hatred of idolatry and reaffirms the need to place absolute trust in God's power. This version is translated from Beza.

13–18 *God my only portion is . . . partage got?*: the references to *portion*, *child's part*, *lot'* and *partage* implicitly recall how plots of land were measured out and allotted to families, to be passed down to succeeding generations.

Psalm 17

In the depths of distress, the Psalmist protests his innocence and devotion and pleads for support in escaping the persecution of his enemies. The Psalm ends with a confidently expressed faith in the Lord.

25–6 *apple of an eye . . . wings' shade*: traditional images of God's loving care and protection, the former entering into common usage from the Bible.

33–6 *Now like a lion . . . those watching paws*: in a vivid extended metaphor, the Psalmist's enemies are depicted as ravenous lions.

47–8 *When waking . . . in likeness thine*: the morning awakening was traditionally the time for God's favours and deliverance of justice. It is sometimes taken as the context of this Psalm that David had taken sanctuary for the night within the Temple at Jerusalem.

Psalm 18

A royal thanksgiving Psalm for a military victory, appropriately for its heroic subject cast in hexameters in rhyme royal. David praises God for his many and generous blessings (cf. 2 Samuel 22). The first part of the Psalm utilizes the ancient language of mythic battles of floods and earthquakes to represent God's heroic rescue of David from his enemies.

2 *my strongest rock*: in BCP, God is frequently referred to as the 'Rock of Israel' and especially the bulwark of David's people.

4 *my ever-saving horn*: the horn of the bull is a traditional symbol of strength and fertility.

10 *winding sheet*: in which the corpse is wrapped for burial.

15 *And so the earth did fall* . . .: here begins the description of God's epic and triumphant intervention to save the Psalmist.

22 *cherubims*: cf. Exodus 25: 18–20 and 37: 6–9 for the cherubs above the Ark, inspiring the prophet Ezekiel's vision of the Chariot of God (Ezekiel 1: 5–13). Cherubs were winged creatures derived from mythology and cherubim were God's throne-bearers.

63 *iron bow*: a hyperbole, suggesting the extraordinary strength required to bend a bow made of metal.

Psalm 19

A hymn in praise of God's heavenly creations for the world, particularly the sun, and a celebration of the potency of his laws. It may have originally been two distinct psalms, one in praise of Shamash, the Babylonian sun-god, adapted for Hebrew use; and the second an ode in praise of the law as a reflection of God's wisdom.

9–14 *There is no speech* . . . *proceeding*: an allusion to the ancient idea that the stars are the silent 'writing of the heavens'. The regular alternation of the heavens between day and night also silently reminds humans of God's power and wisdom.

37–8 *Of him the fear* . . . *for ever*: Geneva: 'The fear of the Lord is clean, and endureth for ever.'

Psalm 20

A prayer to support the king in all his exploits and for Divine protection to be granted to him. It was perhaps originally composed as a prayer for success in one of David's military encounters.

22 *his own anointed*: the king of Israel.

27 *chivalry*: replacing 'horses' in both BCP and Geneva, perhaps to echo the Sidney family's long tradition of chivalric military service to the monarch.

Psalm 21

A royal and messianic Psalm in two parts, offering ecstatic praise to God (lines 1–24) and then giving thanks for a victory and expressing confidence in future success (lines 25–52).

Psalm 22

An intensely passionate lament of the persecuted and innocent man, concluding with thanksgiving and an invitation to praise God. This Psalm is of great importance to the New Testament since its opening words recall those spoken by Christ on the cross (Mark 15: 34; Matthew 27: 46). They are also reminiscent of the lament of the suffering servant in Isaiah 52: 13–53: 12.

11 *Our fathers . . . did bear*: Geneva: 'Our fathers trusted in thee'.

15 *I a worm*: the Psalmist's sense of dehumanization is especially strong in this Psalm.

28–30 *mighty bulls . . . lions*: the enemies of the Psalmist are depicted in dehumanized forms as wild animals.

38 When the body is reduced to dust.

48 *doggèd might*: a pun, playing against the literal *dogs* (line 40).

57 *hid from him his face's fair oppearing*: God turning his face away is a traditional metaphor for the withdrawal of his grace and favour.

61 *Th'afflicted then shall eat*: an allusion to the messianic banquet in Isaiah 55: 1 ff.

Psalm 23

This Psalm, perhaps the most famous in BCP, celebrates the Psalmist's confidence in God's infinite love and grace which is focused here on the figure of the good shepherd. God as a good shepherd is central to both the Old and New Testaments (see Ezekiel 34: 11–16 and John 10: 11–18).

4 *green pasture*: fresh-grown grass prompted by vitalizing rainfall.

5 *waters still*: tranquil waters to rest beside.

19 *Thou oil'st my head, thou fill'st my cup*: a traditional eastern gesture of hospitality.

Psalm 24

A hymn of praise, celebrating God's Lordship over the world and exhorting the listener to receive him. This Psalm was perhaps penned for the use of the Hebrews when David brought up the Ark of God to Jerusalem or when Solomon brought it into the Temple. See 2 Samuel 6 and 1 Kings 8. The temple was regarded as a physical affirmation of the Creation and worshippers were required to affirm their fidelity before entering the sanctuary.

7 *hurtless hands*: clean hands free from the stain of sin.

17 *Lift up your heads, you gates*: a difficult line to interpret literally since portcullis gates, which were raised and lowered, were unknown in the ancient world.

Psalm 25

An acrostic Psalm in the original Hebrew, confirming the Psalmist's commitment to prayer for remission from sins and help in affliction. In the Hebrew text each verse begins with a successive letter of the Hebrew alphabet.

25–6 *remember not / Sins brewed in youthful glass*: unlike the Bible's general reference to sinfulness here, Philip focuses upon drunkenness.

60 *I am poor and least of all*: I am poor and all have left me; cf. Geneva: 'For I am desolate and poor.'

Psalm 26

The Psalmist protests his innocence to God as a true believer. He asserts his own integrity, his aversion to sin and sinner, and his dependence upon God's mercy.

12 *That from . . . depart*: metrically defective line, lacking two syllables in most of the early authoritative manuscripts.

20 *washèd*: the washing of hands was of liturgical importance, symbolizing outer cleanness and inner purity (see Exodus 30: 19, 21; 40: 31–2; and Isaiah 1: 16).

30 *blood-seekers' case*: BCP: 'blood-thirsty', Geneva: 'the bloody men'.

Psalm 27

In an especially close paraphrase of their original, Philip's Psalmist reasserts through prayer his trust in the power and protection of God. It has generally been read as comprising two distinct sections. The first (lines 1–36) is confident of God's guiding light and intervention but the second (lines 37–60) is much more fraught.

10 *My very flesh for to devour*: the enemies of the Psalmist are again dehumanized as ravenous beasts. Cf. Psalm 22. 30.

17–18 *In this I would / My trust still hold*: Geneva explains this trust in a note: 'That God will deliver me, and give my faith the victory.'

39 *'Seek ye my face'*: to seek to know God and to dwell in his presence or commune with Him in the Temple.

Psalm 28

A prayer prompted by the Psalmist's great distress and tribulations. It begins with his fear of death but concludes with thanksgiving for God's support.

8 *sanctuary*: the innermost area of the Temple containing the Ark.

11 *selfsame chain*: an original image, not in any of the usual sources for the Sidney Psalter.

24 *But let me give praises high*: there is here a marked shift of tone from distress into earnest thanksgiving, sometimes attributed to the receipt of a priestly or prophetic oracle.

Psalm 29

An exhortation to give glory to God for his all-pervasive powers and presence. This is the ancient Psalm for Pentecost, celebrating the day of God's coming in power and might.

7 *His voice*: the insistent repetition of the phrase *His voice* in this Psalm suggests the elemental power of God's authority.

16–18 *Like young calves . . . like young unicorn*: he made Leban (Lebanon) skip like a calf and Shirion (the Phoenician name for Mount Hermon, see Deuteronomy 3: 9) skip like a unicorn.

20 Deserts trembling have experienced his voice.

21 *Ev'n deserts*: the desert of Kadesh, probably to the north of Palestine.

25 *He sits on seas*: the Flood was the first great manifestation of God's absolute power over the earth. Alternatively, it may indicate the primeval sea of chaos upon which order was imposed by the Creation.

Psalm 30

A thanksgiving Psalm in praise of God's merciful deliverance after mortal danger, perhaps composed for the dedication of David's new palace at Jerusalem (2 Samuel 5: 11) or for its dedication after it had been polluted by Absalom (2 Samuel 16).

2–4 *foes' . . . woes*: internal rhyme, connected by sound as well as sense.

28 *earth*: substituted by Mary for Philip's *'dust'*, presumably to avoid the repetition of *dust* (line 30) in the same stanza but also perhaps to contrast the animated *earth* with lifeless dust.

Psalm 31

A prayer to God for help in times of ordeal, reasserting the Psalmist's absolute trust in God's righteousness. Despite the unjust accusations of his enemies and a fear of death, the Psalmist makes a solemn commitment of himself to God's mercy and loving care.

6–7 *forteress*: trisyllabic spelling for metre and rhyme, reflecting the Old French origin of the word.

13 *Into thy hands . . . my sprite*: Jesus utters these words on the Cross with his last breath (only included in Luke 23: 46). The verse is used as an antiphon in the Office at Compline, the last prayer of the day.

36 *broken pot*: *un pot cassé* in Beza; 'broken vessel' in Geneva and BCP. This is a common biblical comparison for something shattered or useless (Isaiah 30: 14 and Jeremiah 19: 11; 22: 28) and is echoed in *bake* (line 42).

57 *pavilions*: Philip's rendering here of the Bible's 'tabernacle' shifts the contexts towards courtly pageantry.

Psalm 32

The second of the Penitential Psalms and an individual thanksgiving, advocating the candid confession of sin as a means of easing the conscience and avoiding sickness.

22 *flood of straying streams*: a metaphorical representation of the dangers surrounding humanity.

Psalm 33

A joyous praise of God for his infinite goodness, power, and providence. This Psalm celebrates the productive union of song and prayer in the Psalms.

It confirms God's absolute powers, as manifested in the works of the Creation, and his sovereign dominion over the whole world.

12 To witness you rejoice.

23 *all that host*: the stars in the heavens.

Psalm 34

A Thanksgiving Psalm, offering the Psalmist's praise of God's infinite powers and Divine justice. It was probably composed when Achish (or Abimelech), King of Gath, drove David, who feigned madness, from his court (1 Samuel 21: 10–16).

41 *children*: the traditional term in wisdom literature for students and others who wish to learn rather than merely infants and the young.

Psalm 35

The earnest lament of a virtuous man, suffering from oppression by his enemies. The persecuted figure of the Psalmist in this Psalm is sometimes compared by Christian readers to the figure of Christ. He supplicates that God will espouse his cause and defeat the expectations of his enemies.

Psalm 36

This Psalm condemns the grievous wickedness of the sinner and then celebrates the excellency and goodness of God's mercy.

8 *hatred get*: receive punishment from God.

21 *shadow of thy wing*: a common metaphor in the Psalms for Divine protection, perhaps referring to the winged cherubims in the Holy of Holies of the Temple (1 Kings 6: 23–8, 32; Ezekiel 1: 4–9).

Psalm 37

In this heavily didactic Psalm the Psalmist compares the different fate of the virtuous and the wicked. The Old Testament often poses the question as to why the wicked seemed to prosper and the innocent suffer. Here it is argued that God's power will ultimately reverse things, granting rewards to the virtuous and punishing the evil. Cf. Psalm 73 for a similar argument.

5–6 *grass . . . wither*: cf. Isaiah 40: 7.

29 *meek men shall the earth possess*: the Beatitudes of the New Testament (Matthew 5: 3–12; Luke 6: 20–6) are heavily influenced by this Psalm, especially in the reversal of the present in the hope of a happy and rewarded future.

73–6 *the righteous minds . . . within his limits binds*: Geneva: 'The righteous men shall inherit the land, and dwell therein for ever.'

Psalm 38

One of the Penitential Psalms and the moving prayer of a devout man in dire sickness and distress. The Psalm reveals a remarkable patience and resignation in the face of physical troubles and a fervent hope that God will mitigate human sufferings.

Psalm 39

The Psalmist focuses on the insignificance of man before God and as a sinner pleads to be saved from his transgressions. It evokes a violent struggle in the Psalmist's own mind between grace and corruption and between passion and patience.

15 *thou a span's length, mad'st my living line*: you made my life (*living line*) equivalent to a *span* (a stretch of time or life), perhaps alluding to the Fates spinning, measuring, and cutting the thread of life.

32 *thy handy strokes*: strokes given by your hands.

Psalm 40

A thanksgiving Psalm combined with a personal lament. It confirms the benefit of confidence in God's compassion and mercy, offering both a hymn of thanksgiving and a cry of distress; cf. Psalm 70. *All the French Tunes with English Words* (1632) contained possible adaptations of Psalms 40–2 of the Sidney Psalter.

12 *New song*: a song prompted by the new action of God.

25–7 *Thou sacrifice nor off'ring . . . didst crave*: God prefers loyal obedience to mere sacrifice and offerings. Cf. Psalm 51.

70 *make no stay*: cf. Psalm 70.24.

Psalm 41

The prayer of the sick man oppressed by his enemies who turns to God for succour and a merciful deliverance.

11 *sick*: Philip eliminates the poor who are usually included in other translations.

29–32 *my friend . . . Did kick against my state*: see John 13: 18 for a comparable description of Judas, drawing on this Psalm, as a false friend to Jesus.

Psalm 42

This and the next Psalm were originally one Psalm in three sections with chorus. The Psalmist is exiled in the north and cannot attend the Temple in Jerusalem, perhaps because of the rebellion of Absalom (2 Samuel 13–18). He encourages his soul to trust in God and hopes once again to join the worshipping crowds.

26 *Hermon's dwelling*: Mount Hermon is situated at the southern tip of the Anti-Lebanon mountain range and was regarded as the northern boundary of the Promised Land (Deuteronomy 3: 8). It has also been identified as the possible site of the Transfiguration of Jesus in the presence of Peter, James, and John.

28 *Mizar's hilly head*: an unidentified hill, presumed to be in the same range as Mount Hermon.

29 *noise of his fall*: this suggests a waterfall among the deep waters.

Psalm 43

The Psalmist prays to return to the Temple, laments his ungodly and unjust oppressors, and promises his loyal service to God.

13 *thy truth and light*: these two Divine attributes are often personified as guides for the pilgrimage.

17 *Tabernacle*: the Temple at Jerusalem.

Psalm 44

The translations of Mary Sidney Herbert, Countess of Pembroke, begin here.

The speaker knows of God's previous deliverance when Israel was empowered to overcome its enemies. Now God seems to have deserted them to be enslaved and mocked, even though they have continued to obey the covenant.

5–8 *How thy hand . . . wanting*: God makes *that branch*, i.e. *the pagan foe*, to be *Leafless*, while this branch, i.e. *thy folk*, brings forth green leaves, i.e. *verdure*.

17 I stand under your authority.

28 The sword (i.e. God) by which I should make myself safe.

37 *that*: we who.

50 *as balls of scorn*: cf. Isaiah 22: 18.

60 *blush*: cf. Psalm 40. 52: 'blush for shame'.

77 Would not God have been able to detect any duplicity or apostasy on our part?

Psalm 45

This Psalm, traditionally read as an epithalamium or wedding poem for Solomon's marriage to a young Egyptian princess, was often allegorized by Christians as a metaphor for Christ and the Church as his bride. From line 37 the song is addressed to the bride herself, emphasizing the experience of a young woman facing an arranged marriage, and promising that if she obeys her husband, then she will command many others. Mary draws on her own experience both of an arranged marriage that brought her increased wealth and status and also of her days at Elizabeth's court in her description of the duties of the 'maids of honour' (line 54) with some hint of competition among the ladies for 'more favour' (line 55).

13 *right hand*: metaphorically, righteous hand. Cf. lines 22–4.

17–20 *Sharp . . . to undergo thy hand*: God's power, as demonstrated in the way he deals with those who even contemplate rebellion, also makes those without noble rank (*the meaner people*) glad (*fain*) to submit to his rule (*thy hand*) with willing hearts.

36 *Ophir*: a biblical place name, unidentified except as a source of gold.

42 The queen's beauty will produce and maintain the king's delight.

45–6 *both Tyrus . . . and richest nations mo*: Tyre and still more of the richest nations will be glad to offer gifts.

54–6 *Her maids of honour . . . their happy days to spend*: Mary elaborates on the biblical text by seeming to claim that the maids of honour gain favour by their association with the queen herself, with whom they will spend *their happy days*. Some of the women are nearer to the queen than others, which opens up the potential for envy. Cf. the reference to honour derived from the king in lines 33–4.

60 *left*: left behind (when the queen marries the king). Cf. line 40.

Psalm 46

A song of thanksgiving, sometimes attributed in Geneva to the deliverance of Jerusalem from Sennacherib or to some other intervention by the hand of God.

18 *kings with siege her walls enround*: Mary adds the idea of the besieged city to the biblical text.

Psalm 47

A song of praise for God's infinite power and mercies.

6–7 *From whose almighty grace . . . oppressed*: it is through God's grace that nations are oppressed by our power and humbled under our feet.

14 *you judgements sound*: probably a synecdoche for 'you people who have the capacity to judge, to make sound judgements'.

18–19 *The folk . . . great princes gains*: he gains great princes to befriend the folk of Abraham's God.

Psalm 48

A celebration of Mount Zion, the ancient nucleus of the holy city of Jerusalem which God protects.

13 *it*: the city.

19 *Tarshish*: Tartessus in Spain, representing distant lands attainable only by heavy-draft vessels. Cf. Isaiah 23: 1.

27 *both*: *fame* and *name* (line 28).

Psalm 49

The poet calls together an audience comprised of people of all social classes before singing the Psalm. The theme of the Psalm is the mutability of wealth and power.

15 *he*: *death* (line 14).

16 *tomb*: this substitution for the biblical word 'grave' underscores the futility of attempting to escape death by means of wealth; a glorious tomb does not prolong life. Cf. line 30.

26 *pit*: 'grave' in Geneva (verse 14) and 'hell' in BCP.

carrion food: Mary omits here both the comparison, 'Like sheep they lie in grave' (Geneva verse 14), and the promising metaphor of death as shepherd (BCP, verse 14).

29 *far his prince*: far above his lord.

Psalm 50

This Psalm explains that true faith in God and salvation lies not in outward ceremonies but in loyal praise and obedience.

3 *his word*: Mary's rendering of the biblical 'hath spoken' (verse 1) connects the giving of the law and the coming of Christ, the word as Logos. John 1: 1.

4 God shines out of beauty's beauty, Zion.

5 *ear and tongue*: Mary adds God listening as well as speaking (as in the biblical text).

13 *Then when*: at the time when the *eternal league* (line 12) was formed.

33 *Oh, no*: added to emphasize God's rejection of animal sacrifice (verse 14).

Psalm 51

The Septuagint headnote links this Psalm to King David's penitence after his rebuke by the prophet Nathan for adultery with Bathsheba and the murder of her husband Uriah (2 Samuel 11–12), alluded to in line 41. Usually known by its Latin incipit, '*Miserere mei*', it is the most influential and beloved of the seven Penitential Psalms (the others are 6, 32, 38, 102, 130, and 143) and has been frequently turned into poetry and sometimes set to music. Cf. versions by Petrarch, Thomas Wyatt, Anne Vaughan Lock (quoted in line 40), Mary Queen of Scots, Archbishop Matthew Parker, Richard Rowlands (also called Verstegan), George Sandys, and Thomas Carew. Mary emphasizes the Psalm's importance by using rhyme royal, seven lines of iambic pentameter rhymed *ababbcc*. Her version was set for high voice and lute in the seventeenth century (BL Additional MS 15117), possibly for a woman's private devotional use.

8–14 *For I, alas . . . may be regarded*: this verse of the Psalm was crucial to Luther's development of the Protestant doctrine of justification by faith.

13–14 *Thy doom . . . regarded*: God is presented as the offended party, judge, and witness. The general sense of the passage is that God's judgement (*doom*) as judge and evidence as witness with regard to the speaker's guilt (*awarded* with a just verdict) will be acknowledged as both righteous and true.

15–17 *My mother . . . she cherished me*: in Mary's paraphrase the mother cherishes her child even though she inadvertently transmits original sin.

23 *hyssop*: a herb used for cleansing lepers in Leviticus 14 and to give Jesus his last drink in John's account of the Crucifixion (19: 29).

52 *Salem's*: Jerusalem's. Salem also means 'peace' and thus plays on the *peace* and *peaceful place* of the next line.

56 *whole calves on altars be consumèd*: the apparent contradiction between verse 16, where God rejects burnt offerings, and verse 19, where he accepts them, has been variously interpreted. Sixteenth-century Protestants usually interpreted this final verse metaphorically, so that the offering is 'the calves of men's lips', as Calvin says (i.e. praise of God). Others (like Thomas Wyatt) simply omit the calves altogether, leaving the sacrifice a figurative one.

Psalm 52

An address to the wicked, depicting their destruction, and rejoicing in the security of those who trust in God alone.

1 *Tyrant*: either Saul or Doeg. Saul, who conspired against David and was told by Doeg the Edomite that David was at the house of the priest Ahimelech (1 Samuel 22: 9–23).

29–32 *I as an olive tree . . . My roots to nourish*: cf. Psalm 1. 7–8.

Psalm 53

An almost exact duplicate of Psalm 14 in the biblical text but given very different paraphrases by the Sidneys. This Psalm meditates on the folly of the wicked, who are oblivious to God's oversight as they devour the godly, and ignorant of their own impending judgement and destruction. God is imagined speaking in lines 9–16 and the Psalmist addresses God directly in lines 17–19.

3–4 *This fancy . . . on loathsome ill*: *rotten deeds* and *studies fixed on loathsome ill* are the subjects of *bewray* (reveal); *This fancy*, its object.

Psalm 54

A prayer for Divine favour and protection against enemies. Geneva identifies the Psalm with David, when he and his men hid out in the land of Ziph and were betrayed to Saul by the Ziphims (1 Samuel 23).

4 *heavy . . . light*: Mary adds the wordplay in the plea that *heavy*, or mournful, words not be taken lightly.

14–15 *with happy flight / Above my evils*: Mary adds an image of flight to the biblical text.

15 *evils*: monosyllabic.

Psalm 55

A prayer for deliverance from and vengeance against the treachery of a false friend and betrayer. Geneva identifies this Psalm as David's complaint against Saul. Henry Howard, Earl of Surrey, translated this Psalm just before his execution while he was in the Tower of London. It was his last poem, as well as the first in unrhymed English hexameters. His example seems to have prompted others to follow suit since it was also translated by Sir Thomas Smith while he was in the Tower. The Sidneys' uncle John Dudley, Earl of Warwick and Duke of Northumberland, also penned a poetic version when imprisoned in the Tower for supporting Lady Jane Grey as queen (BL Arundel MS 290). See also Psalm 94.

6 *My body . . . torment and tear*: Mary adds the idea of tearing the body, an ancient form of lamentation.

20–30 *Confound their counsels . . . bears the sway*: Mary expands the biblical personifications, adding the image of the masque and creating a mini-allegory. Cf. Proverbs 7–8.

45 *buried breathing in their bier*: Mary's alliterative phrase explains that they have been buried alive and that the earth has therefore become their bier.

56 *but kindness mere*: anything but kindness.

60 *than balm from wounded rind*: than soothing oil from the cut bark of a tree.

70–2 *who their thirst . . . in sunder shear*: Mary adds an allusion to the female Fates of classical mythology, who spin, measure, and cut the thread of life.

Psalm 56

The Psalmist prays for deliverance from his enemies and declares his trust in God, promising to praise him. Geneva identifies this Psalm as David's complaint before Achish, King of Gath (2 Samuel 21: 12).

3 *spies*: with relevance to courtly intrigues and conflicts, Mary adds to biblical 'enemies' (verse 3) the concept of being spied upon. Cf. Psalm 71. 32.

27 *these*: i.e. *These matters* (line 25).

37 *that*: thou that.

45 *light of life*: cf. Psalm 55. 69.

Psalm 57

A lamentation against the treacherous assaults of enemies with a plea for deliverance and a concluding song of praise. In the biblical text, the verses paraphrased in lines 31–54 (Psalm 57: 7–11) are virtually identical to the verses paraphrased in Psalm 108. 1–16 (Psalm 108. 1–5).

4 *Hide me, hive me*: Mary leaves implicit the bird imagery from BCP (verse 1): 'under the shadow of thy wings shall be my refuge', but seems to transform the creature from bird to bee.

10–12 *He shall down . . . love and verity*: Mary omits part of verse 3 that refers to 'the reproof of him that would swallow me up'.

12 *His love and verity*: the direct objects of *send* (verse 10).

14 *hands*: added to parallel the teeth and tongues in the biblical text.

34–5 *Wake my tongue . . . the consort make*: cf. the courtly despair of Sir Thomas Wyatt's 'My Lute Awake'. Mary develops the musical figure well beyond the original.

31–6 *My heart prepared . . . Myself will bear a part*: cf. Psalm 108. 1–8.

44–5 *far . . . star*: added to biblical 'heavens'. Cf. Psalm 10. 1–2.

49–54 *As high . . . of thy face*: refrain repeated from lines 19–24, as in biblical verses 5 and 11.

Psalm 58

A Psalm, including a series of curses against enemies (lines 17–28), in which the Psalmist denounces those wicked judges who had falsely condemned him as a traitor. Cf. Psalm 21.

3 *sons of dust*: Mary's original use of the biblical metaphor from Genesis 2: 7 (the creation of mankind from the 'dust of the ground'), is a subtle reminder of the tree of the knowledge of good and evil in Genesis 2: 9.

1–5 *And call ye this . . . Oh, no*: Mary emphasizes the rhetorical structure of question and answer, as though in a trial. Cf. a similar series of questions asked of unjust judges in Psalm 82.

8 *Just to yourselves . . . to none*: line added by Mary to underscore the partiality of worldly judges only to themselves, not to others.

9 *But what could they*: but what else could they do?

15 *aye missing of his end*: always failing in his purpose.

16 *she self-deaf*: the serpent is female in BCP, as in many medieval and Renaissance pictures of the serpent in the Garden of Eden. The image recalls the claim in bestiaries that asps supposedly stop their ears with their tails.

20 *ere past the shooter's hand*: before it moves past the shooter's hand.

22 *vital band*: probably a physiological reference to the umbilical cord but perhaps also incorporating a reminder of the mythological thread of the Fates.

25–8 *a brood of springing thorns . . . off by tempest blown*: Mary revises her original from flesh cooked over burning thorns to young thorns uprooted, allowing further development of the echoes of the tree and forbidden fruit.

31–2 *'The just . . . to each his own'*: cf. lines 1–4. God gives each person what that person deserves.

Psalm 59

Another personal prayer for deliverance from enemies and vengeance upon them, notable for the emphasis on God's *free grace* (lines 43, 89), and for the vivid dog imagery, expanded by Mary (lines 25–30, 67–78).

5–6 *Who make a trade . . . for blood do long*: Mary amplifies the biblical 'bloody' (Geneva verse 2) or 'blood-thirsty' (BCP) men, to explain that they have been raised in the family profession of murder.

13 But what does it matter if I am free from fault?

25–6 *When golden sun . . . Returned again*: the dog-like foes return at sunset.

41–2 *wait . . . wait*: wait as planning entrapment and as patient expectation.

43–4 *with thy free grace / Prevented*: an interpretive reference to the doctrine of Prevenient Grace (verse 10), derived from Paul and Augustine and developed by Luther and Calvin. This doctrine states that God's grace is bestowed on humans prior to and independent of any action they may take. It was held to establish that humans, though fallen, still had free will.

73–8 *Abroad they range . . . will lie*: expands dog metaphor, contrasting the barking of the dogs with the singing of the Psalmist.

Psalm 60

A national prayer for an end to God's wrath, demonstrated by defeat on the battlefield, and a request that God will once again inspire the armies of Israel to overcome their enemies, leading to the restoration of an enlarged and unified kingdom.

18 *I*: King David, speaking for the people.

21–40 *Then make a merry stay . . . for war to train*: God will triumph over Israel's traditional enemies, taking over their territories, and establish his

kingdom in Israel. Gilead, Sichem, and Succoth were territories con-
quered by Israel, Moab, Edom, and Philistia more recent enemies of Israel,
and Manasses one of the twelve tribes.

Psalm 61

The exiled Psalmist prays for God's protection and offers perpetual service to
Him.

   5 *From country banishèd*: Geneva notes: 'From the place, where I was
banished, being driven out of the City and Temple by my son Absalom.'

Psalm 62

A didactic song of confidence in God, instructing the people to rely on God
only, not on fraud, on force, or on riches.

  20 *Remove . . . move*: Mary's characteristic wordplay and rhetorical question
add emphasis and a sense of the speaking voice. Cf. line 4.

31–2 *lightness . . . lightness*: i.e. lightness's . . . lightness's (uninflected posses-
sive).

  35 *when*: cf. BCP and Geneva (verse 10): '*if* riches increase'. A revealing class
statement by Mary.

Psalm 63

The exiled Psalmist longs for God's sanctuary, praises God even in the wilder-
ness, and prophesies the destruction of his enemies.

   5 *this waterless, this weary waste*: the Argument and title in Geneva state the
occasion as David's exile 'in the wilderness of Judah' or 'Ziph', when he
was 'in great danger by Saul'.

  15 *here*: an allusion to the speaker's presence in the desert (verse 5). Even
here, in the wilderness, the Psalmist will praise God.

  21 *right right*: not a redundancy but rather an intensifier: just or righteous
right hand. Cf. Psalm 45. 13–14.

  27 *all that God adore*: the king will conceive high joy in God and in all those
who adore God.

Psalm 64

A prayer for personal deliverance against slanderers who were always active in
the world of the court.

   1 *entertain*: admit into consideration, but also with a figurative and/or
allegorical overlay of 'receive, give reception to' (i.e. at court).

  23 *sound and try*: take the measure of (as by sounding the depths) and find
out.

33–6 *Not one . . . entertain*: there is no one who shall witness this event and not
tell of it.

37–8 *In who . . . joy and hope*: the just shall joy and hope in God, who reigns
timeless.

Psalm 65

A Psalm of thanksgiving for God's protection after a good year and a bountiful harvest.

5–6 *There thou my sins . . . sacrificing flame*: Mary adds the metaphor of sins turning into the smoke of sacrifices, apparently derived from paying vows in verse 1, connected in Psalm 51 with animal sacrifice.

10 *of thy check-roll number makest*: Mary intensifies the courtly imagery in the biblical 'dwell in thy courts' (Geneva verse 4) by adding that they will be enrolled on the court payroll.

18 *cradle . . . of restless wavy plain*: the sea (verse 5).

23–4 *stormy uproars . . . That civil sea*: Mary equates God's stilling of the storm with his calming of the people.

28 *Both houses of the sun*: 'the East and West' (verse 8).

36 *buried seed . . . doth grow*: cf. John 12: 24 (Geneva): 'Except the wheat corn fall into the ground and die, it bideth alone: but if it die, it bringeth forth much fruit.'

44 *hedge of mirth*: BCP, 'the little hills shall rejoice' (verse 11). Mary's sense of celebration is amplified throughout this stanza.

46 *clotheth*: the inexact rhyme with *encloseth* (line 44) seems to be intentional, adding a clothing metaphor for the valleys.

Psalm 66

A Psalm of praise for God's deliverance, first of Israel and then of the speaker; the speaker presents a sacrifice to fulfil an earlier vow.

19 *Jordan's*: Mary supplies the name for the 'river' (verse 6).

34–8 *pinching saddles . . . did rudely roar*: Mary complicates the biblical metaphor of the ungodly riding over the top of the ungodly, suggesting the godly are actually saddled and ridden on like horses.

43–4 *To pay my vows . . . my body bowèd*: a development of the biblical phrase (Geneva verse 13): 'and will pay thee my vows'.

61 *what is left me*: what remains for me to do but to give praise to Him?

Psalm 67

A Psalm of praise for God's blessings, a prayer that they may continue, and a promise that all nations will praise God.

24 *of*: on.

28 *The father of the year*: the sun

Psalm 68

A Psalm of liturgical praise recalling God's past favours to his people, particularly in leading them from Egypt and providing them a new homeland in Canaan. The specific occasion of the Psalm has traditionally been thought to be David's taking the Ark of the Covenant to Jerusalem. Mary emphasizes the role of women in the celebration of God's power and protection of his people (lines 25–32, 66–7).

6 *dance*: traditionally taken as an allusion to David's dancing with joy when the Ark was brought to Jerusalem (1 Chronicles 15: 25–9).

7 *named of eternal essence*: Mary is following a source like the Geneva gloss on 'Jah' or 'Jehovah' as referring to God's essential and eternal being.

28 *We share . . . in house did lie*: we who remained weak at home share the spoils. Mary substitutes the first person plural for the second person in her sources and thus seems to identify here and in subsequent lines with the women. She transforms the domestic, or at least passive, biblical image into the *virgin army* (line 26), a feminized version of the Church militant.

32 *wavy*: along with *feathered oar*, *wavy* is part of Mary's metaphorical paraphrase of the Psalmist's description of the dove as silver and gold.

33 *that this may not seem strange*: the character of the conquered land (lines 35–6 describe the land, not the atmosphere) changes to accord with God's expulsion of the kings and their armies (lines 33–4), and Canaan thus becomes more habitable and less threatening to its new possessors, the Israelites.

36 *Salmon*: Mount Salmon (Calvin) or Canaan (Geneva).

37 *Bashan*: a mountain in the area east of Galilee.

41 *This mountainet*: the little mountain of Zion, not noted for its height.

49–56 *Ascended high . . . free*: possibly a reference to the traditional reading of verse 18 as Christ's harrowing of hell, although not usually so designated in Protestant commentaries.

66–7 *The rearward loud . . . ring*: Mary, unlike most of her sources, has the instrumental music played solely by the women.

71 *little*: the youngest of the sons of Jacob.

77–8 *their ending . . . shall take*: the subject of *shall take* is *their ending*.

89 Then acknowledge God the source (*well*) of all strength.

Psalm 69

An individual prayer for deliverance from enemies. Mary does not make explicit either the attribution to David or the Christological application present in many of her sources.

35–40 *In my teeth . . . winy taste*: Mary emphasizes both public and private mockery. The biblical text, however, speaks of drunkards, not feasters; hence, *winy taste*.

45 *from such, and mirèd*: *such* refers to the drunken, jesting, *prating* enemies of the preceding stanza. The sense of lines 45–6 is thus: keep me safe from such people, and, mired as I am, keep me safe from foes surrounding me like a flood.

52 *told by none*: innumerable.

65 *not seen before*: I had not previously seen such behaviour in them.

89–92 *Then by me . . . hoof and horn*: thanksgiving is superior to animal sacrifice. Cf. Psalms 40, 50, and 51.

98 *thine . . . yours*: your inhabitants, creatures.

Psalm 70

A prayer for deliverance of the godly and punishment for the wicked. According to Calvin, this Psalm is identical to Psalm 40. 13–17.

15 *them thy paths ensue*: them that follow thy paths.

Psalm 71

The speaker recalls having trusted in God even from earliest infancy (lines 16–21) and, now in old age, prays for renewal of God's help and favour, ending with a promise to sing in praise of God's deliverance of one who relies on him. Cf. George Herbert, 'The Flower', and Lady Mary Wroth, 'Forbear dark night, my joys now bud again'.

10 *feignest*: in *A Defence of Poetry*, Sidney underscores a difference between God as Maker (thou who *never feignest*) and mere makers (i.e. poets who offer but 'a feigned example' (in *Miscellaneous Prose of Sir Philip Sidney*, ed. Katherine Duncan-Jones and Jan Van Dorsten (Oxford: Clarendon Press, 1973), p. 89).

32 *my spies*: the addition of the spies to the biblical text was perhaps influenced by Mary's awareness of intrigues in the Elizabethan court.

52 *cradle*: the addition of this image reinforces the speaker's lifelong reliance on God.

58 Let me present an account of thy might.

69 *my lute, my harp shall sing*: reminiscent of a Renaissance courtly context, cf. Wyatt's 'My Lute Awake'.

Psalm 72

A prayer that God will bless the king's son and teach him to rule justly. Mary focuses exclusively here on the son, not the king, perhaps following Geneva and Beza who describe this Psalm as parental advice. Alternatively, she may be adopting Geneva's emphasis on Solomon as a type of Christ (i.e. the Son of God).

4–7 *poor men's right . . . The mountains proud shall fill*: Mary makes explicit the connection between the treatment of the poor and the prosperity of the land.

23 *many-formèd queen*: a reference to the triple goddess (Diana, Lucina, and Hecate) of classical mythology, all located in the moon, which is figured as feminine.

29 *Pison's*: Pison (Pishon) is the first of the rivers of Eden (Genesis 2: 11).

35–40 *all ev'n all . . . sceptres bear*: Mary sets up a parallel between the kings falling prostrate and those that *stand*, or maintain their positions at court, at their command.

Psalm 73

Like the Book of Job, this wisdom Psalm focuses on the suffering of the godly in the face of the temporary prosperity of the wicked. The speaker begins with a complaint concerning God's apparent desertion of the righteous while the unrighteous prosper (lines 1–42), then pleads for a hearing (lines 43–8), and finally realizes that God will continue both to show favour to the godly and to punish the wicked. Cf. Psalm 37, in which the speaker also learns not to be disquieted by the temporary prosperity of the wicked, and George Herbert, 'The Collar'.

1 *most true*: Mary quotes from the opening phrase of *Astrophil and Stella* 5.

4–6 *I fell . . . straying steps declined*: Mary turns a literal slipping in the original Psalm into a figurative, ethical one.

9 *still*: the continuing prosperity of the wicked (cf. lines 29, 36) is contrasted with the speaker's continual reliance on God (lines 67–70).

16–18 *as with a gorgeous chain . . . as if a robe it were*: Mary uses the chain and robes of office as symbols of the wicked.

21 They attain their desires and even more than they hope for.

29 *horn of plenty*: cornucopia, representing the prosperity of the wicked.

28–36 *ev'n godly men . . . still growing less*: the godly, seeing the prosperity of the wicked and their own suffering, question God's providence.

38 *In vain*: the speaker's earlier feeling that his pursuit of righteousness has been in vain is countered later by his understanding of the ultimate vanity of the dreams of the unrighteous (lines 58–60).

38–9 *In vain . . . from filthy stain*: cf. Psalm 51. 4–11.

50 *I did my steps direct*: cf. the imagery of *path* and *way* in Psalm 119.

73 *what is he will teach*: who is there who will teach?

83 *cleave to God*: cf. Genesis 2: 24 for the use of 'cleaves' (i.e. clings) in the marriage service.

73–84 *Oh, what is he . . . while breath shall give me space*: Mary adds an original coda, implying that the ascent will be difficult and require a teacher.

Psalm 74

A prayer for God's deliverance from present distress, traditionally interpreted as the destruction of the Temple at Jerusalem.

29–36 *spoiling . . . remaineth naught*: the Psalmist likens the destruction of the Temple to the felling of a forest. Mary elaborates the metaphor to suggest the destruction of Reformation iconoclasm.

72 *floated dead to every shore*: perhaps referring to Pharaoh's hosts (as noted in Geneva) and drowned bodies from the Spanish Armada. During this emergency of August 1588 Mary's uncle, the Earl of Leicester, and her brother, Robert, had led the mustering of the English forces at Tilbury.

73 *that monster's head*: the Geneva notes interpret verses 13–15 (lines 67–84) as referring to the deliverance of the Israelites from the Egyptians (Leviathan is said to represent Pharaoh).

79–81 *Thou wondrously . . . a fountain flow*: cf. Moses striking water from the rock (Exodus 17: 5–6).

96 *livery*: uniform of an aristocratic household. Another example of Mary's fascination with clothing imagery.

Psalm 75

A national and personal song of praise.

18 *The king his crown . . . bringeth*: Mary adds a specifically courtly context here (Geneva has only 'low' and 'high').

26 *lowly, never-dying rhymes*: added by Mary, a statement characteristically masking self-assertion as self-deprecation. The idea of spending *happy times* (line 25) writing is also hers.

Psalm 76

A national song of praise for God's deliverance in battle. According to the Geneva heading, the Psalm celebrates the 'defence of his people in Jerusalem, in the destruction of the army of Saneheríb'.

3 *Salem*: Mary frequently uses this term, meaning peace, for Jerusalem.

26 *protection*: tetrasyllabic, as is 'affection' in line 28.

28 *loppeth . . . prunes*: following Beza, Mary amplifies the vineyard analogy.

30 God terrifies the kings who terrify the earth.

Psalm 77

The speaker's doubt, presented in the past tense, was allayed by remembrance of God's past blessings. The short lines and close rhymes in Mary's version seem to mirror the restlessness of the Psalmist.

1–2 *crying call . . . calling cry*: polyptoton, used extensively in this Psalm (e.g. lines 19–20).

22–3 *My heart . . . as lamely fares*: personification of body parts is familiar from the Petrarchan tradition and Philip's *Astrophil and Stella*.

25–32 *At length . . . of thee had told*: expands the meditation of the Psalmist as writer, recalling not only God's former blessings but the Psalmist's own earlier writings.

36 *plain*: Mary adds the emphasis on writing formal complaints, a distinctly Spenserian poetic mode.

68 *As when*: Mary makes explicit the simile implicit in the biblical appeal to history.

69–72 *From servitude unjust . . . had sold*: cf. Genesis 37–46.

73 *thee saw . . . saw thee*: an example of Mary's fondness for antimetabole (repetition of elements in reverse order).

85–6 *light of lightnings' flash . . . enclear*: the lightning bolts illuminate the path while the thunder roars and rattles.

89–96 *through dusy deep . . . to glad pastures brought*: Mary adds (from the Geneva note) the path leading through the dry sea bed to *glad pastures*. Cf. Exodus 14: 19–21.

Psalm 78

Beza's 'Argument' praises the usefulness of this long historical Psalm in recalling God's blessings to those who keep his covenant and his 'wrath' against those who break it. Cf. Psalms 105, 106, 135, and 136, which also recall the history of Israel.

2 *renew*: the Psalm recounts God's past blessings in order to encourage God's people to follow his commandments.

15–16 *sons . . . sons*: 'children' in the sources.

21 *anchor*: the image of hope as an anchor, a familiar element of Renaissance iconography, is added from Hebrews 6: 19. Cf. George Herbert's 'Hope'.

33 *And why?*: characteristic addition of rhetorical question. Why did they flee, although well equipped? Because they had abandoned God.

37 *in hard estate*: in difficult circumstances.

40 *Zoan fields*: Zoan was a city in Egypt, called by Calvin (verse 12) 'the famousest place of the Realm'.

42 *There where the deep . . .*: begins the familiar account of God's deliverance from Egypt, necessary to be recounted because it had been forgotten by the Israelites.

67 *Who*: Jacob's race (line 66).

74 *ambrosian manna*: Mary adds the classical term to the biblical manna.

153–4 *Nilus trails/Of his wet robe the slimy, seedy train*: personification of the fertile Nile as a classical river god is added.

158 *Ham*: (Psalm 78. 51 in Geneva, 'And smote all the firstborn in Egypt, even the beginning of their strength in the tabernacles of Ham') or Egypt (based on Genesis 9).

167–8 *his sheep . . . in the waves*: Mary adds the sheep and wolves metaphor, extending the Psalm's metaphor of God as the shepherd.

194 *live despaired*: the description of the young women is given in the passive voice in Mary's usual sources. She makes the verse active, presenting it from the standpoint of the young women, who must live without hope of marrying because the young men have been killed in battle.

197 *a knight*: Mary adds the image of chivalry.

209–16 *And where his servant David . . . did show*: Mary expands the pastoral image that concludes this Psalm. Cf. lines 161–8.

Psalm 79

Prayer for national deliverance and vengeance against their enemies. Mary alternates feminine and masculine rhymes, the former predominating in odd stanzas, and the latter in even.

10 *crows*: taken from the Marot–Beza Psalms.

62–3 *goers . . . knowers*: monosyllabic.

Psalm 80

A national prayer for deliverance, emphasizing God's past blessings, with a prevailing metaphor of the Church as a vine.

7 *face's skies*: perhaps comparing the sun to God's face.

17–32 *A vine thou didst translate . . . ordainèd not to wither*: Mary characteristically expands the gardening metaphor.

20 *her*: the vine's, Israel's.

30 *Review*: see again. Lines 30–1 reflect the biblical parallelism (verse 14).

34 *they*: God's people.

35 *elected*: a charged term for any Protestant reader. In Calvinist theology, the elect were those predestined by God to be saved.

Psalm 81

A liturgical song of praise for a festival.

1–12 *All gladness . . . his praise*: a Geneva note (verse 1) explains that 'for a time these ceremonies were ordained, but now under the Gospel are abolished'. Mary, in contrast, emphasizes the joyful use of music in praising God.

17–18 *There heard I . . . who thus did say*: Mary explains the change in speakers.

20 *bakèd clay*: building blocks produced in the brickpits of Egypt.

44 *lease of bliss*: Mary adds the image of God as the landlord granting bliss.

48 *overfillèd*: Mary exceeds the Psalm's mere 'filling' to superabundance.

Psalm 82

A call to judgement of those who have been given temporal authority by God, the true judge of the world, to rule as his deputies on earth, but who have neglected their obligation to deal justly with God's people. Cf. Psalm 73 and the four poems titled 'Affliction' in George Herbert's *The Temple*.

1–2 *at prince's bar / Who gods . . . are*: the theory of the divine right of kings.

1–5 *Where poor men plead . . . and judgèd right*: Mary emphasizes the duty of magistrates to the poor, stating that God will judge the unjust judges.

13 *to loose and quiet his estate*: Mary's *estate* seems to intend both 'condition' and 'property'; *loose* and *quiet* would then also mean 'rescue' and 'soothe', as well as 'release' and 'settle', as in settle a dispute or *debate* (line 15).

18–20 *the very ground . . . your faults confound*: in Mary's paraphrase, the *ground* seems to be metaphorical: that on which a system is founded. The unjust rule of the princes blurs fundamental moral distinctions and puts all in jeopardy.

23–5 *you as men must die . . . as others lie*: the princes are reminded of their mortality and of the certainty of God's judgement by which the unjust rulers will *fall* (line 25) from their high eminence and lie as low as others stretched out in death.

Psalm 83

A prayer to save the true faith from the machinations of the Amalekites and the Moabites, who were, like the Philistines, identified with the Catholics in Protestant literature but not explicitly here. Most of the incidents cited come from the Book of Judges. Mary develops the bird imagery in the Psalm, showing a struggle between the people hidden under God's wings and the falconer who attempts to ensnare them.

19 *Edom's sons . . .*: most of the nations mentioned in the following section are frequently referred to in the Hebrew scriptures as enemies of the Israelites.

23 *Palestina*: 'Philistia' in the original (Beza is the source for Mary's error).

26 *Lot's incestuous brood*: a reference to Moab and Edom, or the Ammonites, supposedly descended from Lot and his daughters (Genesis 19: 36–8).

27–8 *Jabin . . . Sisera*: cf. Judges 4 and 5.

29–32 *Midian . . . Salmana*: Gideon's victory over Midian (Judges 6–8), including slaying the princes Oreb and Zeb, and the warriors Zeba and Salmuna.

37 *tossèd balls*: Mary borrows the tennis metaphor from Isaiah 22: 18.

45 *paint*: implying whorish or sluttish make-up.

49 *Add fear and shame, to shame and fear*: a line confirming Mary's fondness for antimetabole.

Psalm 84

Traditionally thought to have been composed by King David in exile, this Psalm expresses the joy of serving in God's glorious temple.

3 *far from any telling*: beyond the ability of anyone to describe.

5–6 *the God that liveth, / The God that all life giveth*: cf. Psalm 68. 7.

15–16 *Why should I / From altars thine excluded lie?*: Mary adds both the question and the personal application.

22–3 *mulberries . . . wells they dig*: Geneva notes that 'Bacá' ('of mulberry trees') was a 'barren place', so wells would be required for supplying water there.

46 *The path*: the path that. Cf. the imagery of paths, ways of righteousness throughout the Psalms, especially in Psalms 23 and 68 and the various sections of Psalm 119.

Psalm 85

Corporate prayer that God will deliver them, as He has in the past.

3 *Jacob's servitude*: cf. Genesis 29.

8 *wounds . . . darts*: Mary adds these Petrarchan images.

11 *as heretofore*: Mary characteristically connects the revelation of God's past actions with the prayer for present mercy.

17 *thread*: Mary's syncretism prompts her to add here a reference to the mythological thread of life, spun by Clotho, measured by Lachesis, and cut by Atropos. Cf. note to 55. 71–2.

31–8 *Truth shall spring . . . we till*: Mary expands the agricultural metaphor, suggested by the biblical phrase (Geneva verse 11) 'Truth shall bud out of the earth', and adds the characteristic clothing metaphor (*earth's attire*).

Psalm 86

A personal prayer for deliverance. Mary adds a courtly context to this Psalm, not present in her biblical sources.

7–8 *sadness . . . gladness*: the rhyme, used also in 48. 29–30 and 51. 27–8, sums up a major theme in the Psalms.

15 *if gods be many*: Mary adds this parenthesis, hedging away from polytheistic implications perhaps with Catholic/Protestant disputes in mind.

40 *of thy handmaid*: by eliminating the 'son' in the biblical phrase, Mary maintains ambiguity in the gender of the speaker.

47 *Eye-taught*: the oppressors will see with their eyes how God delivers the faithful; also a pun: eye-taught and I-taught.

Psalm 87

A celebration of Zion, God's city, which includes people from all the world.

2 *who*: God.

7–8 *'I will' . . . my knowers*: God desires that Egypt and Babylon be added to the list of nations that know him.

17–20 *this account shall make . . . as born in Zion namèd*: continues the idea of God's adoption of Gentile peoples, who will be treated as though they were native born.

Psalm 88

A personal prayer, full of agony and despair, complaining of the suffering endured because of God's punishment and apparent alienation and because of the desertion and disaffection of former friends. It provides a notable example of Mary's virtuosic handling of verse line and rhyme.

4–5 *Both when . . . doth display*: an inversion for the sake of the metre; *his* in line 6 also refers to the sun.

7 *Admit to presence*: a metaphor perhaps drawn from the royal presence or audience chamber.

42 *and fail no day*: the speaker does not fail to make his supplication to God each day.

43 *will then be time*: *will* there *then be time* to spread God's truth when men are dead (lines 44–5)?

55 *Good reason*: Mary characteristically supplies a connection between the lack of praise in the grave and the speaker's entreaty.

Psalm 89

The Geneva heading says that 'the Prophet' praises God's 'testament and covenant, that he had made between him and his elect by Jesus Christ the son of David'.

8 *periods*: oxymoron, since 'period' also means 'end'.

13 *wheels*: either a classical (Apollo's chariot) or biblical (Ezekiel's wheels) reference (or both).

24 *armour-like apparel*: Mary adds the reference to the armour of faith (Ephesians 6: 11–17), but here God's own faithfulness is his armour.

30 Everything that the earth encompasses belongs to God.

35 *Tabor and Hermon*: mountains west and east of Jerusalem, signifying God's power over all parts of the world.

40 *Truth with Mercy goeth*: cf. the similar allegory in 85. 29–30.

49 *Jehovah's shield*: the ruler. Cf. 47. 20.

52 *Aid I will you bring . . .*: God is imagined speaking in these lines, which recount what God said to the prophet Samuel (1 Samuel 16).

71 *my first-born's room*: the room (in the palace) intended for my firstborn child. The image, unique to Mary's Psalms, is of a king honouring his eldest son with the choicest lodging he can provide.

75–6 *My bounty . . . in years*: God's bounty will not cease, nor be bound by a term of years.

79–80 *A steadfast throne . . . they never breathèd*: David's kingdom will endure until the spheres of the Ptolemaic universe grow weary. Their circling becomes a measure of time, as in lines 73–4. Cf. 139. 24, 148. 13–14.

94 *their enduring*: the enduring of the sun and moon. The heavens shall last no longer than the faithful seed of David.

97 *And yet . . .*: rom here to the end of the Psalm, the prophet bewails the present state of David's descendants, caused by their sin, and prays that God will nevertheless honour his covenant with them.

105–8 *Takes he his weapon . . . Ascend his throne?*: rhetorical questions characteristically added to provide immediacy.

109–10 *His age's spring . . . Winter of woe*: the seasonal imagery is added to the biblical text (verse 44).

115–20 *think how short our age's measure . . . no age protecteth*: Mary expands the meditation on mortality. Cf. Geneva (verse 48): 'What man liveth, and shall not see death? Shall he deliver his soul from the hand of the grave?'

125 *many a*: metre requires elision.

126 *and at thy Christ*: Mary's Christological addition.

Psalm 90

A meditation on mortality as contrasted with God's eternity and a prayer for God's protection. Attributed to Moses in the biblical sources.

9–12 *man by thee created . . . to earth he goes*: as people were first created of the dust of the earth, so will they return to the earth as dust (*In equal state*) when God has determined the length of their life.

13 *and saying mak'st it so*: Mary adds this reference to God's speaking Creation into being. Cf. Genesis 1: 1.

14–16 *Adam's heir . . . Dust*: emphasizes the Hebrew pun on 'Adam' as dust. Mary here alludes both to Adam's creation from dust (Genesis 2: 7) and to Adam's punishment after the Fall (Genesis 3: 19).

23–4 *fancy . . . substance*: Mary develops the idea of the dream from the biblical 'sleep' (Geneva verse 5) and from Beza, 'their life seemeth to be like a dream that suddenly vanisheth away'.

34 *his*: its, life's (measure of days).

Psalm 91

A wisdom Psalm, meditating on God's protection of his people.

4 I, for one, dare affirm.

9–13 *From snare . . . with wing and plume*: Mary expands the bird imagery of verses 3–4, paralleling her treatment in 57. 4 and throughout 83.

41–4 *To bear thee . . . Against the stone misled*: quoted in Gospel accounts of the temptation of Christ, Matthew 4: 6 and Luke 4: 10–11.

Psalm 92

A Psalm of praise (or encomium). The Geneva heading declares: 'This psalm was made to be sung on the Sabbath, to stir up the people to acknowledge God and to praise him in his works.'

1–2 *lovely thing . . . sing*: there is prominent use of internal rhyme in this Psalm, cf. *ear . . . hear* (line 33).

7–9 *so to sing . . . and voice consent*: Mary makes no apology, as does the Geneva note on verse 3, for using music to worship God.

13 *What wit can find*: it is conventional in praise poems to express that the object of praise is beyond expression.

15 No one can understand thy thoughts.

16 *blind*: Mary's addition.

20 *flow'ry grass*: the biblical text has grass but not flowers. Mary develops the plant metaphor here to connect with the rest of the Psalm, particularly lines 34–42, which expand the biblical metaphor in verses 12–14.

32 *spies*: Mary revises the original 'enemies' to suggest a more courtly context.

36 *For green and growth*: with regard to greenness and growth (the righteous shall be like the cedar and the palm).

38 *his*: the just man's.

Psalm 93

A Psalm praising God as King. Mary's paraphrase emphasizes the eternal, unchanging nature of God's reign.

1 *Clothed . . . girt*: Mary's allegorical apparel here is more detailed than the Psalmist's.

9–12 *Rivers . . . Lord of skies*: the lines conform to Beza's interpretation (verse 3): Even though rivers roar and roaring waves rise, trouble the sea, and break upon the shore, God on high is more powerful than them all. Mary does not read the storms allegorically as a reference to the wicked, however, as does Beza (verses 1 and 4). The unusual phrasing of line 9 seems to be an attempt to match the Geneva translation: 'The floods have lifted up, O Lord: the floods have lifted up their voice.'

Psalm 94

This prayer for vengeance was frequently applied to contemporary situations. Mary's uncle, Robert Dudley, wrote a poetic version when imprisoned for supporting Lady Jane Grey as queen (BL Arundel MS 290, see also Psalm 55) and Beza's 'Argument' applies the Psalm to Europe 'at this day'.

3–8 *How long, O Lord . . . thy possession lies*: here and throughout the Psalm Mary renders more of the text in the interrogative than do the biblical sources, making the Psalm a dramatic monologue.

16 *From whose first workmanship the eye did grow?*: cf. George Herbert, 'Love III' ('Who made the eyes but I').

19–20 *who reigns above,/He knows*: He who reigns above knows.

21 *in thy school*: on God's school, see Psalms 51 and 119.

his age: his life. Cf. 89. 120 and note to 104. 112.

35 *quailèd in mind-combats*: Mary adds the martial imagery.

39 The unjust judges pretend to administer the law, but intend only to injure the righteous.

Psalm 95

A Psalm, praising God as King and calling on the people not to repeat past mistakes, and a liturgical canticle, sung at Morning Prayer.

4 *rock*: Mary's addition may be inspired by the rock in Exodus 17.

24 *Masha . . . Meriba*: Mary's addition from Geneva. Refers to the account of the Israelites' dissatisfaction with their wanderings in the desert. Cf. Exodus 17: 7 and Psalm 78. 49–56.

25 *God doth say*: Mary explains the switch from the Psalmist's voice to that of God in the biblical text.

Psalm 96

A Psalm praising God as King. Mary's version is notable for its emphasis on sacred song and dance.

10–12 *For Jehovah . . . throne*: because Jehovah, who alone is great, doth hold his throne for awe and glory far above all the (false) gods.

23–6 *get you thither . . . Where his pomp is most displayèd*: Mary expands the courtly imagery of verse 8 (Geneva): 'into his courts'.

34 *Leafy infants*: a double play upon the Latin etymological sense of *infans* (without speech) and the idea of trees as old, but compared to God they are only *infants*.

35 *fieldeth*: obtains food in the field; predating *OED*'s first citation (from Charles Darwin).

Psalm 97

A Psalm praising God as King, using the image of thunder and lightning to demonstrate his vengeance on idol worshippers.

12 His flashing maketh lightnings.

27 *angels*: biblical translations all have 'gods'. Mary is perhaps hinting here at the Christological emphasis of the Geneva headnote.

31 *towns in Judah*: Mary's omission of the metaphor of towns as daughters is uncharacteristic, given her usual interest in women.

34–5 *they all by thee / Be ruled who rulers be*: God is the ruler over the rulers. Cf. 82, where God is presented as the judge of judges.

Psalm 98

A Psalm calling on God's people and all nature to praise God as King.

2 *newness*: Mary's rendering of the familiar biblical text, 'Sing unto the Lord a new song' (Geneva verse 1), may be self-reflexive, for that is what she is doing in these Psalms.

5–6 *He that salvation . . . hath set in open view*: God has revealed that long-hidden salvation for which his elect wait.

7 *taught*: Jehovah has taught the nations his justice.

9 *the motives were*: the motives for God's revealing his salvation.

15 *lute*: Mary replaces the biblical 'harp' (verse 6) with the lute as accompaniment for vocal music.

21 *you*: the sea and rivers, etc. The command to the heavens and the earth to rejoice parallels Isaiah 44: 23.

22 *Who*: the Lord.

Psalm 99

A Psalm praising God as King, recounting past blessings to Israel.

4 *He that on the cherubs rideth*: in the biblical texts God sits between the cherubs.

18 *There*: at God's footstool.

20 *their suits*: Mary adds the courtly imagery.

Psalm 100

A Psalm of praise for God's creation and for his adoption of the Church, originally intended as celebration of God as a king who cares for his people as a shepherd cares for his flock. It is presented as part of a temple entrance liturgy. One of two sonnets, this one Scottish or Spenserian, among Mary's paraphrases. See also Psalm 150.

2 *merry shout*: the exuberance of Mary's rendering surpasses both the BCP (verse 1), 'come before his presence with a song', and Geneva, 'Sing ye loud unto the Lord.'

Psalm 101

The *appointed* king, traditionally thought to be David, vows that when he receives the crown he will rule righteously and will not tolerate unrighteousness and that he will prepare for the part with study of virtue. Cf. the description in Psalm 82 of the unjust rulers who fail in their duties as God's *vicegerents*. The courtly context of Mary's paraphrase is unmistakable, particularly in her use of words like *counsellors* (line 16) and *officers* (line 17). This Psalm thus becomes part of the tradition of the 'mirror for princes' or instructions for the monarch. Mary emphasizes the cluster of images on hearts and tongues (6, 11 ff.).

6 *pure in heart*: begins a series of allusions to hearts, particularly contrasting David's pure heart with the *Malicious hearts* (line 11) of the slanderers and the *puffèd hearts* of the *proud ambitious band* (lines 13–14).

11 *never will admit*: will never allow into my presence.

16–21 *Such men . . . accepted well*: the speaker acknowledges his obligation both to govern virtuously and to surround himself with others who will fulfil their responsibilities honestly and justly.

Psalm 102

The second of the four Penitential Psalms paraphrased by Mary, Psalm 102 is a complaint concerning the speaker's *woes* (line 13) that are so severe as to cause *sharpest pain* (line 10) and emaciation (lines 13–14, 19–20). Isolated and despairing, he prays for deliverance, both of Israel (of which he is assured in lines 55–60) and of himself personally (lines 73–8).

9–11 *Mown down . . . grass*: Mary adds the mowing image, perhaps recalling this familiar metaphor from Isaiah or Revelation.

15 *howl*: Mary's addition, perhaps from Job or one of the prophetic books.

17 *desert owl*: Sir Henry Sidney quoted this phrase from the Vulgate in a letter to Francis Walsingham, explaining his wife's isolation after she was disfigured, or defaced, by smallpox (1 March 1583, TNA, SP 12/159, fo. 38ᵛ).

22 *Bereft of spouse, or son*: Mary adds the specific family members.

29–30 *That wishing ill . . . of ills the most*: the speaker's enemies use his condition (*my estate*) as a curse on others and think it the greatest of ills to be wished on anyone.

34 *thou*: God.

50 *she*: Zion (lines 44, 56), linked with *Salem* (Jerusalem) in line 71; interpreted by sixteenth-century commentators as the Church.

 like a carcass: this metaphor is from Beza's 'Argument', suggesting that the Church is 'most like a dead carcass than to a living body'.

61 God's deliverance shall endure in the *record* of his acts.

69 *they*: the *prisoners* and *condemnèd ones* (lines 67–8), who, when released, can serve to *record* God's *honour* (lines 71–2).

73–4 *what is this if I / In the mid way should fall and die?*: what will God's delivering Israel mean to the speaker if he himself perishes in the middle of his life? Cf. *the noontide of my day* (line 77).

79 *stands*: the use of a third-person singular verb with a compound subject is not uncommon in sixteenth-century writings, including Shakespeare's plays.

83 *Till changing still, full change shall them betide*: Mary expands the clothing metaphor to include the resurrection. Cf. 93.1.

Psalm 103

A Psalm of praise for God's forgiveness of sins and care for his people.

1 *heart*: added by Mary (perhaps from Geneva note) to express emotion.

1–4 *My soul, my heart . . . My heart, my soul*: another example of chiasmus (contrast by verbal parallelism in reverse order), one of Mary's favourite devices.

9 *free grace*: Calvin (verse 3) writes of God's grace in 'freely forgiving and wiping away our sins'. Mary also uses the phrase in Psalms 56. 43, 59. 43, and 119D. 40.

19 *He eagle-like*: in biblical versions it is the Psalmist who is renewed like an eagle.

41–3 *For look how far . . . earthly centre bears*: Geneva (verse 11): 'For as high as the heaven is above the earth.' Mary adds the Ptolemaic sphere.

45 *His*: God's.

47 *his sins*: the sins of the one who fears God with *due devotion* (line 48).

65 *potter*: perhaps because of Beza's reference to 'earthen vessels', Mary adds the metaphor of God as potter to the biblical text (verse 14): 'he remembreth that we are but dust'. Cf. Isaiah 64: 8, Romans 9: 21, Jeremiah 18: 1–6.

73–4 *Such . . . in other rate*: Mary characteristically adds a transition.

80 *do . . . not only understand*: i.e. not only understand but also perform.

Psalm 104

An exuberant Psalm of praise of God's creative and sustaining power.

4 *in state*: with great pomp and solemnity. God is portrayed in royal garb, sitting under the canopy of state, like Queen Elizabeth.

10 *In chevron*: in a chevron shape, a beam with a bar bent like two rafters touching one another.

13–14 *Whose wingèd blasts . . . as angels of his train*: God's word finds the *wingèd blasts* of the winds as ready as his company of angels *To post* (go on a mission) from Him. The imagery is further developed in lines 15–16, where the fire is said to be just as glad (*fain*) to do God's bidding.

17 *By him the earth . . .*: a recounting of God's act of creating the earth. Cf. Genesis 1: 9–10.

20–6 *lowly . . . humble*: Mary adds the references to the humility of low places.

28 *bounding*: God's action in fixing limits to the seas.

36 *By these in their self-chosen mansions . . .*: Mary seems to add a pervasive element of socio-political allegory to this Psalm, with references to *mansions* (line 36), *free-born* (line 37), *ploughman* (line 44), *leavèd people* (line 53), *princes* (line 54), and *burgesses* (line 70).

36–40 *By these . . . give attentive heed*: the contrast between art and nature, conventional to pastoral poetry, is added by Mary.

43 *great with young*: the metaphor of pregnancy is intensified by Mary. Cf. Geneva (verse 14).

45 *vulgar grass*: perhaps another element of socio-political allegory, with reference to enclosure controversies.

50 *folded*: wrinkled because of care. Cf. Geneva (verse 15). The oil may have a cosmetic effect on wrinkles.

54 *cedars*: these, the noblest of trees, are God's *princes*. Mary adds the class distinction and also the sense of obligation that the noble cedars show to the humbler birds in providing them places to nest (lines 57–9).

62 *traces*: paths.

65–7 *the empress of the night . . . chariot-man of light*: Mary adds elements from secular poetry and classical mythology in describing the personified inconstant moon (Diana) and the chariot of the sun (Apollo/Hyperion).

69 *he*: the *sun* (line 67). At night creatures of a different sort become active (lines 69–75). Cf. line 73.

78–80 *How I . . . Whereto in me, no wisdom can aspire*: by adding the first person, Mary intensifies the contrast between God's wise governance of his creation and the human inability to comprehend it, except to the extent of acknowledging and admiring it. Cf. 139. 20–1.

81–2 *Behold . . . Look*: by adding the two imperatives, Mary clarifies the structure of the biblical text.

83 *swim, creep, and crawl and go*: seems to prefigure Milton's description of Satan's progress through Chaos ('swims or sinks, or wades, or creeps or flies', *Paradise Lost*, 2. 950).

86 *Sea-monsters*: Mary's description characteristically conflates the 'play' of Geneva with 'pastime' of BCP (verse 26).

89–92 *Thou giv'st . . . Thou tak'st*: the stark contrast between the images of sustenance and mortality emphasizes the absolute nature of God's power over all creatures.

93–6 *They die . . . decays*: the recycling of old substance into new form parallels the process of change depicted in Edmund Spenser's 'Garden of Adonis' in *The Faerie Queene*, 3. 6. 35–8.

99–100 *Who touching mountains . . . earth quakes with quivering knee*: volcanoes and earthquakes also attest to God's might.

104 *be . . . being*: an especially deft use of polyptoton, where *be* and *being* seem different inflections of the same word but, in fact, are not.

112 *time nor age*: *time* and *age* may not be redundant since such apparent synonyms rarely are in Mary's work, but may be distinguished as time in general (in contrast to eternity) and a particular length of human time, respectively.

Psalm 105

A Psalm emphasizing God's goodness, recounting Israel's early history as in Genesis. The Israelites and Egyptians were traditionally the respective descendants of Sem (Shem) and Ham, sons of Noah.

11–14 *His servants . . . no bounds his jurisdiction have*: the distinction is between the special covenant God made with the children of Abraham and his general, eternal lordship over the whole world.

21 *in fee*: a legal term, by heritable right according to feudal law. Mary adds the contractual language.

25–30 *They strangers were . . . Nor to my prophets least offence procure*: although they had no seat, or permanent dwelling, they were secure because God protected them and punished even kings who would molest them.

32 *staff of bread*: bread as the staff or support of life.

33–40 *But he for them . . . of freedom repossessèd*: note the concise presentation of Joseph's story: sold as a slave by his jealous brothers, he was imprisoned, but set free because of his interpretation of dreams (*divining*), and providentially empowered to save his family from famine.

48 *Ham*: or 'Cham', the cursed son of Noah. The Egyptians and Ethiopians were descended from Cush, son of Ham (Genesis 10: 6).

53 *he*: God. It is God who *wills*, not Aaron; furthermore, Aaron is God's choice (line 54), not Moses'.

59 *Late wat'ry*: recently flowing with water (rather than blood as now).

60 *what should I stand to tell?*: Mary adds the personal voice, reluctant to tell these horrors.

61–2 *of noisome frogs . . . where their princes sleep*: Mary vividly images the impact of frogs, lice, and vermin in the royal bedchambers.

Psalm 106

A historical Psalm, emphasizing God's faithfulness and the rebellion of the people, *These mutineers* (line 23).

6–7 *the level straight . . . aiming at the mark of right*: Mary, who learned archery as a child, adds the metaphor to verse 3.

11–12 *kind . . . kindness*: another example of punning polyptoton.

22 *for his name*: recalling the biblical 'For his Name's sake'.

39 *For fully fed, yet fared in pining plight*: explains the reference to *gluttons* in line 38. Even though they are fully fed, they continue complaining on their journey. Mary replaces the biblical lust with gluttony.

45 *Dathan and Abiram*: they were among those who challenged the authority of Moses and Aaron. Their rebellion caused them to perish in an earthquake and then a fire consumed 250 additional men. See Numbers 16: 1–3, 27–35.

50–5 *A molten god . . . hay they should allow*: while Moses was on Mount Horeb (or Sinai) receiving the Commandments, the people convinced Aaron to make a golden calf and then worshipped it; Exodus 32: 1–35. Mary wryly comments that the highest form of worship to such a god would be to make offerings of hay.

56–60 *God was forgot . . . enclose*: they forgot God, who had preserved them through mighty miracles in the plains of Egypt; and wonderful works, like the opening and closing of the Ochre (or Red) Sea, which let them safely pass and then closed over the Egyptian armies.

71 *Peór*: Baal-peór, 'Which was the idol of the Moabites' (Geneva, note to verse 28).

76 *Phinehas*: in Numbers 25, Phinehas, the son of Eleazar, was incensed by an Israelite consorting with a Midianic woman. He killed both of them, thereby ending a plague that had broken out and earned God's special favour of a covenant of perpetual priesthood for him and his descendants.

80 *his*: the brook's.

105 *worthy plagues*: plagues they had deserved (verse 43).

109–12 *So changed . . . tender yielding trains*: they were repentant, and so changed that not only God, but also their captors, had pity on them.

Psalm 107

One of the liturgical Psalms, in which the congregation is invited to praise God's sustaining power. The varied refrain in lines 33–8, 49–54, and 81–6 corresponds to the biblical text (verses 8–9, 15–16, 21–2, and 31–2).

9 *How many, and how many times*: part of the exclamatory construction in 9–12: How many of his people and how often God has delivered . . .!

16 *drought . . . did drown*: Mary adds the paradox of drought drowning, or destroying, them.

19 *error trained*: cf. *Folly's train* (line 42).

33 *They*: the *rebels* (line 29) who, when God humbles them, cry to Him for aid.

36 *bolts*: Mary substitutes *bolts* for 'bonds' in the biblical sources and thus anticipates the imagery of the gates in lines 39–40.

57 *How many mounting . . .*: Mary expands the biblical description of ship-wreck (to line 84).

68 *combat*: the fight between wind and sea. Cf. line 83.

76 *head-lame feet*: feet made unsteady by minds disturbed by fear.

77–80 *What helps . . . naught discern?*: what help is it to have an expert *pilot* when *wisdom*, which is needed to steer the ship but which is now *drowned* in danger-induced despair caused by fear of the storm, can see nothing?

91 *salts the soil*: makes the soil infertile, barren.

109 *Nor strange*: nor is the change of fortune just described strange, surprising.

Psalm 108

A national hymn of praise for God's deliverance, composed of verses 7–11 of Psalm 57 and verses 5–12 of Psalm 60, although Mary's formal variety disguises this repetition.

4 *lute*: in place of 'viol' in the biblical sources (verse 2). Cf. Sir Thomas Wyatt's 'My Lute Awake'.

22–5 *Sichem's . . . Succoch's . . . Gilead . . . Manasses*: cf. Psalm 60. 22–5.

32 *Triumphèd*: when I have triumphed over you.

Psalm 109

A Psalm of vengeance, cursing enemies and praying for deliverance.

6 *Engines . . . batt'ry*: Mary adds the military imagery.

13 *I pray then what? . . .*: from here to line 42, a series of dependent clauses answering the question in line 13, constituting a curse against the enemy.

25 *usurers*: substituted for the biblical 'extortioners'.

38–40 *That neither print . . . remembered not*: a difficult passage, because of the unusual placement of *For* (which may be an error for 'So'). The sense is that the speaker's enemy disregarded even the most basic human impulses to decent behaviour.

77–8 *attire . . . gown*: the clothing metaphor is expanded from the biblical sources. Cf. Geneva (verse 29).

Psalm 110

'David prophesieth of the power and everlasting kingdom given to Christ', according to the Geneva heading and Mary's other usual sources. The Psalm is so interpreted in the New Testament, particularly in Hebrews 1: 13.

1 *to my Lord, the Lord did say*: according to Mary's interpretive sources (verse 1), David here presents God the Father (*the Lord*) as speaking to Christ (*my Lord*). Cf. Jesus' comment on the verse in Matthew 22: 43–5. See also Acts 2: 34–5.

16 *Aurora's*: Mary adds the classical reference to dawn.

19 *Melchizedek*: a priest-king honoured by Abraham in Genesis 14: 18–20 and mentioned as a type of Christ in his eternal priesthood in Hebrews 7, especially 7: 21, which quotes Psalm 110. 4.

Psalm 111

A Psalm of praise that focuses on God's deliverance of his people. The form is an alphabetical acrostic, perhaps symbolizing comprehensiveness. Mary is adapting the form according to differences between the Hebrew and Roman alphabets; there is no 'J' in early modern usage.

3–4 *works of unmatchèd might . . . delight*: judged *of unmatchèd might* by those who *delight* in the study (*search*) of God's works.

5 The honour that pertains to God's power is endless.

6 *From end as far*: endless.

11 Finally he made them (*caused them to*) understand his strength.

13–14 *Now what could more . . . unmoved to be!*: now what could more *confirm* the certainty, justice, and permanence of God's promises, judgements, and decrees than his own acts.

Psalm 112

A wisdom Psalm meditating on God's blessings of the righteous, with a concluding note on the punishment of the wicked. Although this is also an alphabetical Psalm in the Hebrew, it is not so noted by Calvin, and Mary does not render it as alphabetical.

5 *branches*: an adaptation of the plant imagery implicit in the biblical 'seed' (Geneva verse 2): 'his seed shall be mighty upon the earth'. Mary's plant imagery parallels the description of the just man in Psalm 1. 3 (Geneva) as a 'tree planted by the rivers of water'.

13 *he*: God.

17 *He*: the just man.

32 *applause*: an original rendering of the exalted horn of Geneva and BCP (verse 9).

Psalm 113

A hymn of praise for God's providence towards the *needy soul* (line 13). Beza's 'Argument' stresses God's love 'toward the miserable and poor', such as Joseph, Moses, David, and Daniel, and to 'barren women', such as Sarah, Rebecca, and Anna.

13–14 *the needy soul, The wretch*: that God makes kings of *the needy soul* and the *wretch* is not precisely the sense of the biblical text (Geneva verse 8): 'That he may set him with the princes.'

Psalm 114

Praise for God's mercy in delivering Israel from Egypt which, the Geneva heading declares, 'put us in remembrance of God's great mercy toward his Church'. In Dante's *Divine Comedy*, 'Purgatory' (canto 2), the pilgrim spirits arrive singing Psalm 114.

4 *there*: among the people of Israel, *Jacob's race* (line 1).

5–6 *Jordan with swift return . . . did turn*: Jordan participates in the opening of the Red Sea.

Psalm 115

Prayer for deliverance from idol-worshipping oppressors, contrasting the power of God to the weakness of idols. Its first verses were often sung as a hymn of thanksgiving (see Shakespeare's *Henry V*, after Agincourt).

7–12 *You ask . . . of workmen's hand*: Mary clarifies the sense of her originals by setting up parallel questions. The idolaters ask *where* God is, and the godly ask *what* the idols are. The dramatic monologue sets up the contrast between the invisible but powerful Jehovah and the visible but impotent idols. Cf. questions in lines 43–4.

23 *Aaron's house*: priests or instructors.

35 *thrice blest*: Mary adds the number as an intensifier, as in the opening of her poem 'Even now that care' (see p. 5 above).

38–9 *Removèd most . . . With vaulted roof doth rise*: Mary expands the metaphor of the earth as the floor and the heaven as the roof of God's dwelling. God dwells in the upper chambers and gives the *lowly ground* to men.

Psalm 116

A Psalm of praise for God's deliverance from suffering and from doubt.

29 *finding false*: it is false that all men are liars.

33–6 *My cup . . . on thy name will call*: as in ritual sacrifice. Mary adds the detail of throwing the cup into the fire, whereas the sources (verse 13) speak only of lifting up or drinking the cup as part of a thanksgiving banquet. Cf. Exodus 29: 40.

Psalm 117

Another acrostic Psalm (there is no 'J' in early modern usage), in which the first letters of the lines spell out PRAIS THE LORD.

Psalm 118

A Psalm of praise, with the refrain, 'For his mercy endureth for ever', in verses 1–4 and 29 rendered as a chorus in the final couplets of stanzas 1–4 and 20, with different groups being called upon to sing the refrain. Because verse 22 is applied to Jesus in the New Testament (see Matthew 21: 42 and Acts 4: 11) and because verse 26 is quoted in the Palm Sunday account in all four Gospels, Psalm 118 is given a Christological interpretation in Christian sources.

53–4 *Who opens . . . relate*: who opens to me Justice's gate so that, entering in it, I may relate God's praise?

57 *Here, here*: in the Tabernacle.

Psalm 119

This long Psalm is composed in the biblical text of twenty-two sets of eight verses (octaves), each beginning with a different letter of the Hebrew alphabet. Each octave is a separate but related meditation on God's law (*promise*, *word*, *doctrine*, etc.) as a guide to the righteous. Mary paraphrases each octave as a separate poem, using twenty-two different stanza forms, and according to convention, assigns each an English letter (in alphabetical order), which begins the first line in each case. Cf. note to Psalm 111 for the significance of the acrostic form.

Psalm 119 A

1 *course*: like the biblical *way*, which Mary uses in line 7, *course* emphasizes the image of the path that recurs throughout this Psalm.

6 *hearty seeking*: cf. Geneva (verse 2): 'seek him with their whole heart'.

7 For the one who relies on God's way, or commandments, to direct his walk, or behaviour.

8 *no sinful blot infecteth*: Mary adds the metaphor of sin and infection.

Psalm 119 B

1–3 *correcting line . . . level*: Mary uses metaphors from carpentry instead of 'cleanse' (BCP verse 9) or 'dress' (Geneva).

13 *shall . . . declare*: Mary changes the tense in this verse from past to future, making the declaration conditional upon God making her wise.

15 *teach all nations*: Mary adds the quotation from Christ's instructions to the apostles in Matthew 28: 19: 'Go therefore, and teach all nations.'

Psalm 119 C

13–14 *Thou proud and high . . . lowly make*: God will make those who are high become low, and the proud lowly, or humble.

21 *thoughts shall walk*: Mary carries through the image of the godly life as a journey on the path depicted in God's word, so that thoughts and speech also *walk*.

Psalm 119 D

28 *My tongue to tread*: this image of the tongue treading appears grotesque if taken literally but it is a literal paraphrase of Parker (verse 3): 'To talk thy wondrous steps'.

Psalm 119 E

Throughout this Psalm Mary seems attracted to images of abstracted and individuated body parts.

14 *falsèd face*: an original addition to 'vanity' (verse 37).

Psalm 119 F

This Psalm begins with a plea for grace to see the defeat of the speaker's enemies (lines 1–12) and continues with an assertion of trust in God's *doctrine* (lines 13–24) and a promise to persist in studying and following the way of righteousness (lines 25–32).

Psalm 119 G

2 *My trust*: either God or the *promise*.

11 *in exile*: Mary follows Beza's phrase (verse 54) 'being an exile', instead of being on pilgrimage (Geneva, BCP) or 'among the strangers' (Old Version). The metre in this section recalls Sternhold and Hopkins.

Psalm 119 H

4 *Hot and hearty suit*: this image of the courtier comes from Calvin (verse 58): 'made suit unto thy face'.

11–12 *But to keep . . . tell*: but [I] contend speedily to keep what thy precepts are. Cf. Geneva: 'I made haste and delayed not to keep thy commandments.'

13–15 *By lewd robbers . . . proceed*: He was robbed, but his losses did not result from neglect of God's laws. Here, as occasionally elsewhere, Mary uses a Latinate structure with the verb at the end of the sentence.

Psalm 119 I

13 *on me lie*: lie to me.

16 *fat in mind*: Mary adds the figurative to the literal fatness.

23 *mines*: added to the biblical image of gold and silver (verse 72).

Psalm 119 K

The speaker, certain of God's justice from past experience, asks both for full understanding of God's commands and for vengeance against enemies so that others may acknowledge and joy in the favour shown to him.

1–2 *Knit . . . every part of me*: cf. 139. 43–56, where God's fashioning of the embryo is more elaborately developed.

4 *Conceiving*: a pun.

10–12 *When thy scourges . . . thy promise overthrow*: even when the speaker was being punished by God, he saw nothing that might counter the fundamental justice of God's dealings with him.

19 *Whose*: the speaker's (the antecedent is *me* in the previous line).

Psalm 119 L

8 *wine*: added to the biblical metaphor of the smoked bottle in verse 83, connecting it with the wine of the Gospel that cannot be contained in old bottles (Matthew 9: 17).

Psalm 119 M

The repetition of the odd-lined rhyme words from stanza to stanza may be intended to reflect the Psalm's focus on *stay* as support.

5 *they*: earth and sky.

Psalm 119 N

23 *true wisdom*: in opposition to the *false ways* (line 24).

Psalm 119 O

The speaker swears, as before, to follow the light of God's law, even when subject to treacherous enemies, and promises offerings of praise for past blessings.

10–11 *this unforcèd praise/I for an off'ring bring*: Geneva stresses offering sacrifices of praise instead of animals. A Geneva note and Calvin's commentary on verse 108 both mention the 'calves of my lips'.

13 *naked*: added by Mary, probably from Beza.

Psalm 119 P

1–2 *People that inconstant be . . . from me*: Mary adds the emphasis here upon constancy rather than wickedness.

5 *closet*: the biblical 'refuge' (verse 114) is rendered here by the usual term for an aristocratic woman's private room.

15 *pillar*: Mary's original, metaphorical addition to the biblical prayer to 'stablish me' (verse 116).

Psalm 119 R

6 *babes*: the biblical sources have 'the simple', which Geneva interprets in a note as 'the simple idiots' (verse 130), rendered by Old Version as 'the very idiots'.

10–12 *As erst . . . thy name embrace*: as ordained and taught by thee, I see that
thou hast earlier had pity for them whose hearts embrace thy name.

Psalm 119 S

11–12 *Whose dooms . . . remain*: follows Beza (verse 142) in contrasting God's
eternal laws with the laws of men that 'are subject unto change, and . . .
come to nought'.

15 God's judgements are everlasting and not acknowledging any time limit.

Psalm 119 T

9–10 *My cry . . . Doth daily rise*: a convoluted rendering of the biblical text
(Geneva verse 147): 'I prevented the morning light, and cried: *for* I waited
on thy word.'

29–30 *Now . . . long ago*: I know now, although I also knew it long ago.

Psalm 119 V

5–6 *Then be . . . my soul's redeemer*: the Psalmist prays that God will serve both
as his *deemer*, or judge, and as his *redeemer*, or his advocate, against those
who falsely accuse him.

10 *health*: Mary frequently uses this rendering (Latin *salus*, health) of the
biblical 'salvation' (verse 155).

14 They are without number.

16 *Revive*: Mary's usual rendering of the biblical 'quicken' (verse 156).

32 *no date defineth*: without any time limit.

Psalm 119 W

1 *men of might*: Mary's substitution for 'princes', perhaps for alliterative
purposes.

Psalm 119 Y

11 *thy scholar*: cf. Geneva note (verse 169): 'As thou hast promised to be the
schoolmaster unto all them, that depend upon thee'. As in Psalm 51, Mary
emphasizes the sequence present in her biblical sources: God will teach
the Psalmist, and then that Psalmist will be empowered to speak God's
praise.

Psalm 120

This is the first of a set of fifteen liturgical Psalms, called 'Songs of Ascents',
'Songs of Degrees' or, in the Catholic tradition, 'Gradual Psalms', that were
apparently used in temple celebrations. Mary paraphrased the first eight of
this subgroup, Psalms 120 to 127, in quantitative metre, without rhyme. Beza's
lengthy 'Argument' for Psalm 120 terms Psalms 120–34 'Psalms of Ascensions',
although the common Hebrew title is literally interpreted (by Calvin and
Geneva, for example) as 'songs of degrees'. Beza notes that they 'were pecu-
liarly consecrated to celebrate the return of the Israelites out of Babylon' and
that they were usually sung by those who 'went up to the temple at solemn
feasts'. Calvin rejects Beza's interpretation and interprets them as songs about

David's wanderings, sung in the temple after his return. In either case, the theme of exile made them particularly relevant to the Genevan community, as Beza notes: 'now also there is great use of this Psalm, seeing that the Godly are compelled often times to flee into far countries by the cruelty of the wicked'.

1–4 *As to th'Eternal . . . to receive an answer*: Mary adds to the biblical text the idea of repeated past answers as an indication of future answers.

19 *Kedar . . . Mesech*: the Psalmist, exiled from his homeland, wanders in remote regions of northern Arabia and Asia Minor.

20 *In a tent*: emphasizes the nomadic life of the speaker.

22 The furious enemies to friendly peace.

Psalm 121

A Psalm of praise, interpreted in Beza's 'Argument' as the song of the people as they come within sight of the hills of Judaea. God's protection of them in their long journey from Egypt has application to 'all the Godly'.

1–4 *What? . . . my comfort*: Mary's dialogue format clarifies the sense of the biblical text, interpreting the biblical 'whence' interrogatively and supplying a reason for looking to the mountains of Judaea and the site of the Temple.

5 *March, march*: added by Mary following Beza's 'Argument'.

13 *boldly*: God's people should set forth boldly, knowing that God will protect them as He has done in the past.

Psalm 122

A Psalm of praise for Jerusalem and the Temple, rendered *Salem* (peace) by Mary, thereby emphasizing the theme of the Psalm.

8 *justiced*: Mary adds this idea, emphasizing that more than judgement shall be given in Jerusalem.

Psalm 123

A prayer for God's deliverance. This highly original treatment stresses the court context.

5 *erected face*: implies that the speaker, like a servant or courtier, is on bended knee looking up.

Psalm 124

This Psalm is in iambics; hanging indentation and rhyming of lines 1 and 11 indicate structural divisions.

5 *had*: would have. Cf. lines 8, 10.

7 *If not*: a continuation of the parallel construction begun in line 2: If the Lord had not assisted us . . .

9–10 *That in the deep . . . our dead carcasses*: If God had not assisted, our corpses would have been buried (*tombed*) in the *deep* water, or at least would have *tumbled* (been thrown down in confusion) on the water.

Psalm 125

Praise for God's protection of his people and a prayer for the punishment of the wicked.

13–17 *As the well-workers . . . Lord him abjected*: The Lord will *favour, further*, and give *peace* to those who believe and act rightly, but the *vain deceiver* (or hypocrite), who wanders from the way, whose doings are lawless and bent to mischief, he has *abjected*, or rejected.

Psalm 126

A celebration of the return from Babylonian exile and a prayer that God will bring home the rest of the exiles. After the conquest of Judah (the southern kingdom of Israel) and the destruction of Jerusalem in 586 BCE, many of the surviving Jews were taken into captivity in Babylon. The Exile ended with the return to Jerusalem in 537 BCE, after the conquest of Babylon by Cyrus of Persia.

2 *Lord's conduct*: Mary adds this metaphor of a *conduct* or passport that was necessary for travel abroad.

3–4 *We . . . Thought mere visions moved our fancy*: Mary adds the idea of visions produced by fancy, or the imaginative part of the brain, to 'dream' in the biblical sources (verse 1).

9 *Most true*: the reassurance that this is truth and not a dream comes from Beza (verse 3), 'and surely so it is', but the wording comes from *Astrophil and Stella*, Sonnet 5. Cf. Psalm 73.

Psalm 127

A wisdom Psalm describing home and family as God's blessings.

Psalm 128

A wisdom Psalm on children as God's blessing.

4 *By him first trodden*: the idea that God (in the person of Christ) has already walked the path the godly must follow is Mary's Christian reading of the Hebrew text.

10 *parlour*: Mary adapts the biblical metaphor (Geneva verse 3), 'Thy wife shall be as the fruitful vine on the sides of thine house', sensibly placing the wife in the parlour.

18 *race*: Mary adds the biblical topos of life as a race (1 Corinthians 9: 24–6 and Hebrews 12: 1). Cf. 145. 63.

Psalm 129

A prayer that God will deliver his people, as He has done in the past.

5 *their force*: the force of Israel's enemies.

13–14 *Tell me . . . your end?*: Mary characteristically adds questions here and at lines 19–20 to make the poem a dramatic monologue, addressing enemies of the godly.

17 *the wheat on house's top*: Mary follows Calvin's interpretation of verse 4 ('But the righteous Lord has cut the cords of the wicked'), which connects

it to the ploughing metaphor: by cutting the lines that bound the plough to the oxen.

24 *Common kindness*: supplied by Mary as a transition to the following stanza, taken from Beza's explanation (verse 8) that the wicked, like the herb on the housetop, will not be harvested.

Psalm 130

Another of the Penitential Psalms and one of the most popular for poet-translators, such as George Gascoigne, Francis Seagar, John Hall, and Henry King. This Psalm acknowledges the speaker's faults, but, trusting in God's justice tempered with mercy, prays for forgiveness. This paraphrase was also set to music: BL Additional MS 15117, which also contains a setting of Psalm 51.

1 *depth of grief*: Mary provides a psychological depth to the more concrete 'deep' of the original.

12 And mercy makes thy worship more excellent.

30 *often, often*: Mary usually avoids empty repetition; thus, the sense may be that God has often redeemed the current nation of Israel just as He often redeemed it formerly.

Psalm 131

The Psalmist uses the image of a weaned child to express his humility and trust in God.

Psalm 132

Mary follows Beza's interpretation of the Psalm as Solomon's consecration of the Temple to God, rather than making it the generalized speech of 'the faithful', as in the Geneva headnote. The connection to Solomon is scriptural; 2 Chronicles 6: 41–2 reports verses 8, 9, 10, and 16 as Solomon's words. Mary has Solomon speak in lines 1–40, with an embedded quotation of David's earlier vow in lines 7–18. The rest of the Psalm is God's response.

3 *oath and vow*: cf. line 40. David vowed to build God a house (temple), but God made an oath to build David's house (lineage) instead (2 Samuel 7). David's son Solomon was directed to build the Temple (1 Chronicles 17; 2 Chronicles 2–7).

24 *Jear*: a transliteration of a disyllabic Hebrew word (sometimes also spelled 'Jaar' in English) translated as a place name in Beza (verse 6), although it was also rendered as 'forest' (Geneva) or 'wood' (BCP), a double sense captured in Mary's phrase 'woody Jear'.

25–6 *here / We find . . . what we sought*: we have found what we sought here (Mount Zion in Jerusalem), not in either Ephrata or Jear. Cf. lines 49–54.

32 *Ark*: of the Covenant.

36 Who have had thy graceful bliss.

64–6 *tenants . . . fields of bliss*: Mary adds the metaphor of God as landlord who gives tenure to his *fields of bliss*.

68 *sceptre*: choosing this word rather than the usual 'horn', Mary alludes to Aaron's rod that bloomed to indicate that he was chosen to be the chief priest (Numbers 17: 8). Aaron's rod was thereby a rod of office, and thus a synonym for sceptre. The rod was placed in the Ark of the Covenant, mentioned in line 32.

73–8 *But as for them . . . With fame and glory rise*: God will cast down the wicked but will crown Christ.

Psalm 133

A wisdom Psalm, praising 'brotherly amity' (Geneva heading).

5–9 *oil . . . tears the morn doth shed*: the images of oil and dew are interpreted variously in the sources. The oil represents the Holy Spirit (Beza's 'Argument'), 'the graces, which come from Christ' (Geneva note, verse 2), or 'the peace which issueth from Christ' (Calvin verse 2).

11 *Impearlèd*: formed into pearl-like drops. A neologism coined by Pembroke to parallel *Embalms* (line 8).

12 *Hermon's*: a mountain in Syria.

13 *therewith*: with brotherly concord.

15 *it*: concord.

Psalm 134

The priests are exhorted to praise God and to bless the people.

20 *of naught*: Mary adds the emphasis on creation *ex nihilo*, not present in her usual sources (verse 3).

Psalm 135

An exhortation to praise God for his works and his providential care of his people.

9 *domain*: demesne, in the original sense of a lord's lands or possessions, emphasizing a courtly context.

12 *inviolate*: not violated. The heavens, earth, and sea do not violate God's decree.

17 *incorporate*: the mists and vapours take corporeal form as clouds and then as rain.

20–1 *Of breathing blasts . . . his pleasure wastes*: God in his pleasure lays waste (causes destruction) by the breathing blasts drawn forth as wind.

26–8 *Not only meaner men . . . the king among the rest*: Mary emphasizes the courtly context and class distinctions between the *meaner men* and *the best*.

30–1 *Sehon . . . who Basan's crown enjoyed*: Sehon, King of the Amorites, refused to give the Israelites permission to cross his land. When Sehon attacked them, Moses and the Israelites were victorious, as they were when they were attacked by Og, the King of Bashan. See Numbers 21.

38 Time may well fulfil his message to the world.

40–5 *how should be forgot . . . their gods?*: questions characteristically added to create a dramatic monologue.

Psalm 136

An exhortation to praise God, strongly reminiscent of Psalm 135, for his creation and for his salvation of Israel. The long series of *Who* clauses matches the biblical original. Throughout this Psalm the biblical refrain that concludes each verse, 'for his mercy endureth forever', is rendered in the second and fourth line of each quatrain, retaining the antiphonal quality of the original.

25 *rushy sea*: the Red Sea (originally deriving from the Septuagint, which mistranslated the Hebrew 'reed' (or 'rushy') into the Greek for 'red', and followed by the Vulgate and other vernacular versions.

37–9 *Sehon . . . Og*: see note to 135. 30–1.

49 *each feeding thing*: the biblical sources (verse 25) have 'all flesh' and Beza, 'all living creatures'.

Psalm 137

A lament of the Israelites in exile in Babylon and a plea for vengeance against their captors, who have taunted them about their songs in praise of distant Zion, God's holy hill (see headnote to Psalm 125). This Psalm, with its focus on singing, was understandably popular with poet-translators, such as Francis Davison, Thomas Campion, Richard Crashaw, and Thomas Carew.

10 in whose captivity we lay.

19 *his*: its, my hand's.

24 Or if I do anything (*aught*) except sing of Jerusalem (*Salem*).

26 *To quit the pains of Edom's race*: to repay (*quit*) the efforts of the Edomites, who were thought to have been in league with the Babylonians.

31 *it*: God's holy city, Jerusalem. Lines 31–2 are the war cry of those who laid the city waste.

Psalm 138

A Psalm of praise, which Mary adapts to emphasize the personal vow of the speaker to praise God in his court.

3 *I will . . . tell*: Mary adapts the biblical 'I will praise thee', which occurs in verse 1 only, into a series of promises to praise God (lines 7, 10), and to tell the story so that *all kings* will understand God's grace and *sing* with the speaker (lines 13–15).

4 *palace*: Mary again emphasizes a courtly context in this rendering of the biblical 'Temple' (verse 2), as did Beza.

14 *contract*: Mary adds the legal metaphor to the biblical phrase, 'the words of thy mouth' (Geneva verse 4).

17–18 *With humbled look . . . espieth*: Mary expands the eye imagery, present in the biblical text only in the verb 'beholdeth' (verse 6).

18 *aspiring things*: 'the proud' (verse 6). Cf. 140. 18.

Psalm 139

The Psalmist meditates on God's omniscience and the mysteries of creation. Protesting his trust in God's personal care for him even from the womb, he prays for deliverance from his enemies. Several unusual renderings in this Psalm indicate the translator's perspective as a Renaissance woman: *closest closet* (line 6, Geneva has simply 'my thought') suggests a private, domestic space, and *embroid'ry* (line 55, 'fashioned' in Geneva) involves God in a craft practised by early modern women.

1–2 *naught . . . lies*: nothing except what lies *revealèd* to thy *search*.

4 You take note of it.

13–14 *not one word . . . thou dost know*: there is *not one word* I intend (*cast*) to speak, except you *know* it, still *unuttered*. A statement of God's omniscience.

15–19 *If forth I march . . . thy hand I find*: not only does God go before and follow behind, but He also guides the speaker with the touch of His hand.

20–1 *Well I thy wisdom . . . with earthy mind*: the speaker can admire, but never fully comprehend God's wisdom. Cf. 104.78–80.

24 *starry sphere*: a reference to the theory of the spheres in Ptolemaic astronomy. Cf. 89. 79–80 and 148. 13–14.

22–8 *To shun thy notice . . . in vain I should assay*: there is no way to avoid God's presence or all-seeing eye.

29 Nothing can *match* the *light* or *flight* of the *sun*.

34–5 *west . . . western*: Mary's addition of the *west* to what Geneva renders as 'the uttermost parts of the sea' suggests the contemporary context of exploration and trade. The Pembrokes, like Sidney, were involved in financing New World exploration.

40 My *night* shall be *unmasked* with the coming of *day*.

42 *father of all lights*: cf. James 1: 17.

56 *wrought in shop both dark and low . . .* : Mary's elaboration of the Psalmist's statement that God formed him in his mother's womb is drawn from details in several of her sources, but the tone and intensity of the passage are her own.

61–3 *All these . . . enrolled did lie*: God, creating the embryo, is described as a craftsman who plans a project in his order book, indicating appropriate times for each task.

64 *these studies*: Mary here develops the speaker's study as scientific exploration of God's *hidden workings* (line 65).

67 *No sum so much*: no number can express God's numberless works. Cf. line 68.

71–4 *if thou but one wouldst kill . . . Inured to blood*: the sense is that if God would demonstrate his power by killing one of the speaker's pursuers, then the whole group, accustomed (*Inured*) *to blood* (violence, murder), would cease chasing him any further; *my . . . chase* means *chase* (pursuit) of me.

Psalm 140

Prayer for deliverance from enemies, with concluding assurance that the wicked will be punished and the godly delivered.

10 *foul*: cf. also 141. 28–9 for Mary's fondness for 'foul'/'fowl' puns.

15 *In thee my stay*: my stay (support) is in thee.

18 *they will aspire*: i.e. 'the proud'. Cf. 138. 18.

22 *shall*: shall be stung.

23 *flames shall fling them low*: as by lightning.

24 *to drown*: Mary adds the idea of drowning where the biblical text (Geneva verse 10) has the wicked cast 'into the deep pits'.

Psalm 141

A prayer that God will watch the speaker's words, will help him to accept just words of rebuke, and will deliver him from the enemy.

12 *flatt'ring baits*: beguiling refreshments, used as a lure or trap.

13 *But let the good man wound*: but if the righteous rebuke.

21 *quarry*: a punning play on the source of the mason's stone and the pursuit of the *worthless* Psalmist.

Psalm 142

A prayer for deliverance. A freer translation than most of Mary's paraphrases, adapting the past tense of the biblical sources to the present.

10 *Lights*: the eye lights, but may also be directed by lights, or lighthouses, developing the travel metaphor implicit in *map* (line 4) and *coast* (line 9).

Psalm 143

The last of the Penitential Psalms. Acknowledging his sinfulness, the speaker appeals to God that He will act out of *honour, justice, mercy* (line 51) and deliver him from his foes and the torment they cause him.

1–6 *entreaty . . . suit . . . audience*: emphasizes the courtly context of the paraphrase.

3 *is*: see note to 102. 79 for use of a singular verb with a compound subject.

26 *thy handwriting*: the sources have some form of the expression 'thy handiwork'.

31 *his*: the speaker's; *one* (line 34) also refers to the speaker.

37–9 *My hope . . . My help*: God.

40 *I may not wand'ring stray*: an elliptical construction: 'So that I may not . . .'

48 *Meander*: a winding, labyrinth-like river in Phrygia.

50 Stand guard, so that I do not stray.

55–6 *in destruction's river/Engulf and swallow those*: Mary continues the water imagery introduced by *Meander* (line 48) to render the biblical phrase, 'slay mine enemies' (verse 12).

Psalm 144

A Psalm of praise, usually attributed to David, and a request for future blessings.

8 Because of whom my realm obeys me.

29–32 *Whose mouth . . . As aptest instrument*: Mary supplies the explanation, that their mouth forges the intent that is carried out by their sword hand. Cf. line 39.

41–8 *O Lord . . . instrument*: virtually repeats lines 25–31, as verse 11 repeats parts of verses 7 and 8.

53–6 *As pillars . . . embellish shall*: the daughters are described as caryatids, both bearing and garnishing the palace.

63–4 *such the sheepy press . . . shall scantly hold*: such will be the crowd of sheep that the streets will scarcely hold them.

Psalm 145

A hymn vowing and giving praise to God for his kingdom, his power and his mercy. Like Psalms 111 and 112, this is acrostic in the Hebrew original.

6 *praise past-praise*: an instance of the topos of inexpressibility.

11 *all excel*: which excel all excellences. An instance of the topos of outdoing.

29–35 *all creatures thou hast wrought . . . state*: as in the biblical text, there are two levels of praise, the sound made by dumb creatures, and the highest praise from those who have *special bonds* to God.

39–41 *age's close . . . procure*: the sense generally is that time (*age*, line 39), in spite of its mutability (*unsteadfast change*) cannot bring closure to God's kingdom.

63 *race*: an instance of the topos of life as a race. Cf. note to 128. 18.

Psalm 146

A hymn, beginning with 'Hallelujah' (as do Psalms 147–50), vowing perpetual praise to God.

1 *Up, up*: like Beza, Mary begins with the imperative.

5 *this decree*: the speaker's declared intention to praise God continually.

9 *for not himself he can*: added to the original, stressing the prince who cannot even save himself.

15–17 *levelled . . . built*: Mary adds the carpentry metaphor. Cf. 119B. 1–3.

Psalm 147

A hymn of praise for God's providential care of his people and especially for the lowly and oppressed.

1–2 *what can better be . . . the honour sing?*: questions are added here and throughout the Psalm to make a dramatic monologue.

15–16 *What great to him . . . Whose pow'r no limits stay?*: what is great compared to God, whose greatness knows no limits, whose power is without restraint?

29–30 *From whom young ravens . . . their diet take*: God feeds the croaking young ravens who are forsaken by the careless old ravens. Cf. Job 38: 41, where God also provides food for the ravens and their young.

60 Except Israel, there is no nation that is not blind to his light.

Psalm 148

A celebration of God as creator and a call to all created things, but particularly God's people (lines 51–4), to acknowledge their dependence on him and to sing his praises.

5 *careful*: full of care, to do God's bidding. Compare the angels as heralds and soldiers here with the more general reference to their function in 104. 13–14.

9–10 *sun . . . light of sea*: the *sun* is the source (*sea*) of light; the reflected light of the *moon* lights the *sea*.

13–14 *Thou sphere . . . emball*: a reference to Ptolemaic astronomy: *Thou sphere* is the sphere of fixed stars, which contains all the others that surround (*emball*) the earth in the centre.

18 *eternal being*: cf. 68. 7.

22 The heavens will endure till the end of time.

25 *When heav'n hath praised, praise earth anew*: after heaven has praised God, then the earth should *praise . . . anew*. There follows a roll-call of all creation, including dragons who live in deep caves; sea creatures and plants; the four elements of fire, water, air, and earth; trees; wild and domesticated animals; reptiles; birds; and people of both sexes, all ages, and all social ranks.

39–40 *And you . . . By what you bear, than be*: the reference in the biblical text is to cedars, in contrast to fruit trees, which have more *renown* from *what* they *bear*.

Psalm 149

An exhortation to praise God through music and dance for his love for the Church.

3–4 *Make his favourites . . . with cheerful noises*: make his praise be sounded with cheerful noise among his favourites.

10 *Dance Jehovah public dances*: Geneva (verse 3) omits the sacred dance. Beza's 'Argument' meditates on the power of music but concludes that such forms of worship are inappropriate.

16–17 *Swords . . . that they may*: so that they may plague and chastise with the two-edged swords.

Psalm 150

Final doxology (an expression of thanksgiving to God), concluding BCP and exhorting musical praise by all living beings; written as a Sidneian sonnet.

13 *Conclude*: added to the text to provide closure, summing up the entire Book of Psalms with an admonition of praise.

air or life: maintains Calvin's distinction between humankind and other sentient beings (verse 6).

EMENDATIONS

This list includes selected emendations of punctuation (*J* and *A* readings in parentheses). as opposed to instances of modernization not affecting meaning: e.g. 'soul' for 'soule', etc., and the substitution of semicolon or comma for a colon according to modern conventions, etc.

'Even now that care': 22 reft (rest); 25 sighs (signes) 40 Unwealthy (unwalthy); 85 vanity's (vanity).

'To the Angel Sprit': 14 the (thy); 34 in me (im mee); 89 the highest (thy highest).

The Psalms: 2.1 these (this); 2.19 The heath'n (Th'heath'n); 3.27 hast (hath); 8.8 ever-hating (ouer-hating); 9.5 high, (hie); 9.38 stay (stray); 10.47 hoodwinked (hud-winck); 10.75 prepared'st (prepar'd); 11.4 a-flying? (a flyeng,); 12.2 do (doth); 15.3 of life an (a life of); 17.40 best, (best.); 18.52 lift'st (lifts); 18.80 enchain (enchain'd); 21.30 have hated (hated); 22.28 Basan's (Basan); 22.32 wried, (wri'd.); 22.65 remotest (remotedst [*altered from* remoued); 25.43 name's (name); 27.18 hold. (hold:); 28.28 safety (safely); 29.15 be; (be.); 29.17 Leban's (Liban); 31.6, 7 forteress . . . forteress (fortresse . . . fortresse); 33.7 harp (hart); 34.61 approach (approach); 34.67 true sight (sight); 38.43 thee, Lord (the lord); 39.35 mak'st (makes); 47.5 king, (king.); 48.30 sadness. (sadnes^); 51.5 Oh, cleanse (clense); 55.11 death's (death); 57.35 harp (hart); 58.5 Oh, no (no); 59.32 They (their); 59.78 lie. (lye^); 65.17 doth (doe); 66.54 from (in); 69.45 such (sūck); 71.28 Do (No); 71.50 march^ assured? (march? assured^); 71.69 sing (ring); 72.76 earthy (earthly); 72.83 All (and); 74.6 flock (folk); 74.23 oft (eft); 74.53 hated (hatred); 75.11 heavens (heav'ns); 77.80 way, (way.); 77.84 earth's (earth); 78.40 fields, (fields.); 78.49 rived (rift); 88.43 will (wilt); 89.106 mak'st (makest); 91.16 affy (affy.); 95.20 pasture's (pasture); 96.13 For but (But for); 96.14 besides (bsides); 96.20 Give (O giue); 104.68 know (knowes); 105.75 folk (flock); 106.28 hater's hands (hands); 106.69 with (their); 107.13 who (how); 108.16 face^ (face.); 108.34 strongest (stronget); 109.69 thou, thou (thou); 112.25 stayèd (staid); 112.27 displayèd (displaid); 116.14 esteemèd (esteem'd); 116.16 redeemèd (redeem'd); 117.7 H is (H his); 118.20 enlarging (unlarging); 119F.4 thee; (thee.); 119F.29 with (will); 119H.10 dwell, (dwell^); 119H.11 keep, . . . speed, (keepe^. . . speed^); 118M.3 earth (Eearth); 119Q.24 shake: (shake.); 119T.22 pursue (pusue); 121.10 Whom but (whome? but); 121.15 night: the^ (night^ the:); 130.12 excelleth, (excelleth.); 131.6 Oh, did (did); 139.61 with (~~which~~); 142.8 danger (dange); 142.10 on one (one); 144.58 fullness^ find, (fullnes, finde^); 145.58 destroy: (destroy^); 146.12 him, his (his, his).